XENO FICTION

Borgo Press Books by DAMIEN BRODERICK

Adrift in the Noösphere: Science Fiction Stories
Building New Worlds, *1946-1959* (with John Boston)
Chained to the Alien: The Best of ASFR: Australian SF Review (Second Series) [Editor]
Climbing Mount Implausible: The Evolution of a Science Fiction Writer
Embarrass My Dog: The Way We Were, the Things We Thought
Ferocious Minds: Polymathy and the New Enlightenment
Human's Burden: A Science Fiction Novel (with Rory Barnes)
I'm Dying Here: A Comedy of Bad Manners (with Rory Barnes)
New Worlds: Before the New Wave, 1960-1964 (with John Boston)
Post Mortal Syndrome: A Science Fiction Novel (with Barbara Lamar)
Skiffy and Mimesis: More Best of ASFR: Australian SF Review (Second Series) [Editor]
Strange Highways: Reading Science Fantasy, *1950-1967* (with John Boston)
Unleashing the Strange: Twenty-First Century Science Fiction Literature
Valencies: A Science Fiction Novel (with Rory Barnes)
Warriors of the Tao: The Best of Science Fiction: A Review of Speculative Literature [Editor with Van Ikin]
x, y, z, t: Dimensions of Science Fiction
Xeno Fiction: More Best of Science Fiction: A Review of Speculative Literature [Editor with Van Ikin]
Zones: A Science Fiction Novel (with Rory Barnes)

Borgo Press Books by VAN IKIN

Warriors of the Tao: The Best of Science Fiction: A Review of Speculative Literature [Editor with Damien Broderick]
Xeno Fiction: More Best of Science Fiction: A Review of Speculative Literature [Editor with Damien Broderick]

XENO FICTION

MORE BEST OF *SCIENCE FICTION: A REVIEW OF SPECULATIVE LITERATURE*

DAMIEN BRODERICK &

VAN IKIN, EDITORS

THE BORGO PRESS
MMXIII

I.O. Evans Studies in the
Philosophy and Criticism of Literature
ISSN 0271-9061

Number Fifty-Eight

XENO FICTION

Copyright © 2013 by Damien Broderick & Van Ikin
The "Chapter Sources" pages shall constitute an extension of this copyright page.

FIRST EDITION

Published by Wildside Press LLC

www.wildsidebooks.com

DEDICATION

For John Betancourt, Michael Burgess,
and Rob Reginald

CONTENTS

Introduction 1, by Damien Broderick 9

Introduction 2, by Van Ikin. 13

Science Fiction and the Plight of the Literary Critic, by
    Kirpal Singh. 17

The Other in Its Own Home: Aliens in Speculative Fiction,
    by G. Travis Regier 26

Strangers in an Alien World: Weinbaum's "A Martian
    Odyssey" and Le Guin's *The Left Hand of Darkness*, by
    Barbara Bengels. .54

Hermeticism as Science: *Rats and Gargoyles*, by Mary
    Gentle, by Yvonne Rousseau 61

A Thought-Experiment: *Solution Three*, by Naomi
    Mitchison, by Helen Merrick. 67

The Camera Speaks: *An Unusual Angle*, by Greg Egan,
    by Veronica Brady. 73

Hacking the Spew: Technology and Anxiety in Neal
    Stephenson's *Snow Crash* and *The Diamond Age*, by
    Talia Eilon. 80
Science Fiction, Parafiction, and Peter Carey, by George
    Turner 132
Carey Goes Cybersurfing, by Marie Maclean 142
Postmodernism vs Postcolonialism, by Elizabeth Hardy . 148
The Art of Xenography: Jack Vance's "General Culture"
    Novels, by Terry Dowling. 156
Vance Fiction Cited. 253
Chapter Sources in Chronological Order 255
Contributors 256
Index 260

INTRODUCTION 1
BY DAMIEN BRODERICK

If there's one trait that marks the literatures of the fantastic—especially science fiction—it's an emphasis on *the strange*.

Traditional fantasy appeals to a taste for the strangely *fanciful*, while horror horripilates our gooseflesh with the *uncanny*, the frighteningly strange. But sf, when it's done right, speaks to an appetite for the strange at the edge of the known, or well beyond the edge.

A taste for such strangeness is the polar opposite of *xenophobia*, the tribalistic fear and distrust of strangers, which evolutionary psychologists tell us is deeply stamped into our genetic inheritance. Us versus Them, those dreaded, despised Others. Some science fiction does appeal to that atavistic dread, but for fifty or even seventy years the best sf has been *xenophilic*. "Xenos" is the Greek word for "stranger," and I'm proposing (here, and in an earlier book, *Unleashing the Strange*) that one of the key characteristics of science fiction is its tendency to seek out the stranger, to roam far from home, to watch with a certain avid eagerness the ways of the Others, human or alien, and even to participate in their strange lives.

Yet the strangest thing about the way science fiction in its popular "sci fi" mode is regarded is the reverse spin put on its portrayal of the strange by marketers and mainstream critics. "Terrifying! Disturbing! Outlandish!" Or, scornfully, "Childishly unrealistic! Irrelevant! Invented poppycock!" A grudgingly positive *Washington Post* review by Patrick

Anderson, of the James Renner serial killer novel, *The Man from Primrose Lane*, comments: "too often, we simply don't know who's doing what to whom.... I can imagine young readers making [it] a cult favorite, but it may be too demanding for the mainstream audience." How so? Well,

> ...about 110 pages along, in a flashback to 1986, a local policeman, investigating strange sounds outside town one night, confronts a red-eyed, frog-like alien that is equipped with a weapon that emits "brilliant sparks of blue-white light," which has emerged from an egg-shaped spaceship. The patient reader will in time learn what in the world this apparition has to do with Neff and his problems.... Renner jumps back and forth in time and raises questions he doesn't immediately answer.... I hope that next time he'll discipline his free-wheeling imagination and give us a more accessible, more satisfying story. [1]

Too strange! Too difficult for adults! Avaunt!

It's not that non-fantastic literature always insists on the polite or even challenging portrayal of here-and-now middle class verities, although that remains a safe course if a writer hopes to be taken seriously. Increasingly, Anglophone writers explore the hinterlands of their own ever-more insecure world, taking their protagonists into Africa (as Saul Bellow did more than half a century ago in *Henderson the Rain King* and Graham Greene before him) or the Ukraine or India or Brazil or Indonesia. But their true locale is inner space, the tormented territory of consciousness and conscience. Any steps beyond can be taken only in the form of allegory; any presentation of an Atwood-like future is just there for the simplifying chiaroscuro lighting it casts upon the present day.

---

1. http://www.washingtonpost.com/entertainment/books/the-man-from-primrose-lane-by-james-renner/2012/03/06/gIQAf4bCLS_story.html (March 2012)

Science fiction, as the essays in this book show again and again, and in varying focus, dotes on the strange. In its flagrantly lustful *xenogamy*—a step farther than exogamy, or marrying outside the tribe—it relishes oddities unavailable to us even in our global cornucopia.

The major piece in this volume, by Terry Dowling, closely examines the artful, whimsical, sardonic xeno fiction of a Grand Master of sf, Jack Vance. Gail Travis Regier looks at some classic examples of how sf represents the alien, not as a ghastly intrusive visitor to our familiar world but in its own habitat. The thematically and stylistically diverse Australian writer Peter Carey, several times winner of the Booker Prize and US National Book Award finalist, is scrutinized here by three observers for work that goes beyond the postcolonial and allegoric into the realm of free imagination. Other chapters explore a range of xeno fiction approaches by sf writers to the topic of the strange, and the stranger, including the technologically-mediated strangers in our midst or in our future.

All these chapters are drawn from Professor Van Ikin's long-running journal *Science Fiction: A Review of Speculative Literature*. It is our second selection, a companion to *Warriors of the Tao* (Borgo Press, 2011). As I noted in my introduction to that book, Van is a connoisseur of all the odd flavors of sf's menus. His first anthology, *Australian Science Fiction*, in 1981, was an early and exemplary sampling of the best sf from the island continent. Published by University of Queensland Press, it delved back into the roots of fantastika in Australia in 1845, and forward to brilliant writers such as Peter Carey who were opening out literary fiction in this formerly despised direction. In 1990 he edited the anthology *Glass Reptile Breakout*, published by the Centre for Studies in Australian Literature, and two years later he and Terry Dowling compiled the excellent anthology *Mortal Fire: Best Australian SF*.

This background of knowledgeable scholarship is the basis for the most important historical study to date of Aussie sf: *Strange Constellations: A History of Australian Science Fiction*, from

Greenwood Press in 1998, co-written by Van with Dr. Russell Blackford and Dr. Sean McMullen.

Van's chief contribution to the sf mode, though, is his distinctive and long-running (if sometimes belated) critical magazine, familiarly known by the iconic initials *SF*. With its cleanly printed pages and a trademark yellow or white stiff cover, always a cut above the traditional mimeograph-copied sf fanzines, *SF* is not quite an academic literary review nor a wildly anything-goes celebratory or controversy-fuming fanzine. The voices in Van's magazine engaged in a long conversation, with no stuffily imposed tone beyond civility and a willingness to cite sources, usually good-humored, sometimes naive, sometimes hair-raisingly hieratic.

I should perhaps stress that I am responsible for the neologism *xeno fiction*, so Van should not be blamed—although, in turn, I put the blame on Dr. Terry Dowling, whose excellent "Xenography" essay, first published more than three decades ago, made me realize how much the fear, loathing, and fascination for the strange is central to science fiction. One request, though: please don't start calling it "xee fee" or "xi fi," or I'll never forgive myself.

INTRODUCTION 2
BY VAN IKIN

Yes—to start with what is most important: "xee fee" or "xi fi" are ruled *out*.

But let's track further back into Damien's Introduction, returning to those two opposed responses to strange fiction: "Terrifying! Disturbing! Outlandish!" or "Childishly unrealistic! Irrelevant! Invented poppycock!" Kirpal Singh also addresses this dichotomy in his lead essay in this book, where he observes that for some critics sf is associated with "Superman, Bug-Eyed Monsters, and Spaceships" and that this association leads to "a profound mistrust" of the genre, its readers, and its critics..."a suspicion that we ourselves are wayward in our literary inclinations."

Maybe this is the moment to confess that, as a youngster, I was first attracted to the genre because of—well, Bug-Eyed Monsters, terrifying or outlandish aliens, and the disturbing but also thrilling scenarios of a future that used spaceships to bring all this right to the front door. (I had an interest in Superman too, but that was on a different basis; to me he was a social crusader, trying to right wrongs, and when Marvel introduced its grittier and more committed caped social crusaders I gravitated to them and left Kal El to play with his kryptonite.)

Was all this a wayward literary inclination?

Given that my chief schoolyard academic rival was wrestling with *Anna Karenina* while I was still enjoying *Superman*, maybe the answer is yes—so let's leave the question open and ask a different one instead: What became of that literary inclination?

For me as one reader it led to a lifelong interrogation of the deeper meaning/s of BEMS, spaceships, and so forth. Much of that engagement was reflected in the editing of *Science Fiction: A Review of Speculative Literature*—and so you have before you the hard evidence of this.

One of the joys of editing the journal has always arisen from the diversity of the material arriving from contributors. It was rare for us to "commission" a piece of writing (beyond occasionally soliciting reviewers for particular books) and so we rode a wave of excitement every time a manuscript arrived in an envelope. It was like an intellectual lucky dip to read a new submission: it was interesting to see what authors and issues were attracting the interest of those who cared enough about the genre to write about it, and it was fascinating to see their differing approaches. Each contributor, in his/her own way, was interrogating "the deeper meaning/s of BEMS, spaceships, and so forth". Yvonne Rousseau's review of Mary Gentle's *Rats and Gargoyles* tracks patiently through the world Gentle has built, noting its reliance upon Renaissance Hermetic *magia*, and then confronting the sf reader with the significance of what Gentle has achieved: "The kind of science fiction plot in which an ordinary individual can save the universe becomes only natural when Hermetic principles rule." By contrast, Barbara Bengels uses her discussion of Le Guin to draw a social message: "through Genly Ai's painful journey toward self-knowledge, Le Guin shows us that the burden of distrust toward women is society's burden." Taking a different approach, G. Travis Regier assesses the achievement of sf in its handling of "one of the most durable motifs of speculative fiction"—aliens—and finds it wanting:

> The ideal alien would be both a complex character and an icon of strangeness, and these two goals are inherently in conflict to an extent that few writers have really tried to pull it off. At the one extreme, aliens are

presented as ravening, destructive monsters, without the capacity or desire for communication with humans. [...] At the other extreme, the alien is anthropomorphized [...] in effect, humans dressed up in Halloween disguises.

Regier's essay sounds especially disturbing in the context of my candid confession of youthful attraction to BEMs and Kirpal Singh's observation that critics so strongly associate sf with aliens. If sf is weak in this crucial area, does it deserve the attention we pay to it? For me the Regier essay is immensely optimistic and reassuring on this point, for it steadfastly sets out the grail to be sought in portrayal of aliens—"a complex character and an icon of strangeness"—and in this provides a standard for reader and writer alike. We know where we should be going and we're participating in the journey to get there. Some of the other pieces in this collection will point to scenes and works in which the Regier criteria may already have been met.

This collection also collects a series of pieces on Australian writer Peter Carey: George Turner's "Science Fiction, Parafiction, and Peter Carey" and two perspectives on Carey's 1994 novel *The Unusual Life of Tristan Smith*—Marie Maclean's "Carey Goes Cybersurfing" and Elizabeth Hardy's "Postmodernism vs Colonialism". Carey's career has run parallel with that of *Science Fiction: A Review of Speculative Literature*: he published his first collection, *The Fat Man in History*, in 1974—the year in which I made the decision to begin publishing the journal—and the first issue (published June 1977) featured an interview with Carey which the author said at the time was his first non-newspaper interview (though production delays meant that ours was not the first such full-scale interview to appear in print). By 1981, with the publication of his first novel, *Bliss*, Carey had moved away from science fiction, and the pieces by Maclean and Hardy mark his 1994 return to the genre. Once again, the approach of these two critics displays the diversity of possible responses to sf, with Hardy exploring Carey's manipulations of postmodernism and colonialism whilst Maclean considers his construction of "alternative worlds and virtual realities" and "the way he boldly tears the monstrous and grotesques from their comfortable repression, confronting us [...] with the knowledge that, until we can inspect, accept, love or detest the monstrous in ourselves, we can never be truly human."

I should probably conclude my Introduction on that rousing note...but forgive me if, instead, I end with a footnote for history. Issue 3 of *Science Fiction: A Review of Speculative Literature*, which featured Terry Dowling's "The Art of Xenography: Jack Vance's 'General Culture' novels", sold over 3,000 copies and continues to generate a trickle of annual back-issue sales. Unfortunately, that huge (and never again repeated) print-run was achieved through a series of cautiously small reprintings (sometimes only 150 copies at a time) and as a result there were no economies-of-scale that might have led to a profit: our best-seller barely broke even. Let's hope that the reappearance here of Terry's superb essay, providing *Xeno Fiction* with both its *raison d'être* and its capstone, will be greeted with similar applause by a new generation.

SCIENCE FICTION AND THE PLIGHT OF THE LITERARY CRITIC
BY KIRPAL SINGH

Even in countries such as England and America, where science fiction has long flourished, people keep asking the question, "How do we approach sf?" The fact that such a topic should even be raised suggests that we are not sure about the meaning, role, significance and relevance of sf. We do not ask (at least, we do not ask in the same tone and with the same set of questions in mind) "How do we approach history?" or "How do we approach literature?" The traditional disciplines of history and literature have by now assumed familiar positions and so our approach to these subjects is governed by an understanding which prompts the necessary responses. But when it comes to a subject like sf, we seem to be in troubled waters.

Various factors have conspired—and I use the term deliberately—to create problems for sf. As is usual in most areas of human intercourse whenever an apparently new and vigorous subject offers itself for exploration, human beings are wont to put up resistance. The literary fraternity—who of all people ought to know better—have time and again given scant attention to sf. Some critics see sf as an inferior form of literary expression and so do not think it worth their time and energy; sf in their minds is associated with Superman, Bug-Eyed Monsters, and Spaceships. They find all this very irritating, or at best amusing.

There is here a tendency—very often expressed in no uncertain terms—to regard sf as juvenile, something good and exciting that children ought to read and enjoy, but not quite the thing for adults and certainly not suitable fare for the literary critic.

Those of us who have tried to engage the serious literary critic in a discussion of sf have often found not only a shocking ignorance but also a profound mistrust, a suspicion that we ourselves are wayward in our literary inclinations. "Given Shakespeare, Dickens, Lawrence, Henry James, Joseph Conrad and the lot, how could one *possibly* spend so much time and effort on sf?" This is a question which the sf devotee frequently encounters in his meetings with his literary peers or superiors.

This is, needless to say, an unfortunate attitude. Before we can make up our minds about a topic we ought to give it a fair hearing. How can we make judgments without first attempting to understand and familiarize ourselves with the case as much as possible? The kind of bigotry—there is no other word for the off-hand dismissals—displayed by some literary critics, a bigotry which prevents them even from reading a good sf book, reveals a deep-seated sense of insecurity parading itself shamelessly. There is no doubt that today sf does, indeed, pose a considerable challenge to the more received and traditional forms of literary expression, but it does so not because it is an enemy but because it is a friend, a friend who is earnestly knocking at the door and whose each knock helps to open the door slightly. Traditional opponents of sf are fighting a losing battle because people everywhere are reading and enjoying sf. But because these opponents are still in charge of disseminating standards of "taste" and "quality" they exercise a certain amount of clout and we, the lovers of sf, have to reckon with them.

On the other end of the scale we have to reckon with the crusaders. These are people who are so passionately devoted to sf that they forget there are other things in life. Their intentions are good and they work with tremendous zeal and energy, but sometimes their emphasis is misplaced or they come on too strong and too loud. Being crusaders, they look upon everyone as being a potential convert or a potential enemy. These crusaders masquerade under all kinds of banners, but chiefly under the banner of fandom. And fandom is both a curse and a blessing. If a bigotry opposes sf, there is also a bigotry which *possesses* sf. What these super-fans do not seem to realize is that blind devotion does not really help to put sf on a sound footing; rather it has the opposite effect of making it appear like some strange cult.

Given these two polarities that dominate the world of sf, I suggest it is best to approach the subject with an open mind—willing to receive knowledge, information, persuasion, and understanding. An open mind provides the necessary corrective balance for both extremes.

Proceeding with an open mind, the first thing that strikes one about sf is the curious fact of its origins. In their book, *Science Fiction: History, Science, Vision*, the scholars Robert Scholes and Eric Rabkin state:

> The history of science fiction is also the history of humanity's changing attitudes towards space and time. It is the history of our growing understanding of the universe and the position of our species in that universe. Like the history of science itself, the history of this literary form is thin and episodic until about four centuries ago, when the scientific method began to replace more authoritarian and dogmatic modes of thought, and people at last could see that the Earth is not the center of the universe with the sun, moon, and stars all spinning round it for the edification of mankind.

What Scholes and Rabkin suggest—and they demonstrate it quite admirably in their book—is that the history of sf is akin to the history of science itself. As science developed, so did science fiction. It is sf's curious kinship with science that is both its strength and its weakness. The hybrid title—and no hybrid title that I know of can boast of its comfortable acceptance—at once points to the tension as well as the consummation between science and fiction. Science and fiction may be seen to be two lovers, and, like lovers, they have their periodic ups and downs. But when they are in perfect harmony, when they can balance themselves on the precarious expression of complete fusion, then the results are exquisite.

The kinship between science and sf creates further problems for sf. On the one hand, sf is commonly and popularly seen to be a sign of things to come. The prophetic or predictive element in sf allows it to enjoy a certain appeal, for readers are curious to find out how the world might be in the future. However, it is interesting to observe that an sf novel containing a predictive element often meets with awkward responses at the time of publication. H. G. Wells's stories about voyages to the moon, Huxley's *Brave New World*, and Arthur C. Clarke's *Imperial Earth* are just three examples of sf works which met with incredulity arising from a refusal to endorse the vision. I wonder how opponents of sf would react today to *Brave New World* since test-tube babies have become an accomplished fact? Newspapers today are full of statements such as, "No longer is X science fiction, it is now science fact." Are we to take these statements as compliments to sf or as dismissals?

Where the predictive element is proven right, sf takes on a new appeal. Statistics reveal that more and more people are consuming sf, and part of the reason seems to be that sf's status has been enhanced by its proven ability sometimes to foresee the future. But if an sf work is read as a kind of prophecy, no great service is really done to the author. Very few sf writers, I think, produce sf because they feel they can see the future. If the situation portrayed comes true, it should come as an added bonus, not as a primary reason for the legitimization of the work. Whether or not the kind of monster envisaged in Mary Shelley's *Frankenstein* becomes a fact ought not to detract from the worth of the novel itself. Sf writers try to dramatize as imaginatively as they can situations which could conceivably arise;

but the eventualization of these situations is less important than their imaginative portrayal. Whether or not a device such as that described in *The Time Machine* ever materializes hardly affects (or will affect) the quality of that superb work.

I have labored an obvious point because many people in approaching sf confuse themselves by imagining that sf is prophecy. It may prove prophetic, but it most certainly is *not* prophecy. The critical reception of such works as H. G. Wells's *The First Men in the Moon*, Čapek's *R.U.R.*, and George Orwell's *Nineteen Eighty-Four*, has amply and ably shown that frequently sf's merit is decided by extra-textual considerations. If a work is found to be a blatant lie, in the sense that the situation portrayed is deemed to be "never possible," it is usually dismissed. But our approach to sf ought *not* to be conditional upon the scientific validity or otherwise of its visions.

Here we come to the tricky question of definition. Sf is, as I have already said, a hybrid art-form. Its chief, though by no means exclusive, framework is provided by scientific and technological data. Most sf is *extrapolative* in nature: working on the assumptions of current scientific and technological possibilities, sf tries to fashion worlds in which these possibilities have either become realities or have been pushed to their logical limits. Harry Harrison's *Make Room! Make Room!* did not itself have the impact of the film version, *Soylent Green*, but the novel does imagine a future society where unemployment and scarcity of food have imposed a kind of cannibalism on human beings once again. But whether or not the possibilities are real, the fact remains that *Make Room! Make Room!* does involve the reader in its dramatization of a terrifying vision of the world. Fiction, as Melville pointed out long ago, is *not* truth, and does not therefore rely upon conceptions of truth to authenticate it. We have come to believe that science is truth. Put science and fiction together, simplistically speaking, and you get truth-untruth. In many ways the label science fiction is oxymoronic, but it does lend itself to a very significant and profound understanding of the world we live in. Sf is about us, and reflects our meanderings in a world with which we have not come to terms.

Sf explores and dramatizes human nature against a scientific and technological background. This is its main strength. It is the only major form of literary expression that takes our scientific and technological environment seriously. I feel that those who decry sf are often the old-fashioned among us, the sentimental ones, who want desperately to cling to a notion of the world where science and technology play a minimal role. If true, this is most ironic, for a good deal of sf is actually concerned with the dehumanizing tendencies inherent in an ever-increasing stress upon science and technology. Indeed, it is alarming that so much sf should be so conservative and old-fashioned. The settings may be new (though those of us who are familiar with the field will know that much sf uses stereotypic, idyllic settings), the inventions and the gadgets may be new, the labels may be new, but the situations are as old as humanity. How do I come to terms with my surroundings? That has been, and will continue to be, the focal point of all good sf. Like the other more readily accepted branches of literature (such as poetry, drama, mainstream fiction), sf deals with human beings, and the stress is always on the human factors. Where sf differs is that it no longer takes for granted the environment, for the environment is seen to impede human nature and human existence. To put it simply, sf writers feel that they cannot ignore or neglect the science and technology which alarmingly and increasingly shape human existence. Where a D.H. Lawrence or a Thomas Hardy were content to use the technological environment as a backdrop, sf writers have pushed science and technology to the foreground.

Readers of traditional novels have not always approved of this, for they feel that in highlighting the environment rather than the individual, sf has betrayed the most sacred task of literature: to visualize human conflict and dramatize human nature. And certainly, if literature is to prove both the mirror and the lamp—that is, if it is both to reflect and illuminate society—it has to have a sound basis founded upon human experience. But what we are witnessing today is that human experience is very largely shaped by science and technology and writers can no longer afford not to take this into account. Hence the need for sf.

I may, at this juncture, be immodest enough to quote from my own book on sf, *Wonder and Awe:*

> It will be appreciated that in science fiction man is still at the center of things but in an altogether different form from his central position in non-sf literature. Thus the center stage occupied by Emily Bronte's Heathcliff in *Wuthering Heights* is very different from that occupied by Wells's protagonist in *When the Sleeper Wakes*. While the traditional protagonist seeks within himself for answers to the riddles in his life, his counterpart in science fiction looks outside himself to arrive at solutions to his problems. It follows therefore that the protagonist in science fiction is often a man who is constantly aware of everything around him and one who is always in the process of some mode of interaction with his surroundings. He is neither isolated nor insulated; he views himself as part of a bigger and larger whole to which he makes his small contribution and from which he receives his particular share of comforts and conveniences of life. If he is sometimes presented as a man ridden by conflicts, his conflicts have their genesis in his identity. Frequently he may be presented as the person who tries to be the detached observer of events which sweep all around him into a new pattern of existence, not fully comprehending the processes by which such a state of affairs could occur. At other times he is so impressed by the great strides made by man that he finds himself musing at his own insignificance as an individual. And yet at other times he is trying desperately to see how he could fully belong to the new pattern of life being created without

causing any great harm either to himself or to those around him.

When approaching sf we must be aware that science fiction is a different kind of literature, *not* that it is something other than literature. In fact, more and more critics are now coming to believe that sf is the dominant mode of literature in the 20th century and beyond, that it offers a serious and profound exploration of the human condition at the present time. Ironically, numerous critics are now discovering what sf readers knew all along: that some of the greatest writers of our times have at some point felt the need to attempt science fiction writing. The names of Poe, Henry James, E.M. Forster, H. G. Wells, Aldous Huxley, and Doris Lessing, all come to mind. As more and more contemporary writers turn to sf to find a more viable means of expression, it becomes apparent that sf is gaining strength and popularity. The movement is unavoidable. Literature has always been a sensitive response to the prevalent ethos—and in our time the prevalent ethos is, fortunately or unfortunately, technocratic.

It may be advisable to end by quoting one of today's best sf writers: Brian Aldiss. In a small book called *Science Fiction as Science Fiction*, Aldiss writes:

> By uniting fantasy with reason, by extending its own artistic frontiers, sf can quintessentially become what it potentially is, the art-form of our time, time-haunted. I see the ideal sf novel as prodromic, free from clock-time, and perhaps more gnomic than explanatory; the reason in it will see that it is in some way related to our days and problems, and not mere wish fulfillment.... Science fiction is capable of achieving a status by which our epoch can be interpreted anew to itself and light what would otherwise be darkness "for want of moral faculty."

Approaching science fiction is approaching the fictions we create for ourselves and those that are created for us through our science and technology.

THE OTHER IN ITS OWN HOME: ALIENS IN SPECULATIVE FICTION
BY G. TRAVIS REGIER

1.

One of the most durable motifs of speculative fiction is the encounter of humans with intelligent extraterrestrial organisms, or aliens. I would submit, though, that these encounters are generally among sf's less successful moments. The ideal alien would be both a complex character and an icon of strangeness, and these two goals are inherently in conflict to an extent that few writers have really tried to pull it off. At the one extreme, aliens are presented as ravening, destructive monsters, without the capacity or desire for communication with humans. There is nothing complex about their character, nor any attempt to draw the reader into empathy with them. The alien is presented as an object rather than a character. At the other extreme, the alien is anthropomorphized; while its physical structure may be as bizarre as the author is able to invent, its psyche has little or nothing of the Other about it. The aliens are, in effect, humans dressed up in Halloween disguises.

Most of sf's aliens fall into one of these two extremes, though the author may try to mitigate the situation with vague or expository discussion of their alleged strangeness. In Clifford Simak's *Way Station*, for example, we are told repeatedly that the confraternity of races includes beings whose patterns of thinking are radically different from those of humans and of one another. Yet the conflicts that result are solved rather easily with the lubrication of some coincidences and a little rural Midwestern common sense. In E. E. Smith's epic Lensman cycle, the myriad races of Civilization are said to vary enormously, not only in their physical structures but in their mental structures as well. In particular, we are told, it is hard for the cold-blooded races and the warm-blooded, oxygen-breathing ones to understand each other. Yet, in specific situations, these races show less variation in personality and behavior than a sample of individuals from various human cultures. There is much rhetoric of difference, but little of that sense of profound strangeness one feels on reading the accounts of anthropologists recording tribal customs or naturalists the habits of animals in the wild—though one would suppose that a species produced by a separate evolutionary path would seem to us far stranger. In fact, Smith's aliens are able to fit themselves easily into the Overgovernment of Civilization—an uncomplicated extrapolation of Anglo-American democratic capitalism. They are so compatible, we are told, that no race that has ever joined Civilization has ever withdrawn from it. As in so many alien encounter stories, we feel that the aliens are merely humans playing dress-up, generic heroes and villains and damsels and confidantes under their fur and robes.

Sometimes Smith is able to make us feel the aliens' strangeness, by putting a human in the alien environment—for example, in Virgil Samms' recognition of how the Rigellian's non-human sensorium (they have an etheric sense of perception in lieu of sight and hearing) contours their culture—their cities are built with no attention to physical appearance, and no concession to noise levels. Elsewhere we are told that species have different values, and this difference extends beyond the cultural level to the biological. We are told that certain species lack the emotional capacity for such human values as courage and altruism. (What they have instead, we are not told—though certainly, radical moral theorists such as De Sade or Nietzsche could readily have been drawn on to supply alien value systems.) Yet this information never goes beyond the level of abstract generalization or of a scene involving an individual character, and these value systems don't seem to interfere with economic, military and cultural cooperation—which seems impossible. At any rate, human and alien morality is superseded, among the Lensmen, by their mysteriously unexplained "incorruptibility."

This summary may not be entirely fair to Smith simply because his story-cycle is an epic. The heroes are types rather than characters, idealized soldiers of Western techno-militarism bearing the White Man's Burden out to the stars. Their foes are demonic invaders from an unspecified "other realm of being," their allies a species so advanced—both cognitively and morally—that they are in effect gods. Smith rewrites human history and evolution, revealing that humans (and most extraterrestrial species) are descendants of the godlike Arisians, sprung from spores which that species disseminated throughout the galaxy and carefully bred over eons for a particular destiny. Smith's aliens seem "really" human, but then, his humans aren't really human either, as we define the term, and anyway they're all in some sense "cousins," descended from the Arisians. Go figure.

It is a part of sf's positivistic heritage, perhaps, that intelligence itself should be supposed to bridge the enormous gaps between species. But this idea seems increasingly implausible in the light of current ideas from sociobiology and cognitive science. The theorists of modernity, from Descartes to logical positivists such as Rudolf Carnap and A. J. Ayer, imagined Reason as the core of consciousness, a sovereign and autonomous faculty that enabled human beings to make direct contact with "reality" and to model this reality with language, which is imagined as an entity separate from thought and yet the mirror of it. Current thinkers, representing the "postmodern" paradigm, imagine that reason, or disciplined abstract thought, is only one facet of consciousness, and derives from certain particular (*not* "universal") constructions of the body, history, and culture. In particular, they deny the existence of "pure" thought independent of language, a distinction essential to Smith's idea of a universal non-linguistic telepathy which renders meaning comprehensible, unambiguous, and reliable (i.e., one cannot lie while using telepathy) and thus makes possible his intragalactic, interspecies culture. In this respect, Smith's "science fiction" is based on a philosophy of science that has become obsolete.

Some authors have written from the point of view of the alien species, but this generally reads as a fairly artificial convention which keeps the reader at a considerable aesthetic distance. It is as if the high school principal, trying to be one of the boys, began talking in their hip-hop slang; everyone is left uncomfortable. Hal Clement's *Mission of Gravity* is considered a classic rendition of an alien point of view, but rereading this book, I can't say that the characters are more than stereotypes, nor see any significant differences in thought or emotion between the human characters and the alien ones. The main character is a resourceful merchant captain straight out of a Yankee clipper saga, and the supporting characters are defined and limited by their functions in the plot. Clement's account of these beings' physical existence on a high-gravity world is brilliant, but his picture of their inner life and their culture is, by comparison, thin and unconvincing. Who are these aliens? Do they have a health care system—or even the concept of health? Do they have a generation gap, or an avant-garde? In many works that attempt the alien point of view, the author is forced to intrude on the narrative with blocks of explanatory exposition—a style that was accepted in much early sf, but for which sophisticates of the genre now have scant patience. Sometimes, as in Arthur C. Clarke's "The Second Dawn," the author attempts to get around this problem by casting the entire story in the omniscient mode. But this is a form of narrative that has inherent difficulties when used in an sf text, principally the difficulty that an omniscient narrator is not perceived as inherently outside of the narrative (as in naturalistic fiction) but might just as likely suddenly enter the text as a character. Thus the omniscient narrator lacks the special authority readers grant it in other genres.

Given these difficulties, why do so many sf writers turn time and again to the motif of the alien? For one thing, the alien is the perfect image of what literary critics call the Other—that which is different from ourselves. We define or understand a thing based not only on what it is but also on what it is not. If, as Brian Aldiss has said, sf is primarily about defining the human, then this definition will involve understanding the nonhuman as well. We cannot understand what something is without understanding also what it is not. Naturalistic fiction defines the human by setting human beings against the natural world, particularly other animals, and by closely examining situations in which humans perceive others as less than human, particularly in texts that focus on marginalized ("subhuman") populations such as women, minorities, the poor, and the insane. Epic presents the hero as the ideal type of humanity and the villain as the antithesis of the human. In the mythic fictions of theistic cultures, the human may be defined by its relationship with the divine or the demonic, while in modern high fantasy, there are often no humans as we understand them; even the human characters have been made, through a subtle alchemy, creatures of the eldritch realm.

Mostly, sf avoids genuine confrontation with the nonhuman. It confronts the human, as we ordinarily understand it, with analogues of itself: humans in the future, who have evolved to live on other planets (sometimes these mutations are quite radical, as in Robert Silverberg's *To Open the Sky* or Clifford Simak's "Desertion"); humans mechanically modified (cyborgs) or human-like constructions (robots, androids, intelligent computers); extraterrestrials who are descended from the same genetic stock as ourselves but have evolved in other environments, as in Theodore Sturgeon's "Claustrophile" or the Hainish novels of Ursula Le Guin; terrestrial animals who have been "upgraded" (from Wells' *The Island of Dr. Moreau* to Cordwainer Smith's "Underpeople") or clones (as in Gene

Wolfe's circuitously Oedipean *The Fifth Head of Cerberus*). In all of these, the figure of the human is reconfigured, but that figure is not set in stark contrast to the nonhuman, not illuminated by the chiaroscuro blaze that only confrontation with the Other casts. The figures described are human in essence, however bizarre their modifications, or human in origin, in the case of androids and robots. Technology has created what we find hard to comprehend, yet we know at least its history and the moment it dropped from our hands.

I can think offhand of only one story in which an alien writes in the first person, Sonya Dorman Hess's "When I was Miss Dow." In this story, the alien is a shapeshifter who has imitated human form and brain structure and then "gone native" by refusing to return to her previous form or activities. She takes on human gender and experiences emotions unknown to her species: sex, love, the need for privacy, bereavement. She speaks to us in human language, after these experiences have "humanized" her. Quite different is the true extraterrestrial, the Other in its own home, the alien who waits for us in the vacuum of spacetime we have not yet entered. For this alien, we have no template, no way to form an expectation. How can we draw close to such a narrator?

2.

At the hinge where Other meets Other, power is the language spoken. The most common relationship between *Homo sapiens* and the alien species they encounter is colonial: Humans expand out into space in a kind of Manifest Destiny, terraforming planet after planet, bringing the "benefits of civilization" to the "natives." This situation is hardly surprising, considering how deeply sf is rooted in the industrial/colonial tradition of Western Europe. Historically, sf began as a supplement to nineteenth-century realistic fiction, a grudging nod to the suppressed imagination ("Okay, you can have your fantasies, but only as long as you offer a scientific explanation to make them plausible") and like realist fiction it is profoundly rooted in materialism ("Science can solve all our problems") and imperialism ("Someday we will conquer Outer Space"). Even when sf struggles against these values, as it often does, they are the baseline that defines the genre. The very idea of realism, after all, is essentially colonial—all of life's mysteries will lie down now and accommodate our view of reality—and sf is tolerated only because it tacitly accepts this assertion of privilege. Unlike fantasy, sf does not suggest that the prevailing conception of reality may be wrong, only that someday, far off in the future maybe, it may have changed. And even this speculation has to pass the test of whether our own science accepts it as plausible. Sf is a closed system disguised as an open one.

In Stanley G. Weinbaum's "A Martian Odyssey," the ostrich-like Tweel is a thinly-disguised version of one stereotype of the native—the faithful scout who guides the explorer through the dangers of the new landscape. Tweel quickly learns to communicate with the Earthman ("Let the wogs learn English!") and in the climactic battle with a "bad" native species (i.e., noncooperative with its colonizers), risks dying beside him rather than using his superior leaping ability to flee to safety. Tweel is a "good" native, a Gunga Din who recognizes the natural superiority of the colonizer and gives him his loyalty.

Sometimes, of course, the model is reversed, and humans are invaded (or even conquered!) by aliens. It is safe to say that most alien invasions have been beaten off, unlikely as this may seem given the technological and numerical superiority always ascribed to the aliens. Here, as in other areas of sf, H. G. Wells set the prototype, in *The War of the Worlds*. In this story, Wells reverses the colonial model to cast humans as the Native. (To some extent, he analogizes us to the lower animals as well.) The Martians are described as an older race, physically feeble but possessed of powerful mechanized weapons, including walking tanks, a heat ray, poison gas, and flying machines. They set out from their smaller planet to conquer a larger, in the same way that the British and other Europeans used their ships and guns to conquer much larger and more populous countries in Africa, Asia, and the Americas. Like these colonial peoples, the Earthmen lack the weapons to fight the invaders or vehicles to counterattack them on their own planet. Ironically, we are saved by bacteria destroying the Martians; though in the history of colonialism it was the "native" populations who were decimated by European diseases.

Some sf writers have written stories that condemn the colonial model, particularly by constructing allegories to the history of the European conquest in Africa. Examples include Edmund Cooper's *The Last Continent* and a series of novels by Mike Resnick that are based in detail on the conquest of the tribal states in the areas now known as Kenya, Zimbabwe, and Uganda. But sf seems unwilling to imagine alternatives to imperialism, despite the critiques of even "benevolent" colonialism by Marxists, Liberation Theologists, and the so-called multicultural movement, and despite the likelihood that planets suitable for one species would not be useful to another. (As far back as the 1940s, Poul Anderson made this observation re the heavy-gravity species of his Dominic Flandry series. He postulated further that we would not be able to exchange culture or even language with such beings except in the most elementary way, since our sensory environment would be so different that we would share few referents. Side by side with this impasse, however, Anderson imagined myriads of Earth-analogs, populated by the usual humanoid aliens ruled by a galactic empire based on the model of ancient Rome.) In many stories, the planet is placed under an "embargo" that limits cultural and (especially) technological diffusion, giving the Natives a chance to "catch up" to the more advanced spacefaring race. In real human history, of course, such embargoes are imposed by those within, to limit contamination of their culture by outsiders. I can think of no reason why the achievement of spaceflight should invert this pattern.

If we view sf purely as an adventure genre—as space

opera—then all this does not create a problem. In thrillers, morality is simplified to Us against Them (the demonization of the Other) and verisimilitude is streamlined out of plotting so as not to interfere with the headlong pace. But if we take seriously the claim that sf is, or can be, serious literature (as sf readers, authors, and critics have been insisting for decades now), then we must note that, in this respect at least, sf has by and large taken the easy and undistinguished path.

In stories describing alien domination of humans, the focus falls not on the aliens but on human revolutionaries. The story typically ends with the liberation of humankind and perhaps the subjugation or xenocide of the alien race. The aliens are usually presented as physically repellent and/or morally disgusting, without any balderdash about value-neutral differences among species. They are usually described as an older race, as if their technological superiority has been achieved unfairly, and as a race in evolutionary decline, implying that the humans' turn to grasp power may be just around the corner. Unlikely as it seems, the aliens are fairly often depicted as having sexual desires for human women, though never for men. Even when the alien regime is benevolent or indifferent, as in Roger Zelazny's *This Immortal* or Gene Wolfe's *The Book of the New Sun*, the aliens who actually appear in the text are presented as decadent tourists. The humans seem to retain their own traditions and cultural integrity in a way conquered peoples seldom do.

In its extreme form, the colonists may regard the "inferior" species as slave, domestic animal (the faithful dragons of Anne McCaffrey), or even a food source (in *The War of the Worlds*. the vampiric Martians seem to anticipate using humans in all three ways). They may exterminate the natives, as in Orson Scott Card's Xenocide trilogy (and as Europeans destroyed indigenous populations in the Americas and elsewhere). They may become parasites on the native species, as in Heinlein's hysterically paranoid *The Puppet Masters*, or enter into symbiosis with them, as in Clement's *Needle* or Ted White's *By Furies Possessed*, two books which strikingly parallel Heinlein's in concept and plot but present the symbiosis as voluntary and beneficial. In William Tenn's *Of Men and Monsters*, the humans are vermin of the superior race, like rodents or cockroaches on human beings. Remarkably, Tenn's humans learn to accept this role, and even regard it as the discovery of the race's proper ecological niche. This vision of humans as a non-dominant species is a rare moment of courage in the history of sf.

Occasionally the alien is presented as, essentially, a god—as in Arthur C. Clarke's *Childhood's End*—though sf is more fond of gods who turn out to be aliens. Authentic gods are even harder for sf to handle than authentic aliens (as J.G. Ballard has said, sf is "profoundly atheistic at its core") so that gods are usually left to the writers of the genre known as "high fantasy." Humans, of course, may become deified; one thinks of A. E. van Vogt's *The Book of Ptath*, Roger Zelazny's *Lord of Light*, and Frank Herbert's *God Emperor of Dune*. But the "gods" in these books are better regarded as superhumans who have run their bluff on the masses; they retain not only feet of clay, but legs and torsos of it as well. An interesting case, for our purposes, is Valentine Michael Smith, the Christ figure of *Stranger in a Strange Land*, because the doctrine and miracles he founds his church on is the heritage of his being raised by Martians. Yet I don't find his Martians exceptions to anything said here about the vagueness of alien cultures. The Martians are always described in abstract terms, like the saints in a stained-glass window, or perhaps more like the angels in heaven. We are told that they lack such human frailties as hate and ambition (though they do practice warfare—it was they who created the asteroid belt by destroying an inhabited planet). The Martian life-cycle consists of two bizarrely different metamorphic states: as babies they are carefree beachballs, bouncing randomly about the planet; and as adults, tripod beings the size of sailboats, whose social order is a placid utopia, and who regard a well-timed suicide and the eating of their dead as the most solemn and joyful of all occasions. In any case, most of the population consists of Old Ones (ghosts, in our terms) who dwell side by side with the living and are the true rulers of the planet. These aliens are extremely promising characters, but Heinlein tends to throw them away in order to pursue a rather naive and clumsy moral allegory. (Doubtless this summation is somewhat heretical, given the book's vast popularity both within and outside sf circles. But in any case, one must agree that the alien culture is left relatively undeveloped, and that the Martians remain shadowy background figures.)

Another possible relationship is that of master to pet, as in Heinlein (*Red Planet* and *The Star Beast*) or in two of my own short stories, "A Thief in Heaven" and "Relics." Each of these works opens with a master/pet or pet/master relationship between the human and the extraterrestrial, though in each case the nature of the relationship becomes more complicated during the course of the story. A straightforward master/pet relationship is presumably too simple a dyad to build a story on, though there seems no absolute reason why this should be so.

3.

One of the most ambitious, and in some ways successful, attempts to take the alien point of view is the "alien" section of Isaac Asimov's *The Gods Themselves*. This book is composed of three related novellas, one of which describes an alien species inhabiting a planet of a parallel universe. These aliens have free-flowing amoebic bodies and three distinct sexes. Each sex possesses a distinct personality type, and all three must "melt" together to create children. These beings enjoy a pastoral existence (though on rock rather than pasture), deriving their nourishment from the sun, and having no work other than the tasks associated with each sex: Parentals bear and nurture children; Rationals spend their time learning (though the learning seems to be restricted to science and mathematics); and Emotionals lie in the sun and chatter with each other. They form stable, exclusive family units called triads. We follow the life cycle of a triad that includes Dua, the Emotional; Tritt, the Parental; and Odeen, the Rational. Much of the story concerns itself with explicit description of the physiology and psychology of the alien sexual process; the members of the triad "melt" into a perfect fusion, like Milton's angels. There is a lot of cleverly done comic allegory of human sexual processes; the aliens have their equivalents of human sexual taboos, ranging from the flirtatious to the genuinely shameful and forbidden. Scenes such as Dua's covertly allowing herself to flow into solid rock (the equivalent of masturbation) or Tritt's refusal to do the Deed with Odeen until they find an Emotional for their partner, are presented with a deftness that one could hardly have expected in Asimov.

> One day when she was quite sure her Parental wasn't in the vicinity, she let herself melt into a rock, slowly, just a little. It had been the first time she had tried it since she was quite young, and she didn't think she had ever dared go so deep. There was a warmness about the sensation, but when she emerged she felt as though everyone could tell, as though the rock had left a stain on her.
> She tried it again now and then, more boldly, and let herself enjoy it more. She never sank in really deeply, of course.
> Eventually, she was caught by her Parental, who clucked away in displeasure, and she was more careful after that. She was older now and knew for certain that despite Doral's snickering, it wasn't in the least uncommon. Practically every Emotional did it now and then and some quite openly admitted it.

Soon enough, unfortunately, we must abandon this byplay and return to the plot. We learn that once the Rational has learned enough, and the Parental has raised the three children that will form new triads, the three "melt" one last time and fuse into a Hard One, an adult whose body is fixed in form and whose personality, supposedly, is a combination of the three aspects of the triad. I say "supposedly" because this second point is not made nearly as convincing as is the physical transformation. Before we witness their metamorphosis, we are given extensive descriptions of the aliens' ability to make their outer surface fluid and interface with each others' bodies and with solid matter. How their personalities can fuse is not so clear, nor how the process can occur so quickly, without disorientation or any noticeable vestige of their previous personalities. We are told that when the triad has melted previously, they in fact formed a sort of Hard One, but that they do not afterwards remember this. The problem is that since we have been limited to the Soft One's experience, we don't remember it either, and so have difficulty feeling the continuity of character as Dua, Odeen, and Tritt fuse into Estwald. Intellectually, I understood the concept, but emotionally I felt that they had simply vanished. This seemed especially true because the Hard Ones, we are told, are more like Rationals than like other Soft Ones. They are asexual scientists, who spend their time running experiments in their caves and teaching natural sciences to young Rationals. The Hard Ones we actually see seem all Rational, perhaps even more so than Odeen, who in fact shows a range of emotions, from lust to tenderness to anger. In fact, none of this triad is typical of its type. Tritt, the Parental, steals a radiation source from the Hard One's cave and exposes Dua to it, in hopes that she will have a child sooner; we are told that no other Parental would have done this. In addition, Dua is not a typical Emotional, but a precociously intellectual "tomboy" who badgers Odeen for science lessons. It does little good for us to learn that the triad was meant to be atypical, the result of a breeding program designed to produce a superior Hard One who can help the race out of its current crisis. The result is that the characters do not "come across" as the divided personalities we were led to believe they were; in order to facilitate the plot, they have been presented as more integrated, that is, made anthropomorphic. Despite, then, the strangeness of their physical lives, we have little real sense of psychological strangeness, and none at all of cultural strangeness. We learn very little about the adult culture, and the Soft Ones are, in our terms, children, leading an almost feral existence in a pastoral wilderness. The Parentals spend their time at home, the Rationals in school, the Emotionals hanging out at the beach. The Soft Ones have no culture, and we do not know enough about the Hard Ones to understand theirs.

Though technically asexual, the Hard Ones are referred to as he and given the honorific "sir." It's a Man's World in the parauniverse too; only the Emotionals are regarded as female, and they are prized only because they are necessary for sex; in the adult world there are no females at all. True, Dua herself helps figure out the solution to the crisis facing her species, but then we are told repeatedly that she is not a typical Emotional; she thinks like a Rational (or, as the old saw goes, "like a man"). Both the Rational and the Parental are referred to with masculine pronouns and presented in male terms. The Parental is distinctly fatherly rather than motherly, and Dua when young called her Parental "Daddy." The Emotional is called "she" and is the only one who seems feminine; it is she who must be courted by Odeen and Tritt, and her fluidity that engulfs the other two and makes melting possible. Physiologically they may be a triad, but in thought and behavior they seem just another threesome, two interesting dudes and their wayward chippie on the endless beach of a Truffaut film.

This is one of the most interesting and clever depictions of an alien species, and the author accomplishes it without the device of human observers or, for the most part, omniscient exposition. Nevertheless it must be reckoned an interesting failure, for our knowledge of the alien species founders on two points. One is that we do not learn much about the Hard Ones or their culture; the Soft Ones know little about the Hard Ones, believing that they are a separate species and immortal. (Asimov explains this point handily, with the idea that if Soft Ones learn prematurely what they will be like as adults, it causes a kind of traumatic personality disorder. But this explanation satisfies the plot without removing the deeper problem in character development.) The second point is that the triad he selects as his main characters are atypical, so we get an incomplete feel for what the rest of the Soft Ones are like. In particular, his depiction of the Hard Ones evokes the old positivistic ideal of Reason as a "higher" form of personality development, and his reification of the females as empty-headed dolls strikes us as inadequate and all too familiar. Granted that sexism still pervades the consciousness of us all, it seems a little late for a futurist writer to erect such icons of girlishness. Surely aliens, if they have sex, will have problems between the sexes. But not, one hopes, the same problems we've grown so tired of here.

4.

Little wonder that many sf writers, in their more serious works, imagine a future in which human beings are the only intelligent species. The technical problems of presenting genuinely plausible aliens—ones who remain strangely Other, yet function as developed characters—are daunting. The second requirement can be dodged in a short story, where characters can be suggested in a few strokes and need not be fleshed out. One thinks of Brian Aldiss's "A Kind of Artistry," with its several vividly and convincingly rendered species; of Bruce Sterling's "Swarm," a variation on the instinct-vs-intelligence game so bleak that one of my students once declared, in front of my entire class, that he would like to "beat the shit out of the author"; and of Damon Knight's "Stranger Station," a provocative exploration of (the human side of) the psychology of symbiosis with the Other.

Nevertheless, sf does offer a few novels which create plausible aliens without domesticating or monsterizing them. Two that I would like to talk about here are *Serpent's Reach* by C. J. Cherryh, published in 1980, and *Stars in My Pocket Like Grains of Sand* by Samuel R. Delany, published in 1984.

(Delany described his book as the first part of an sf "diptych," but the second part has not appeared.) Both achieve characterization of the alien by taking several leaps of faith rarely seen in sf: first, they realize that human beings are, as Aristotle said, social animals; we encounter aliens not just as individuals, but as a culture. Second, any human culture which remained long in association with an alien species would be fundamentally changed; presumably, it would take a form no human culture has ever before taken. Third, the authors do not settle for any simple system of domination, colonial or otherwise, but imagine various ways in which humans and aliens might interact.

In *Serpent's Reach*, Cherryh imagines an interstellar culture ruled by an uneasy alliance of a human aristocracy and an insect-like species, the majat. The group of worlds they inhabit, known as the Reach, is sealed off from the rest of normal space, a culture of fifty-odd human-colonized worlds that calls itself the Alliance. Those inside the Reach call everything outside it "the Outside." Limited trade takes place at a single frontier outpost, but no travel or cultural exchange is permitted, even at the highest governmental levels. The reason, we are told, is that normal (that is, Outside) humans are afraid that contact with the majat would disrupt human culture. (See my remarks on the embargo motif above.)

Why is contact with the majat so feared? When humans first landed on the original majat planet, the majat killed all of them, shocked by the concept of Minds-Who-Die—a concept that reflects both the individuality and mortality of humans. Later colonists were allowed to live only because the majat were able to use their biotechnology to make the humans immortal. To the majat, an individual, mortal human was a biological unit of production, not a person. The majat consists of four hives, each known by its dominant color markings (red, gold, green, and red) and having distinct trends in thought and behavior. Red, for example, is the most aggressive hive; blue hive is the most industrious. We might think of these as separate races and cultures, but they are not; each hive is a collective immortal person, and has its own memory (going back millions of years) and personality. The hive divides physically into various colonies, each ruled by a Queen, who gives birth to Drones, Workers, Warriors, and other castes. But these are not individuals in our sense; they constantly exchange memories in chemical form, by touching each other and tasting each other's vital fluids. Warriors sent on suicide missions are sometimes Unminded, so that enemies cannot tell from tasting them what the hive itself is thinking. Their unit of consciousness is the hive, and they think no more of individual death than we do of cutting our nails.

Since the very idea of Minds-Who-Die causes the majat revulsion and trauma, the humans construct a society which is, essentially, a mirror of majat "culture." The immortal Kontrin form an extended family, structured in subdivisions to match the hives. Specific clans are considered "part of" each hive; what that means exactly is clear only to the majat, but members of these clans can sometimes call on units of "their" hive for protection and succor. Through cloning, genetic engineering, and hypnotic conditioning, the Kontrin create "castes" of human workers and soldiers equivalent to the castes of the majat hives.

Cherryh creates this situation not through authorial fiat but as the outgrowth of a particular historical train of events. In an early chapter, a human named Liam, who is old enough to remember life before the majat, summarizes this development and warns of its possible consequences:

> ...I've lived since the first ship came into the Reach, and I'll tell you this: I saw early that men couldn't live here without being corrupted.... We brought in human eggs and the equipment to handle them.... Now do you suppose, fellow Councilors, that the hives didn't know by then what we were about?
>
> Of course they saw. But the human animal is a mystery to them, and we kept it that way. They saw a hive-structure. They saw an increasing number of young and a growing social order which well-agreed with

> their own pattern. We planned it that way. They still had no idea what a non-collective intelligence was, or what it could do. Just one large hive, this of ours, all one mind. They knew better, perhaps, in theory. But the pattern of their own thinking wouldn't let them interpret what they saw....
>
> We've entered into a strange new relationship with our alien hosts.... Humanity's brain, are we not, doing for our kind what the queens do for the hives? And in that process, we've grown *different*....

Cherryh emphasizes here a fact so simple it is easily forgotten: that to our Other, *we* are the Other. Gradually, the humans of the Reach have become more and more like the hives, yet the culture that results is fundamentally out of tune with basic—that is, biologically determined—human needs. Cherryh makes the majat interesting and likeable; their way of life is a product of their evolution, and suits them. Individual units are cheerful to be part of the greater good; queens rule with benevolence and wisdom. But the human culture that mirrors this hive society is a totalitarian nightmare, an interlocking grid of rigid master-slave relationships, where even the members of the ruling class can find no way to express their individuality but sterile hedonism and occasional outbreaks of murderous violence. Liam warns the younger Kontrin of this dehumanization:

> You think you know it all, having been born here, in the Reach, in a new age you think an old Outsider can't understand. But I'm going to go on telling you, because you need to remember it. Because the majat will tell you that a hive that has lost its memory, that has...unMinded itself...is headed for extinction.

Ironically, even as Liam warns of the corruption of human culture by contact with the hives, he uses a metaphor drawn from the majat to express the idea. This fact is perhaps more compelling proof of his argument than anything in the argument itself.

> "We're quarantined. They're all around us, Outside. Human space. These few little stars...are an island in a human sea.... They don't want the majat. They don't want hives in their space.
> "And above all, they don't want us."

Cherryh's protagonist, Raen, as the last surviving member of a House destroyed in assassination intrigues, is a "queen" without a hive. Since her family was affiliated with blue hive, the hive gives the injured Raen refuge. Living in the womb-like darkness of the hive, Raen (and the reader) come to know intimately its Otherness:

> That [Raen] was Meth-maren, and therefore no stranger to majat at close quarters...this saved her sanity. She was naked. She was blind, in absolute darkness, and disoriented. She suffered the constant touches of the Workers the length of her body, wetness which worked ceaselessly on her raw wounds, and over all her skin and hair; an endless trickle of moisture and food was delivered from their mandibles to her mouth. Their bodies shifted above and about her, invisible in the dark, with touch of bristles and grip of chelae or mandibles. They hovered, never stepping on her, and their ceaseless humming numbed her ears as the dark numbed her eyes.

The imagery of these scenes might seem horrific—a teenage girl, naked in darkness, among a swarm of giant bugs. But it is not horrific to Raen, whose point of view we follow closely. Instead, we feel safe and warm and, yes, loved, in this environment. Raen herself seems to regard the blue-hive queen as more of a mother than she did any of her own human family. Her meeting with the Queen is like that of a worshipper with her god:

> Raen hastened, misjudged, almost lost her senses in the warmth and closeness of the place. She gained her balance again, aided and supported into the presence. She filled the Chamber. Raen hung in the grip of the Workers, awed by the sight of Her, whose presence dominated the hive, whose mind was the center of the Mind. She was the one, if there was any single individual in the hive, with whom they of Kethiuy had so long dealt...the legends of all her childhood, living and surrounded by the seething mass of Her Drones, a scene of fever-dreams, males glittering with the chitinous wealth of the hive.
> Air stirred audibly, intaken.
> "You are so small," Mother said. Raen flinched, for the timbre of it made the very walls quiver, and vibrated in Raen's bones.
> "You are beautiful," Raen answered, and felt it. Tears started from her eyes...awe, and pain at once.

The oldest living human, Moth, is "queen" of the entire Reach; she controls an interstellar computer network that controls all aspects of human society in detail even more excruciating than that of cyberpunk novels. This is analogous to the Drones surrounding the majat Queens, who collectively maintain racial memories going back millions of years. Other castes have their equivalents as well. The betas are a petty bourgeois class whose culture and psychology has been deliberately programmed so the betas fear the majat and obey the Kontrin. (The term beta recalls, of course, the hypnotically-conditioned managerial class in Huxley's *Brave New World*.) These are the human equivalent of the Drones, just as the computer network is its electronic equivalent. Various classes of cloned humans, known as azi, are the equivalents of Warriors and Workers. Prenatally stratified by their stereotyped gene patterns, these slaves are further dehumanized by their "childhoods": "Nurtured" in vast tiers of Skinner boxes without parental or social simulation, they are subjected to deepstudy (hypnotic conditioning) tapes that program their later behavior. More specialized than betas, the azi are under normal conditions utterly unable to act against their programming. Without orders, they become virtually autistic. Even in the conditioning barracks, which Raen visits, they simply sit motionless when not given some task. The children do not play, and the azi do not speak or touch each other, even when they believe themselves unobserved.

Given orders, the azi obey literally, and will work or fight methodically but with no particular feeling, even in suicide situations. They are physically insensitive to pain and emotionally numb, lacking even the fear of death. During an aircraft crash, the azi are islands of calm among the chaos:

> They hit a roughness of air, rumbling as if they were rolling over stone, but the lights started winking again to green.
> "Shall we die?" an azi asked of his squad leader.
> "It seems not yet," squad-leader answered. Raen fought laughter, that was hysteria, and she knew it. She clung to the armrest and listened to the static that filled her ear, stared with mad fixation on the hands of the terrified betas and on the screens.

Majat workers and warriors are part of a collective entity, interchangeable as machine parts. Individuals call themselves "This-unit." (Raen herself uses this locution when talking with them, and others such as "my-hive azi." Another time, she tells her azi that "Any Warrior is Warrior," a concept that the azi, with their limited sense of self, accept more easily than we could do.) In the azi, the Kontrin have attempted to recreate majat interchangeability, and though they have not truly done so, both Raen and the reader are horrified by the extent to which this dehumanization has succeeded. Some azi are sold to the majat as slaves, and these hive-denizens seem more insect-like than human; Raen finds it harder to communicate with them than with the real majat.

Just as the majat are revulsed by human individuality (do they feel as we would if our body parts suddenly each became animate and developed a will of its own?), the betas are horrified by the azi's insect-like lack of it.

> There was no beta would get past [the azi commander], no one who would get near controls. Azi lined the room, thirty of them, armed and armored, impersonal as the majat, and that resemblance was no chance. Beta psych-set was terrified by it. There was no one of them about to make a move under those guns.

Even Raen's lover, an azi named Jim, is unable to go beyond his programmed duties without specific instructions, though Raen has placed him in a privileged position and encouraged him to take responsibility. Raen teaches and cajoles him without effect, frustrated by his passivity.

> She looked at him, who sat waiting, looking at her, and reckoned that no azi was capable of going beyond instruction; she had never known one to, not even Lia [her childhood nurse]. Psych-set. They simply could not.

Raen buys Jim presents but they mean nothing to him; she sneaks up on him, only to find him sitting motionless, endlessly patient, awaiting orders. She thinks of him sometimes as a machine, attributing a moment's clumsiness to "a sticking-point in the clockwork." Yet all is not lost, for even Jim in the debased state of his conditioning is eventually provoked by Raen's prodding to a state of cognitive dissonance that is the herald of his birth as a human self. "I am not real," he thinks at one point, feeling real pain at the thought; he catches himself thinking what can only be "born-man thoughts," making plans and feeling desire. In a crisis, his concern for Raen prompts him to perform a taboo act: he deepstudies illicit Kontrin tapes and this develops a more "human" personality—albeit one based on Raen's own psyche. Like a child, he learns from the mirror of his "mother."

One comes to feel, not only intellectually but in one's guts, what it must be like to be a majat, by following the experiences of these humans who have become majat-like. The structure of the text does not ask us to make the vast leap directly from ourselves to the Other, but provides us with beings and a culture intermediate between our own and that of the alien.

5.

In quite another way, Samuel R. Delany achieves a similar effect in *Stars in My Pocket Like Grains of Sand*. His method is in some ways simpler; by focusing on the family unit, he bypasses the chore of describing the overall culture. In the novel, human cultures on various planets are described. These have the breadth of an anthropology text: political and economic systems, sexual taboos, family structures, body language, food and dress—vast differences in beliefs and practices are catalogued. The feeling of the bizarre that one feels when encountering another culture is emphasized repeatedly by the musings of Delany's protagonist, an "industrial diplomat" whose job is to sort out these differences in cultures. (One of Dyeth's multicultural anecdotes tells how he was once served meat with a bone in it—indicating that it came from an animal rather than artificially-grown tissue.) Against this background, Delany presents the interspecies culture of Dyeth's own planet Velm, the one culture that Dyeth, of course, tends to take for granted. Velm has, apparently, two cultures: in the northern hemisphere, humans and the indigenous dragon-like evelmi are engaged in murderous racial strife; but in the south, they live together so harmoniously that they have even formed interspecies "nurturance streams," or extended families. Like Cherryh, Delany constructs for the reader a transitional bridge from human to alien; the human culture has been shaped by the culture of the alien. The concept of the nurturance stream comes from the evelmi, as do other customs Dyeth dwells on: subterranean areas for casual sex, known as "runs," and the elaborate formal "banquet" which closes the novel. Though the two species remain genetically distinct, sex and other aspects of domestic life are shared among the family, and a child thinks of all the adults in the stream, both human and evelm, as its "parents," though it knows who its genetic parents are also. Delany foregrounds this by stealing an image from the archetypal "monster movie" and reversing the meaning of the image:

> Sometimes I think I watched him only a moment; sometimes I think I stared at him an age.
> Then: a black claw descended, like the huge limb of some mechanized sculpture falling into activity.
> The youngster looked up to grin at some hovering parent (like mine): rough and grainy where they emerged from the blue-black hide, becoming metal smooth as they curved to needle tips, iron-colored talons spoke only to me of distance but not of specific origin.
> The child reached up.
> Claw and hand grappled—
> I couldn't have watched that juncture more than a moment. Even then I knew the tussle of a parent picking up a child to go off somewhere into the city—home, for me.
> But for him? Really, then, I knew little of the two kinds of flesh joined there, or of the disparate organic body chemistries that, some places on my world,

sunder the species and at others are the parameters about which everything that is human and everything that is evelm are in play.

They were gone.

I was left, amidst the other children, furred or fleshed, fingered or clawed, to tell myself endless stories over the next years as to why, for a few hours, that child had been there. The most obvious answer? He and a parent had been passing through Morgre and the child had simply been left off at the nursery to play a while. But not a year standard has gone by when, in some lone moment, I haven't enhanced on some recomplication of a human child's and a black-scaled beast's adventuring together across my world, during which, momentarily, I glimpsed an instant of it: their jointed hands within a strange nursery under lead-shadowed light.

The evelmi have three tongues, and so their language is rich in metaphors derived from taste. In response, the language of the human colonists has added such metaphors to their own speech. When Dyeth's

>...mother, V'vish, clasped her forepaws and declared with two tongues at once:
> "Where have you been, Marq?"
> "Where are you, dear! Please, the Thants are here and we don't want to insult them!"

...he tries to alter his voice to approximate this effect, "which is a habit we single-tongued humans here get into in childhood, but which, except when talking to my parents, I've (mercifully) almost broken."

Delany's method is to immerse us in Dyeth's family life without always telling us the species of the characters on stage, or by telling us their species only after we have already learned other things about them. The very simplicity of many scenes, their atmosphere of domestic ordinariness, enhances this effect. As we travel through the text, species as a category is, as it were, "backgrounded" onto the back shelf of our awareness; we begin to think of the characters as persons first, and as human or evelmi second:

> Three of my siblings were playing in the pool by the rocks that turn white down near the water. Spray splattered the olive flags. Tinjo flopped Buchephalus, splosh! Buchephalus wagged her scaled tail, sheeting out meters of droplets. Small Maxa jumped up and down at the pool edge, afroth to her chest.
> Tinjo saw me—or Bucephalus smelled me; Tinjo squealed and the same moment Bucephalus was out of the pool and up by the carved railing on all sixes, shaking her scaly head—Large Max swears Bu is the finest looking of all this generation's children, human or evelm. Bu lolloped across the stones, the wet tufts on her legs dripped about her claws, the scales on her back a glister of purples and browns. She leaped against me, bronze claws hooked over my shoulders (yes, the gold-clawed apprentice in the butcher shop hails from a different continent than Bu), small tongues playing over my mouth. I opened wide, so she could be sure to taste me properly.

The giving of taste reminds us of *Serpent's Reach*. The casualness of "all sixes" rather than "all fours"; the affection Dyeth feels for his siblings of both species; the casually-dropped datum that evelmi, like humans, have ethnicity; the sensual but not sexual open-mouth kiss; and the startling concept of a standard of childhood beauty shared across the species—all these draw us deeply into Dyeth's point of view, away from our preconceptions of the human and the alien. Thus, Delany deconstructs the reader's ideas of human/alien interaction through two techniques: first, he constructs a plot which foregrounds the concept of the great variability of even human cultures. In particular, he introduces a human character, Rat, who becomes Dyeth's lover and tells him how he was persecuted and eventually lobotomized for his homosexuality, on a world where that was the great taboo. Second, Delany presents the human/alien culture through the point of view of Dyeth's first-person narration, so that Dyeth's casual intimacy with the aliens lulls us into thinking of them as persons rather than creatures from a black lagoon. Though Delany does not actually describe human/evelmi sex, he makes us so accustomed to the idea that when the Thants, a family of old friends from another world, voice their disgust at the "miscegenation," the reader sees their attitude as "alien." During an elaborately described "banquet" derived from evelm tradition, the Thants try to insult their hosts in the most profound way they can think of, by mocking their bestiality. But Dyeth does not at first even understand what is meant, and when he does, he is more puzzled than offended. So thoroughly has Delany's textured writing drawn us into the hybrid culture of human and evelmi that we have to think about it for a minute as well. In a limited way, Delany has made us one with the Other here, and made his aliens a real presence in the text. At the same time, he cautions us against thinking we can "become" the Other. Talking to an evelmi, Dyeth feels for a moment the gap between them:

> "Do we humans have a broader notion of religiosity than you?"
> "Merely less refined." Santine arched her upper gum ridge, which was a smile. "Vondramach intrigues me because she had tasted the bitterest sins. Such flavors authorize the highest, the deepest, the widest religious feelings that pull us away from all social centers. But these poems, as you call them, are things made with taloned claw rather than the perceiving tongue."

(Note the imagery of taste which the evelmi employs.)

Dyeth is already uncomfortable with this explicit talk of the differences between the species, as his laughter and then silence in the next paragraph shows:

> "I think," and laughed while I both thought and said it and so probably distorted both processes, "that because you evelmi have more tongues than fingers—or taloned claws—you will never understand us humans, really."
>
> "And that is why you kill us in the north," Santine declared. "Ah, yours is a political statement if I ever heard one. Well, your Vondramach was a mistress of politics as well as art and religion, yes? But in those two fields, she leaves me far behind."
>
> I didn't say (indeed, I probably didn't think): that's why we're killing you in the north. Rather I found myself simply uncomfortable with this, from one of my oldest friends.

6.

From the foregoing, we deduce two points of general theoretical interest: the first is that sf, while loving to invoke the alien as Other, has by and large shied from its Gorgon gaze—as who might not? The second is that this has not always been the case, and that one key to writing about the Other is to focus attention not on the Other as such but on the Perseus' shield of those persons and cultures who are superficially like ourselves, but whom intimacy with the Other has transformed. The first point belongs to the history of speculative fiction. The second point may have an application beyond one literary genre, or indeed beyond "literature" itself.

STRANGERS IN AN ALIEN WORLD: WEINBAUM'S "A MARTIAN ODYSSEY" AND LE GUIN'S *THE LEFT HAND OF DARKNESS*
BY BARBARA BENGELS

"A Martian Odyssey" by Stanley Weinbaum is widely loved by readers and writers of science fiction alike, having been included by both the Science Fiction Writers of America and Science Fiction Research Association in their anthologies of most revered science fiction stories.[2] Isaac Asimov said that it was the first pulp story to withstand critical scrutiny a generation after its publication and that its importance lay in its being "the first example of modern social science fiction" where aliens and setting are "naturally different" and the human characters "acted and felt like people."[3] However, I believe that the focus in "A Martian Odyssey" is not merely on the variety of interesting alien creatures who exist for themselves but rather on the various problems of communications between aliens who are indeed alien and aliens who are members of the human race.

---

2. Weinbaum, Stanley. "A Martian Odyssey", in *The Science Fiction Hall of Fame*, ed. Robert Silverberg (New York: Avon Books, 1970).

3. Asimov, Isaac. "Social Science Fiction," in *Modern Social Science Fiction: Its Meaning and Its Future*, ed. Reginald Bretnor (New York: Coward-McCann Inc., 1953), p.173.

Weinbaum first alerts us to this problem when he introduces his international crew, a common enough device in science fiction to prove that man has accepted himself as a species—but here used for another purpose. Here we are not to be impressed simply by the fact that the crew can function together despite its ethnic or national differences but instead we are to focus upon what the crew-members—cooperative as they may be—cannot do: they cannot truly understand one another. Despite the fact that they're all Earthmen, they remain isolated from each other by language differences. Leroy still doesn't have a grasp of American slang when Harrison confuses him with "Spill it, man" and Putz's translation of "spiel," while to the point, is far from exact (p. 14). Shortly thereafter Putz inquires "Vot iss shenanigans?" and Leroy explains: "He says 'Je ne sais quoi,'... It is to say 'I don't know what'." (p. 17). When Jarvis describes his first encounter with Tweel, we are explicitly told that an alien language is certainly not going to come easy either: Tweel is transformed to Tveel when in fact the reality is more "like [a sputtered] Trrrweerll" (p. 17). If we can't even pronounce an alien language, Weinbaum seems to ask, can we ever fully communicate in it?

How many ways do we fail to communicate in our own human language, even our birth language? Before Weinbaum tackles the subject of communication with an alien he makes us aware of the contrived way description works to convey our feelings and the manner in which we express them. In the first few pages he resorts to a kind of pulp magazine meta-language, showing us how inane our expression of verbal intercourse sounds: Jarvis and Harrison "grunt," Harrison "snaps," "explodes," and "grumbles," while Putz "ejaculates" (only verbally, of course, this being 1934). Perhaps this lack of subtlety is all a function of Weinbaum's inexperience, but it could also be a conscious attempt to define the limits of the writer's capabilities to imitate conversation. Obviously Weinbaum is in control when he has Jarvis say "that's her"—and, lest the reader miss it, he adds "ungrammatically" (p.29). Language—even our own—is not something that rests comfortably with us. We use it sloppily, we use it loosely ("I'll be damned!" [p. 26]) and we use it to comfort ourselves even when no communication is taking place: "We talked—not that we understood each other, you know, but just for company" (p.22).

The fact that Weinbaum is truly interested in this subject of language usage is proven by the way in which the story dwells on the problems of dealing with a uniquely alien language representing an alien mind-set. "We just couldn't connect.... Nothing was the same for two successive minutes.... I couldn't get the hang of his talk; either I missed some subtle point or we didn't think alike" (p. 19). On the other hand, Tweel seems equally surprised and fascinated with the peculiarities of Jarvis's language, but he does find a way to use it successfully with the Earthman's earnest cooperation. It is their desire, their eagerness, and their need to communicate that helps them discover common ground despite their extraordinary differences. Perhaps this is one of the assumptions that makes Weinbaum so likable as an author, his deep-seated conviction that Jarvis—and by extension, the human race—could truly accept and feel affection for a creature so incredibly, even laughably, different: "Somewhere on Mars...is a civilization and culture equal to ours, and maybe more than equal. And communication is possible between them and us; Tweel proves that." (p.32).

What makes this story so memorable, however, is the sense of loss that pervades it, Jarvis's sorrow at having left Tweel behind:

> I went in [to the rocket] laughing and crying and shouting! It was a moment or so before I remembered Tweel.... We sailed out over the desert and put down once or twice. I yelled "Tweel!" and yelled it a hundred times, I guess. We couldn't find him...and all I got...was a faint trilling and twittering drifting out of the south. He'd gone, and damn it! I wish—I wish he hadn't! (p.39)

That failure to say goodbye haunts Jarvis (and provided Weinbaum with a ready-made sequel when fans demanded it, in "Valley of Dreams"); it is a very human sorrow at not having expressed his gratitude and his affection for Tweel. Ironically, what Jarvis finds at the end of this story is that having been "saved" from the desolation of Mars by his crew, he is now more alone than ever before.

His brief and flawed communication with an alien has led to a breakdown in his ability to communicate with his fellow man because he has experienced an "otherness" that they have not—yet their silence suggests that they at least commiserate. Jarvis's distracted sense of isolation increases during the course of his telling of the story; he is never more alone than while he's trying to convey the depth of the experience to friends who simply can't understand the unique camaraderie, the rapport he has developed with Tweel. His crew members have become friend-strangers who can't comprehend that what he has lost is exquisitely more valuable than the wart-cure that he has found. It is this very poignant sense of loss that is communicated to Weinbaum's readers, a loss that reverberates across the decades.

§

Much has been made of the reaction of the one significant "male" character in Ursula K. Le Guin's novel *The Left Hand of Darkness* to the androgynous society he finds himself in on Gethen: his initial revulsion, his sense of alienation, his eventual acceptance and love of Estraven, and his final rejection—*a la* Gulliver—of the first female he sees from his own society. What seems to have been overlooked, however, is his peculiar, even negative response to "normal" women *before* his adaptation to and acceptance of Gethenian mores.

The hard task of wheeling a cart through the rain, for example, is a "bitch" of a job (p.215). His discomfort with what he perceives as effeminacy also fits into the range of our cultural expectations: he is annoyed by Estraven's "sense of effeminate intrigue" (p.8), disappointed that "Argaven was less kingly, less manly, than he looked at a distance" (p.31), distressed that his prison guards were "to my eyes effeminate—not in the sense of delicacy, etc., but in just the opposite sense: a gross, bland fleshiness, a bovinity without point or edge" (p.176).

But this equation of effeminacy and fleshiness is not very different from his displeasure with the female form itself, a form which consists of "more fat than muscle" (p.218). For this reason, he thinks of the superintendent of his island as "my landlady, for he had fat buttocks that wagged as he walked, and a soft fat face..." (p.48). Women, to him, are shrill, deceitful ("Argaven laughed shrilly like an angry woman pretending to be amused," p.31), and sullen ("as an old she-otter in a cage," p.35); in fact, they are frequently seen in terms of animal imagery: Gethenians "behaved like animals...or like women" (p.49) in their inability "to mobilize" (p.49); nothing outweighs comfort if "one is an old woman or a cat" (p.51). Nor does he like their manner of thinking: talking about the Handdara concept of ignorance, he says, "There was in this attitude something feminine, a refusal of the abstract, the ideal, a submissiveness to the given, which rather displeased me" (p.212). Upon his visit to the Fastness of Otherhord, Genly Ai gets caught up in their Foretelling, "obsessed by hallucinations of sight and touch, a stew of wild images and notions, abrupt visions and sensations all sexually charged and grotesquely violent, a red-and-black seething of erotic rage. I was surrounded by great gaping pits with ragged lips, vaginas, wounds, hellmouths..." (pp.65-66). It is here that he mentions the 3-4% of perverts—"normals, by our standard" (p.64)—that dwell on Gethen, none of whom he seems to have sought out for companionship or sexual relief in his two years of virtual isolation on Gethen.

Why, ultimately, is he so prejudiced against and uncomfortable with the idea of relationships with real women on Gethen or on his home planet? For one thing, he seems to equate them with infidelity and betrayal, a subject which he admits to being obsessed by. In the first chapter alone Genly Ai tells us that he doesn't trust Estraven "whose motives are forever obscure" (p.7), that Estraven's house has "a certain air of faithlessness" (p.11), that his performance at table "had been womanly, all charm and tact and lack of substance, specious and adroit" (p.12). A page later he expands on these "womanly" traits: "he was not merely adroit...he was faithless" (p.13). In this first chapter, Genly feels personally betrayed, shocked that Estraven seems to have "no loyalties at all" (p.20) and finally, in the last words of the chapter, tells us "I was cold, unconfident, obsessed by perfidy, and solitude, and fear" (p.21). The dislike and distrust he has of the "soft supple femininity" of Estraven (p.12) grows increasingly confused with his accurate perception of the "fear and betrayal" he feels in "that sunless city" of Ehrenrang (p.50).

What then is Le Guin saying through her "thought experiment"?[4] Almost assuredly she is telling us that even when a normal human male thinks in conventional terms about traditional encounters between the sexes, he is unconsciously consumed by prejudices, misunderstandings, the failures to communicate that plague Genly Ai and Estraven. In Genly Ai's "unrecognized anti-feminism...Le Guin manages to trap us in our own prejudices," notes critic Helen Collins in *The Nassau Review*.[5] The trait that Genly initially dislikes about Estraven isn't merely his androgyny but rather his femininity because Genly simply hasn't come to terms with—he doesn't yet like—that which is womanly. Women are "other" to him and he has no ansible to reach them. To bridge the gap he must first know there is a gap; he must first know what a woman is—or at least acknowledge that he has never known:

---

4. To use Le Guin's own description in her especially commissioned introductory essay for the Ace Books edition (New York, 1984); unnumbered second page of the introduction.

5. Helen Collins, "New Images of Sex in Science Fiction," *The Nassau Review*, Vol. 4, No. 5 (1984), 1-16.

> "Are they like a different species?"
> "No. Yes. No, of course not, not really.... Harth...I can't tell you what women are like. I never thought about it much in the abstract, you know, and—God!—by now I've practically forgotten. I've been here two years.... In a sense women are more alien to me than you are.... (pp.243-45)

He must come to terms with the woman within Estraven, and the woman within himself—and his reward is the new personal dimension that allows him to speak poignantly from the heart, to voice his sense of loss not from an act of infidelity but rather from the greatest demonstration of love, the sacrifice of Estraven's life:

> In such fortunate moments as I fall asleep I know beyond doubt what the real center of my own life is, that time which is past and lost and yet is permanent, the enduring moment, the heart of warmth. (p.240)

Thus, through Genly Ai's painful journey toward self-knowledge, Le Guin shows us that the burden of distrust toward women is society's burden. While men think they like "real" women, Le Guin seems to be suggesting that they secretly—unbeknownst even to themselves—harbor secret prejudices, secret hatreds, which they must first acknowledge and then discard if they are ever to attain the full communication of Genly and Estraven, the fulfillment of perception and love. Through the love that Genly Ai and Estraven learn to feel for one another, Le Guin demonstrates that bridges can be built between the sexes, that man need never again be "alone, with a stranger...in the heart of the Ice Age of an alien world" (p.18).

HERMETICISM AS SCIENCE: *RATS AND GARGOYLES*, BY MARY GENTLE
BY YVONNE ROUSSEAU

Mary Gentle's *Rats and Gargoyles* opens with the judicial hanging of a sow dressed in a robe embroidered with "I" for "Infanticide." Such a scene recalls the past of our own world, where in medieval times (indeed, until the nineteenth century) beasts in Britain and Europe were invested by law with human rights and responsibilities. But in the city at the heart of the world described in *Rats and Gargoyles*, the non-human animal is unexpectedly various. There, Rats walk, talk and dress like humans, are generally taller than them, and have god-given authority over them. At the other extreme from Rats are the daemon-acolytes: carnivorous winged creatures which, if petrified, would be perfect as gargoyles and which kill or carry messages in obedience to the gods' will.

The "god-dacmons" of *Rats and Gargoyles* are the thirty-six "principles that structure the world" and are known as Decans. (In astrology, a decan is one of the thirty-six equal ten-degree arcs into which the zodiac is divided.) They created humans "in Our image," and at first let them live their own lives. Then, thousands of years before the events of the novel, the Decans decided to incarnate themselves on the human world. They chose substances such as brick, granite and marble; for example, the Thirty-Sixth Decan, addressed as "Lady of the Eleventh Hour, who is Lord of the Ten Degrees of High Summer," is incarnated as a sphinx-shape of ochre bricks. The Decans created Rat-Lords to be masters of humans, and the gargoyle acolytes to punish any revolt against the new and seemingly endless human task of building around the Decans a proliferating temple-fortress known as the Fane. The chthonic idols that humans had been worshipping as gods were exiled "beneath the heart of the world," and worshippers of the human Church of Trees (a "*gaia-church*") were "degraded."

As Gentle observes in her acknowledgements, this novel has "treated Renaissance Hermetic *magia*...as one vast adventure-playground." The kind of science fiction plot in which an ordinary individual can save the universe becomes only natural when Hermetic principles rule. Because "deep structures have a power on the universe" and "*magia*-power may be heard and used up and down the Great Chain of Being," the fact that "man's a microcosm, and thus like the larger macrocosm" enables a human being to "draw down power. As above, so below." "Patterns compel, structures compel," and thus in the crisis of the novel when "the great Wheel" of the world "falters, loosens and forgets the unheard cadences of the Dance of all things" and "particles of earth and stone and bone dissolve upon the air," many groups of individuals work in different modes to fend off universal dissolution by reasserting "the deep structure of order and proportion and extravagant flamboyance" which inheres in "particles, cells, souls" and the cosmos itself.

Many individuals have also been involved (unwittingly) in producing the crisis—separately conspiring to alter the balance of power. Some of the Rats have been plotting to force the Decans to retreat to "the Celestial sphere that is Their proper habitation"; others simply want to set up a republic, deposing the traditional Rat King—an unwieldy formation of seven or eight Rats, the ends of whose tails grow together as one flesh. (The Rat King is a much more highly evolved phenomenon than the "seven rats caught in a knot" of our own world's folklore, of which Peter Ackroyd's novel *First Light* reports: "the rat king, so rare a thing in nature, is a warning of disaster and the symbol most feared by those who move from place to place.") Human beings have been plotting both to end their servitude to the Rats (who prohibit them from carrying weapons or even using money) and to end their work of building the Fane.

Above all, several individuals are aware of four unprecedented "true deaths" (where the soul as well as the body dies, thus breaking each time the Great Wheel that souls are fixed to). These have been contrived by the Twelfth Decan, an alchemist ("the Spagyrus"), who employs human servants and has perhaps been corrupted not only by incarnation in matter but also by too much human contact. The Decans tend to disagree with one another (as committee members do), and one of them is concerned enough about the Spagyrus to summon for action in the approaching crisis (beyond which even the Decans cannot foresee) two members of something Rats regard as a "mythical human organization": the Invisible College.

The "adventure-playground" approach in *Rats and Gargoyles* contrasts vividly with another novel concerned with Hermeticism: Umberto Eco's *Foucault's Pendulum*, which illuminates not only the psychological characteristics in human beings that made the Hermetic system attractive, but still more the genuine human evil that responds to the temptation of acquiring immoderate powers. In *Rats and Gargoyles* the supernatural is not (as it is in our history) a matter of doubt and conjecture: the Decans are undeniably there, and one can even view the Boat on which the dead return from their journey through the Night (coming to land speechless at first and without shadows), or see the psyche in the form of a butterfly flutter out from the lips of a corpse. Thus, readers of *Rats and Gargoyles* may feel a little glow of erudition each time they identify a source for phenomena described in the novel, but will not experience any illusion of uncovering mysteries about our own universe or our own nature (as they might, for example, in

John Crowley's novels *Little, Big* and *Aegypt*).

Instead, with her many simultaneous plots, Gentle enacts in this novel the Hermetic idea of the Dance. Two members of the Invisible College may be regarded as the novel's heroes: the female Scholar-Soldier Valentine and the lovelorn Lord-Architect Casaubon. Nevertheless, all characters tend to appear bright and equal, without perspective—their interweaving actions equally vital to the denouement. With everyone in full focus and full light, a painterly rather than a photographic effect is achieved—matching the style of an alchemical illustration to the novel "reconstructed from an illustration in *Apocrypha Mundus Subterranus*...Prague, 1589 (now lost)." But, although the Dance belongs best in the sixteenth and seventeenth centuries (to which all the novel's illustrations are ascribed), Gentle also draws on later eras to stock her adventure playground.

The technology of *Rats and Gargoyles* includes steam trains and internal-combustion engines, and the characters have concepts that in our own world arose in the nineteenth century or later: microbes, bacteria, weak forces, entropy, electrons. Still more confusingly, not only do the authorities cited by Gentle's characters belong to our own past—Cornelius, Paracelsus, Vitruvius, John Dee, Pico della Mirandola—but even our place names occur in phrases like "Bruno the Nolan" (a man born at Nola), and "the old English black bee." Nevertheless, Gentle is not providing a simple projection of an unlikely future for us: her world has five compass points (so that students are instructed: "Now draw the following quadrilateral triangle...") and, under the city, a bridge passes through the sky, with foundations of hills and buildings above it and a burning plain far below. Thus, a reader assessing this gallimaufry may conclude that the Decans ("Who create all in Their divinity") have indulged in some cosmic juggling, in addition to incarnation. As a human reminds one of them, Decans "can forget, can change [Their] nature; it's only Rats and humans that have to live with limitation."

The limitations of Rats and humans described by Gentle

include a propensity to soil one's clothes (especially if one comes near—still more if one is—the Lord-Architect Casaubon). And a woman's menstrual cycle causes her excruciating pain when a Decan chooses to move her thirty days forward in an instant. But the animal aspect of such limitations appears different in a world where divinity looks out from animal eyes: the incarnated Decans are all "beast-headed," as are the chthonic idols (who have human-shaped bodies and serpent heads). Having observed the past patriarchal tendency both to denigrate animality and to project it on to women, some feminists have chosen to investigate past preconceptions about animals, and to question whether behaviors that humans share with other animals do not include traits that we esteem highly (and even regard as uniquely human). Hence, perhaps, Gentle's beast-headed gods—and also the tails on all their new creations: the Rats, the acolytes, and the quasi-human Katayans (who come from a faraway land perhaps resembling Marco Polo's Cathay). Animal status in this novel seems not to have been thought through, however. Although the Church of Trees provides a priest for a sow's execution (described at the novel's beginning), the audience's curse on the criminal—"May your soul rot!"—is inconsistent with the doctrine that the same Church's Bishop delivers, concerning the acolytes, 369 pages later: "Animals are innocent murderers, Divine One."

Another puzzle arises from the way the dead, having passed through the Night, come to land again in physical bodies (all under the age of three) and run off into the city. Does this mean that new brothers and sisters are truly found under cabbages in this world? If there are newborn babies with new-made souls, in addition to the reincarnations returning on the Boat, then overpopulation is inevitable—especially considering that the harem of the present King of South Katay has already produced 973 daughters. (Moreover, the cabbage theory protects one from pondering how an infant Rat King might come into the world.)

Gallantry is the most consistent trait among Gentle's characters—not least in the young Katayan employed as a King's

Memory, Zar-bettu-Zekigal, an up-front lesbian whose amatory advances are made to women too preoccupied and busy to respond to them, even if they had the inclination. Indeed, with god in one's backyard, swagger is a psychological survival mode: speaking with a Decan, the Scholar-Soldier Valentine clings "to wit or a studied carelessness: some scant refuge"—and a Rat-Lord and a Katayan break into laughter (in my view, offensive) when they find that the gigantic serpent-headed idols under the city all have the same speech impediment.

Minor reversals of our own notions of order abound in this novel. Building workers on the site are correctly dressed in silks and satins, and a Mayor is well aware that he is a nobody. Members of the prestigious University of Crime distress people who understand the universe by performing impossible feats: breaking into the Fane at one of the times when it "doesn't *exist*," and dealing tarot cards from the bottom of the pack (only in an emergency, however, and because "readings influence what will come as well as being influenced *by* it"). Females equally with males are shamans, priests and soldiers. There is a strong tendency for the young to lust (unrequitedly) after those a good deal older than themselves. And although the handsome young prince of the novel achieves much that a hero-prince should, he never becomes the center of anyone's interest: this place is occupied, instead, by a man who is overweight, clumsy, and culpably unhygienic.

Despite the unfamiliarity of the novel's happenings, Gentle succeeds admirably in maintaining a sense of urgency. Her hot plague-ridden city and her predominantly wide-awake characters may leave the reader feeling somewhat like an experimental subject deprived of rapid-eye-movement sleep (the novel allows no time to pause and dream), but the constant motion and brightness (even in the Night) are in perfect harmony with the theory of the Dance that holds this world in being. It is a new experience to see Hermeticism treated as a science, rather than a way to make the reader's flesh creep.

A THOUGHT-EXPERIMENT: *SOLUTION THREE*, BY NAOMI MITCHISON
BY HELEN MERRICK

A thought-experiment in psychology and the ethics of tampering with gender and genetics, *Solution Three* could have been written yesterday, and will certainly be read tomorrow. Ursula Le Guin's back-cover endorsement highlights one of the most astonishing features of this reissued novel. Naomi Mitchison did not in fact write *Solution Three* "yesterday"; its first publication was in 1975. Much of the novel's contemporary feel results from the focus on reproductive and genetic engineering, which is such a pervasive and almost commonplace concern in today's society, but was largely hypothetical when Mitchison was writing in 1970. As Susan Squier observes in the afterword, *Solution Three* contains "a remarkable critique of reproductive technologies that would not come into wide use until the 1990s" (pp.161-2).

Mitchison's exploration of reproductive and genetic technologies and engagement with feminist theories and critiques of science ensure this book is more relevant and important to today's society than ever. The Feminist Press (of the City University of New York) is to be congratulated for giving this book a deserved second lease of life, as it was out of print in Britain since 1980. The reissue was even more timely considering the demise of the Women's Press SF imprint which did so much to recover feminist classics, including Mitchison's better known *Memoirs of a Spacewoman* (written in 1962, published in UK 1976, Women's Press, 1985).

Mitchison's background has been similarly obscured; the fact that she was renowned in the 1930s gives some indication of her longevity, as does the existence of some 80 published works ranging from historical and science fiction, poetry, drama and political writings. Whilst curiosity about the author may be slightly unfashionable in these postmodern times, Mitchison's biography is fascinating, little-known and revealing. She was born in 1897 into an educated and privileged family, with a suffragist mother and a circle of friends including Julian and Aldous Huxley and Marie Stopes, so her education and scientific curiosity were encouraged, leading to a lifelong commitment to social reform, birth control education and Scottish nationalism. Mitchison also ran as a Labour party candidate and served as a tribal adviser and "Mmarona" (mother) to the Bakgatla of Botswana in the 1960s (pp.164-5). Her social, scientific and feminist sympathies are obvious influences in her work, especially her science fiction.

Solution Three presents a future where human society has been radically reconstructed in response to the catastrophic effects of overpopulation, famine and war. A world Council has achieved this by implementing various Solutions following "The Code" instigated by prophet-like former activists (a black African male and a woman from Shetland) referred to only as "He" and "She." The population has been controlled by a popu-policy; people live in high density mega-cities designed to equalize living space, leaving the majority of land available for food production which is maximized by genetic engineering. The basic tenet of an egalitarian and non-aggressive society is underwritten by The Code which has mandated homosexuality for all, through hormonal and psychological treatments and media reinforcement. Homosexuality is now accepted as the natural state, representing "the great step in human self-knowledge and control"—the solution of society's ills through the eradication of heterosexuality (p. 14). Future generations will not result from the sexual union of men and women, but from the controlled production of clones from "His" and "Her" genes, incubated by a revered group of "Clone Mums" (the original title of the story) who give them up to communal care when infants. Heterosexuality is seen as abhorrent and unnecessary, surviving only amongst "deviants." Such deviancy persists in some backward regions which are not fully integrated, and is tolerated within this society only among the class of "Professionals." These are the technicians and scientists who, ironically, ensure the very operation of the code by providing the means to manufacture the "clones."

In *Solution Three*, Mitchison explores the possibility of using science and technology in a responsible, feminist fashion to recreate society along more egalitarian, non-aggressive and ecologically sustainable lines. In a sense it could be seen as an experiment in feminist eugenics, what Squier terms a "softer coercion of gentle eugenics" (p. 173) which nevertheless employs science and technology to manipulate human behavior in the name of a better, more humane society. Mitchison's approach is interesting because the resort to a "technological fix" has often been avoided in feminist theory. Among the few exceptions are Shulamith Firestone's *The Dialectic of Sex*, and in fiction Marge Piercy's *Woman on the Edge of Time*. Both these works are actually anticipated by Mitchison, who goes further by examining the social implications of employing such technologies even for feminist ends. Unlike Piercy and Firestone, Mitchison considers the unexpected costs and flaws of pursuing a technological solution to the excesses of patriarchy. Another important difference between this work and *Woman on the Edge of Time* is the overt conditioning of sexuality—the problems of violence and aggression are seen to require a totally new socialization process aided by technology, whereas in Piercy's utopia changes in sexuality (towards a free bisexuality) are seen to flow "naturally" from the technological innovation of exogenetic reproduction.

The relevance and success of Mitchison's writing lies in the fact that she does not provide a static and uncritical Utopian vision but rather what could be described as an ironic utopia. It becomes clear that the society of *Solution Three* is not permanent, indeed its Utopian ideals are interrogated and increasingly found wanting throughout the novel's development.

Solution Three is in many ways ahead of its time, in that it presents not only a critique of the uses and abuses of patriarchal science, but also provides a critical view of future possibilities, of the need to be aware that a feminist (or pacifist or socialist) politics does not guarantee a responsible, egalitarian science and technology. The manipulation of reproductive and genetic engineering, even for benign ends, ultimately faces severe problems—essentially the need to allow for and recognize difference—whether of race, sexuality or generation. The difficulties faced by the Council in implementing the code in regions such as Africa and the Amazon suggest that to enforce a (first world) global solution or Utopian ideal on other societies and races is still a colonial and imperialist act. Mitchison underlines this difficulty through ironic situations where the Council, who are required by the Code to eschew violence, are regrettably forced to use it on occasion, when difficult areas displaying too much "deviance" and aggression need to be contained.

The dangers inherent in genetic engineering form a significant theme in the novel. The process of constructing new plant forms for food has led to a reduction of the gene pool, and food basics are threatened by viruses which new hybrids are unable to resist. The genetic manipulation of plants provides a metaphor for the social and sexual engineering practiced by the Council, with the growing awareness that the eradication of difference is potentially harmful. Miryam, one of the "Professionals," warns "we knock out more and more human genes...and some of them might have values hidden in them which we don't know" (p. 138).

Thus the effacement of individual rights and responsibility is called into question. *Solution Three*'s universalizing of homosexuality for the health of humanity results in the stigmatizing of "deviant" forms of sexuality, resembling the condition of homosexuals in our own society. A growing sense of tolerance towards the end of the novel signals Mitchison's belief in the necessity for self-determination of sexuality. The protagonists themselves begin to recognize that Solution Three is perhaps only temporary, a means to an end, prefiguring a fourth solution where individuality may be allowed more freedom in a society that has successfully become equalitarian and humane. The clones themselves, meant to reproduce exactly and in perpetuity the ideals and actions of "Him" and Her," undergo growth and transformation. Mitchison's message is that we can never totally control our progeny—whether biological or scientific. It is vital to remain open to change.

In the end, Mitchison suggests that we cannot totally rely on "big science" and technology to fix society; that we should be wary of viewing science as the all-seeing, objective savior and not be fooled by the "god trick," as Donna Haraway puts it. When one of the councilors expresses disappointment in the forecasting performance of their computers, she is reminded that "they're only an extension of our brains." Another adds, "what they give us is logic and shape...they take away the passion that hinders us" (p.115). However, the danger of using the myth of objective science to rationalize development lies in this very sublimation of "passion," emotion and subjectivity. Mitchison shows the importance of integrating political and social critiques with the employment of technological programs of constructing a science that is responsive to social and feminist critiques.

The goal of a permeable and "situated" science is referred to in a characteristically ironic passage. One of the councilors wonders if the results of their genetic engineering could have been foreseen in order to prevent the possible catastrophe in food supply they are facing. A council historian replies:

> "It certainly was foreseen earlier...in the second
> half of the twentieth century, to be exact. There was

even what they then called a novel written about it..." (p.115).

Here Mitchison firmly situates her novel as part of the contemporary feminist critique of science and technology. True to her "prediction," *Solution Three* provides us with a fascinating vision, that with ironic humor and compassion emphasizes the vital role sf plays in considering the impact of science on human society now and in the future.

THE CAMERA SPEAKS: *AN UNUSUAL ANGLE*, BY GREG EGAN
BY VERONICA BRADY

Norstrilia Press is up to something, first with Gerald Murnane's *The Plains* (1982) and now with Greg Egan's *An Unusual Angle*. In *The Plains*, a book significantly also about a young film-maker, a group of writers appear some years after the original quarrel between the Horizonites (who "call themselves the true plainsmen, ready to push back the limits of pasturage into regions too long neglected") and the Haremen (who insisted that they were the practical ones, advancing plans for closer settlement). This new group, whose slogan is "The Horizon, After All," attempts to revive the ideals of the Horizonites, "to provoke the intellectuals of the plains to define in metaphysical terms what had previously been expressed in emotional or sentimental language." What moves them "more than wide grasslands and huge skies [is] the scant layer of haze where land and sky merged in the farthest distance." *An Unusual Angle* might have been written by one of them. Egan gets at the old familiar material, schooldays in the suburbs, and provokes his readers to redefine it. This redefinition, moreover, is not in terms of traditional metaphysics, and it certainly involves the "haze between things," the question of perception. In other words, he is pushing back the limits of literary pasturage.

This may make *An Unusual Angle* sound a difficult book.

In fact it is not, not for anyone interested in films or sf on the one hand or in an irreverent review of one's schooldays on the other—I have already met several people who insist that Egan's school is their school or the school they taught in:

> The swimming carnival is an extremely divisive event.
> Firstly, we are split into factions (my dictionary thinks that these are generally subversive, but alas it is not the case): four groups named after worthy local historical (i.e. dead) persons. Each faction is associated with a colour, the idea being that students can perceive the fact of their group identity on a primitive sensory level, without any need for inconvenient and undesirable higher cerebral intervention.
> Secondly, we are split according to function into three groups. Competitors are wonderful, enthusiastic, vibrant, and *alive* people, potential Olympic gold medallists, Rhodes scholars, MHRs, senators. Rotary Club presidents; proud, loyal citizens who *give* unselfishly to their community of their time, effort, and high spirits. Cheering-squad members are quite wonderful, pretty enthusiastic, fairly vibrant, and *supportive* people, potential Oscar winners, law students, senior public servants, company directors. Rotary Club vice-presidents; reliable, sincere citizens who *devote* themselves to their community with commitment, energy, and level-headed vigour.
> The remainder, the unwilling spectators, are unpleasant, unco-operative, dull, and *disruptive* people, potential communists, environmentalists, homosexuals, authors, union leaders, criminals, rock singers; sick, alienated people who either *ignore* or *disturb* the community with their protests, cynicism, and rash actions.

The book is also a grist for the Deconstructionist mill. Since it is difficult to say what it is about, it directs its attention at itself, a tale full of sound and fury signifying, if not nothing, then merely itself, its own organizing principles, its perceptions of itself perceiving. (James Joyce would have been pleased.) The narrator has refined himself out of existence and into a film camera, substituting for personal memory the memory of the films of a decade—*2001* (of course!), *If...*, *American Werewolf*, *Summerfield*, *Slaughterhouse Five*, *The Graduate*, and so on and so on.

> I have been producing high-quality (really) 35 mm films practically since I was four years old (when I grew the camera), and I have not sold one of them to a major (or even a minor) distributor. This is mainly (entirely) because all the film is exposed, developed, printed, and edited inside my head. And I can't persuade any reputable brain surgeons that they should operate and remove a few of the better final prints. I have limited storage space, so I make only two release prints of each film. The brain surgeons say I can't pay them, and I promise them enormous percentages of my takings once I can get some prints out of my brain. But they have no faith.

Heroes and heroines give way to methods of composition—hence the point of the title. It's therefore not a book for the conventional. It's a book for those prepared to acknowledge the dues to be paid to the movie camera, to radio and the magical simultaneity of electronics. But it is a book for those who enjoy Lewis Carroll—*Alice in Wonderland* and *Through the Looking Glass* paid these dues even before their claims were made, and the White Rabbit zooms in and out of Egan's book to remind us what we need to be rescued from, a tyrannical definition of reality:

There is Metalwork, which consists solely of taking large pieces of metal and filing them into large piles of fine shiny dust which adheres to the lubricating grease which is everywhere in the room. I ask why we do this, and I am told that it is training for what goes on in the factories, which is fair enough. I am not permitted to whistle in Metalwork, but I do not ask if whistling is permitted in factories.

This is how I spend my days, in exchange for things I do not need, things I do not want, but what else can I do?

—Duck!

shrieks the rabbit, coming straight out of the sun and passing an inch above my cowering form. What does he want (mean (plan (change)))?

2001 is not far away. The starting point is not the observation and imitation of nature but within the mind.

It is very hard to make lumps when everything is so cyclic and several weeks (precisely) might shoot past in a subjective instant (exactly), and I would notice no change at all. Subjective space-time is a strange place to navigate, but it is the only manifold that really matters (cheer up Minkowski, nobody's perfect) and I need beacons, regions of high experience-density which I can see from afar to determine just where I am and where I'm going. If I wander too far along my world-line without leaving lumps behind like crumbs in the forest, then I will end up with nothing in sight, and the featureless region around me will be free to distort, to expand and contract as it chooses, and living will be like walking blind down a huge intestine with no idea of my speed, position, or destination.

Lumps are very, very important.

> Sometimes I can still detect the lump of my conception, and more often that of my birth, but such sightings are rare and growing less frequent. The lumps of my earliest childhood form a tiny but perfect jewel-like constellation, formed as best as I could to mimic that of my womb-time. I tried to form the pattern a third time, but botched it, which sometimes makes me very sad.
>
> I wonder about the lump of death. Will it be so bright as to obscure all those which came before? Will it be a single point, or an awesome, complex structure? What colour will it be? What colour is death?

Nothing here precedes this perceiving; story-telling becomes, as John Berger says, the art of letting the story unfold in time while letting the listener or reader become aware of what it's like when time is folded. Egan's world may be about things most of us know or have known—schools, films, swimming carnivals, boring holidays, buses, and TV ads—but what he is interested in is that horizon, in Gerald Murnane's sense, the point at which the familiar becomes strange.

> Often unpromising material can be made to stand out by catching it from the right angle to give the greatest contrast and the sharpest relief, but this can only be achieved at the time of experiencing it, because there is no ingenious process or method to alter the angle of a shot after it has been taken.
>   —Ladies and gentlemen....
> says the rabbit, on top of the flag pole.
>   —Mesdames et Messieurs, Damen und Herren....
> says the rabbit, doing a very good Joel Grey.
>   —Allow me to present the one, the only, the sensational, the fabulous....

> Carbon arc spotlight brighter than the sun beams down from the top of the pole, blue dust motes fill the lightcone, all else pales in comparison with:
> —Patch of Lawn!

Crazy? Not if you begin to think about the boundary between reality and illusion—so often ignored or trespassed on. What we see and what we understand or experience are not immutably fixed; the world is as we imagine it to be. Seeing is a transitive verb, it links our notions of the way things are and ought to be with the ambiguous information our senses bring to produce a "picture" of the world:

> If I look at the clouds long enough I am always amazed that primitive people didn't think they were solid structures floating around in the air (perhaps some did, but I have never heard of it). Of course, many types of clouds are obviously intangible, insubstantial...but not all that rarely there are ones which look so solid that I find it hard to persuade myself that they are not enormous floating castles and mountains and creatures. The wind pushes them along without changing their shapes at all, and I can imagine them rushing overhead at incredible speeds like the stone head from *Zardoz*.

It is no accident that both Greg Egan's hero and Gerald Murnane's are film-makers. Film has altered the boundaries between illusion and reality, between mind and sense. As Egan sees it, the alteration is in the direction of freedom. The school, metaphor of the world as prison, becomes metaphor of release. But the way out is imaginary—not as the hero hypothetically essays it, with a *razor*, in the last chapter—through the mind, the peak of consciousness that plays with the contents of "reality" and thus, destroying matter-of-fact activity, produces a new kind of activity—even at a school sports day:

Free will. Mmmm. Lucky for me that I was born after the discovery of quantum mechanics, for the clear impossibility of such a thing under Newtonian mechanics would have depressed me constantly. Maybe the cheering-squad members are just no good at manipulating the wave-functions of the constituents of their brains, and leave everything up to chance and external influences. A brief warm sympathy floods me, then is gone. I will teach you all how to change that; I will ignore you. Despise you. Stay away! They stay away anyway, oblivious. Me and my silly delusions of altruistic grandeur.

A witch meets my eye and cackles hideously. I shudder and divert light around her, making her vanish, almost: an uneasy patch of disturbing distortion takes her place.

An Unusual Angle sets the mind free to pursue a course of discovery of the self and of the world's possibilities. It is also fun to read.

HACKING THE SPEW: TECHNOLOGY AND ANXIETY IN NEAL STEPHENSON'S *SNOW CRASH* AND *THE DIAMOND AGE*
BY TALIA EILON

Introduction

Neal Stephenson's science fiction novels, *Snow Crash* (1992) and *The Diamond Age* (1995), were both published in the wake of the 1980s cyberpunk movement. As is to be expected, his writing forms part of the evolution of the genre of science fiction from that point forward, and displays certain attributes of the cyberpunk style. Bruce Sterling, one of the writers who initiated the movement, describes some of its characteristics:

> For the cyberpunks...technology is visceral. It is not the bottled genie of remote Big Science boffins; it is pervasive, utterly intimate. Not outside us, but next to us. Under our skin; often, inside our minds.... Certain central themes spring up repeatedly in cyberpunk. The theme of body invasion: prosthetic limbs, implanted circuitry, cosmetic surgery, genetic alteration. The

even more powerful theme of mind invasion: brain-computer interfaces, artificial intelligence, neurochemistry—techniques radically redefining the nature of humanity, the nature of self.[6]

Sterling remarks that cyberpunk is fascinated with body invasion and mind invasion, describing futuristic technology as having no respect for human boundaries, neither physical nor metaphysical. Cyberpunk, as well as much of the science fiction that has come since, is fascinated with the permeability of the human, exploring the impact this has on our understanding of what being human means, and what the boundaries of that understanding are. Such questions are framed in futuristic eras in which technology is not only ubiquitous, but also invasive.

In this respect Stephenson's writing draws heavily on the tradition of cyberpunk literature. While it is not always a central theme in his science fiction novels, the relationship between humans and technology is certainly a recurrent issue. The attitudes towards technology displayed in Stephenson's writing are problematic: there is evidence of an enthusiastic technophilia, not unlike that visible in much cyberpunk literature. Yet at the same time there are also traces of uneasiness and anxiety concerning the way that this technology affects what it means to be human.

The reason for this uneasiness, I will argue, lies in Stephenson's understanding of what it means to be human. There is evidence in his novels that suggests an underlying adherence to the presuppositions of humanism, and it is when these are introduced to a futuristic and technologically advanced setting that incongruities come to the fore. The anomalies arise out of an inconsistency of value systems. Stephenson adeptly explores the nature of heavily technologically-mediated societies, investigating the political, cultural and personal ramifications of these scenarios, but in an ideological sense there appears to be little

---

6. Bruce Sterling, "Preface," *Mirrorshades: The Cyberpunk Anthology*, ed. Bruce Sterling (1986; London: HarperCollins, 1994), p. xi.

development beyond contemporary thinking. Because modern values are simply mapped directly onto a future setting, we are left with a situation in which technology has called into question what it means to be human, but the ideological principles providing an answer are conspicuously out of date. The tension which results from this incongruity is dealt with in Stephenson's novels in a number of interesting ways, and an exploration of these tactics is the subject of my discussion.

It is striking that Stephenson's writing reflects conservative values when taken in the context of his upbringing. Stephenson describes himself as coming from "a science oriented family.... My father taught engineering as a professor and his father was a physics professor. My mother is a biochemist and the daughter of a biochemist."[7] Despite this background, his descriptions of near-future, technologically-mediated society are informed by popular attitudes, rather than scientific discourse. Since I am arguing that Stephenson's writing is reliant on popular perceptions of the relationship between technology and humanity, a preliminary examination of these perceptions is in order. The word "technology" can itself be ambiguous, since popular usage can deviate considerably from its more formal definition. Strictly speaking, "technology" refers to anything artificially constructed by humans, which in contemporary western society renders the term extremely broad. In the popular lexicon, however, the word is used in a far narrower sense, carrying connotations of the unfamiliar and the technical. Usually, it tends to refer to inventions which are uncommon, novel or indecipherable, especially those things perceived to be alienated from the human and the mundane.

Taken to an extreme, this sense of unfamiliarity can develop into mistrust, resentment, or even fear of the technological. Certainly there is a palpable undercurrent of luddite sentiment in technologically advanced societies, which is evident in the texts these societies produce. An infamous example is the

---

7. Catherine Asaro, "A Conversation with Neal Stephenson," *SF Site* (September 1999), p1. http://www.sfsite.com/10b/ns67.htm

Unabomber Manifesto, which has attracted interest for its analysis of contemporary industrial society.[8] Similarly, Bill Joy has written an essay on the dangers of technology for *Wired* magazine.[9] Another area which commonly deals with pessimistic visions of the near future is the speculative genre of science fiction, and especially the cyberpunk movement. In fact, the concept of a technologically-fueled dystopia is so widespread in the genre it is almost a defining characteristic. The opening paragraphs of William Gibson's *Virtual Light* provide an evocative example of this dystopian vision:

> The courier presses his forehead against layers of glass, argon, high-impact plastic. He watches a gunship traverse the city's middle distance like a hunting wasp, death slung beneath its thorax in a smooth black pod.
>
> Hours earlier, missiles have fallen in a northern suburb; seventy-three dead, the kill as yet unclaimed. But here the mirrored ziggurats down Lázaro Cárdinas flow with the luminous flesh of giants, shunting out the night's barrage of dreams to the waiting avenidas—business as usual, world without end.
>
> The air beyond the window touches each source of light with a faint hepatic corona, a tint of jaundice edging imperceptibly into brownish translucence. Fine dry flakes of fecal snow, billowing in from the sewage flats, have lodged in the lens of night.
>
> Closing his eyes, he centers himself in the background hiss of climate-control.[10]

---

8. "The Unabomber's Manifesto: Industrial Society and Its Future," http://www.panix.com/~clays/Una/

9. Bill Joy, "Why the Future Doesn't Need Us," *Wired* 8.04 (April 2000). http://www.wired.com/wired/archive/8.04/joy.html

10. William Gibson, *Virtual Light* (1993; New York: Bantam Spectra, 1994), p.1.

Gibson's description of a ruined environment forms a backdrop for the courier's implied sense of alienation. As Veronica Hollinger notes, "Gibson's [writing] invokes a rhetoric of technology to express the natural world in a metaphor which blurs the distinction between the organic and the artificial."[11] Gibson's writing, she says, "evokes the anxiety of this new era" (Hollinger, p.38). The technology surrounding the courier not only seals and protects, with its "high-impact plastic," but also poses a silent and lethal threat in the form of machines like the gunship, ostensibly designed to serve humanity. A common thread in pessimistic predictions such as this one is the way in which technology is depicted as obliquely usurping human potency and self-determination. Sometimes technology is a tool for the spread of political and social decline, as in films like Terry Gilliam's *Brazil* (1985), but often it is the machines themselves which directly threaten the survival of humanity as a species, as in *Terminator* (1984) and *The Matrix* (1999). In these films there is a clear anxiety expressed about the future development of technology and the decreasing agency of humanity. As in the quotations from *Virtual Light*, these films make clear the correlation between the ubiquity of technology and the impotence of humans. Technology can be frightening because it has the potential to one day compete for—and attain—superiority over its creators, leaving us helpless to reassert autonomy and agency.

Stephenson's novels never address the issue of a direct conflict between humanity and technology, but the underlying mistrust of the technological which originates from this anxiety is nevertheless present. Instead of being overtly expressed, the mistrust is repeatedly implied through Stephenson's treatment of key issues. A good comparative example is the construction of "cyberspace," the term coined by Gibson in *Neuromancer* to describe the illusion of space created when the user is interfaced with computer networks. In cyberpunk fiction, cyberspace is often presented as a visual depiction of pure information

---

11. Veronica Hollinger, "Cybernetic Deconstructions: Cyberpunk and Postmodernism," *Mosaic* 23.2 (1990), pp.30-31.

through which the user can move formlessly, as though having transcended the body:

> The matrix is an abstract representation of the relationships between data systems. Legitimate programmers jack into their employers' sector of the matrix and find themselves surrounded by bright geometrics representing the corporate data.
> Towers and fields of it ranged in the colourless nonspace of the simulation matrix, the electronic consensus-hallucination that facilitates the handling and exchange of massive quantities of data...the crowded matrix, monochrome nonspace where the only stars are dense concentrations of information, and high above it all burn corporate galaxies and the cold spiral arms of military systems.[12]

Here, cyberspace is wholly abstract, a set of symbolic representations used to organize information. In *Snow Crash*, however, Stephenson chooses to describe cyberspace as a very literal form of virtual reality. Called the Metaverse, it is modeled on a city and rendered with complete realism right down to the finest details:

> Hiro is approaching the Street. It is the Broadway, the Champs Élysées of the Metaverse.... The dimensions of the Street are fixed by a protocol, hammered out by the computer-graphics ninja overlords of the Association for Computing Machinery's Global Multimedia Protocol Group.... Like any place in Reality, the Street is subject to development. Developers can build their own small streets feeding off the main one....

---

12. William Gibson, "Burning Chrome," *Burning Chrome*. (1986; London: Grafton Books, 1990), pp 196-197.

> Hiro has a house in a neighbourhood just off the busiest part of the Street...people in Hiro's neighbourhood are very good programmers, so it's tasteful. The houses look like real houses. There are a couple of Frank Lloyd Wright reproductions and some fancy Victoriana....
>
> [The Street] is a hundred metres wide, with a narrow monorail track running down the middle. The monorail is a free piece of public utility software that enables users to change their location on the street rapidly and smoothly. A lot of people just ride back and forth on it, looking at the sights. When Hiro first saw this place, ten years ago, the monorail hadn't been written yet; he and his buddies had to write car and motorcycle software in order to get around.[13]

Rather than creating an abstract realm of information exchange, Stephenson uses cyberspace to create a kind of alternative reality. This is striking, considering that cyberspace is a medium that allows limitless creativity in the construction of entire worlds. The Metaverse, "like any place in Reality," is based upon stringent parameters and laws, both social and physical. Even the activities of the people who enter it reflect this realism: rather than manipulating theoretical packets of data in a nonspace, people in the Metaverse spend their time riding the monorail and "looking at the sights" as though they were real tourists visiting a real city.

The primary reason for this realism is its ability to mask the fact that the Metaverse is only a representation. Within such a detailed and internally consistent simulation, it is easy to forget that one's reality is technologically mediated, that this is, after all, a false world constructed by a computer. At moments when this veneer of realism is shattered, "[i]t breaks the metaphor.... It reminds all [the Metaverse's] patrons that they are living in a

---

13. Neal Stephenson, *Snow Crash* (1992; New York: Bantam Spectra, 1993), pp.24-27, ch 3.

fantasy world. People hate to be reminded of this" (*Snow Crash*, p.102). The hatred felt when people find evidence of the inauthenticity of their reality, and the effort expended to avoid that occurrence, indicates an uneasiness about the role of technology in people's sensory experiences. In Stephenson's novels people are willing to be part of the Metaverse, but only if great care is taken to mask the fact that this sensory experience is computer-generated.

An especially telling aspect of this is the way in which people themselves inhabit this space: avatars are "the audio-visual bodies that people use to communicate with each other in the Metaverse" (*Snow Crash*, p.36). In the case of avatars, the user creates their very identity through the computer. One's avatar is not simply a question of sensory experience, but the creation of an identity and all that this entails. It is the users' means of understanding and representing themselves within the Metaverse. Accordingly, the stakes are much higher, and the question of maintaining realism becomes far more crucial.

Stephenson's first description of avatars seems simple and straightforward, belying the complexity of the issues at stake:

> Your avatar can look any way you want it to, up to the limitations of your equipment. If you're ugly, you can make your avatar beautiful. If you've just gotten out of bed, your avatar can still be wearing beautiful clothes and professionally applied make up. You can look like a gorilla or a dragon or a giant talking penis in the Metaverse. Spend five minutes walking down the Street and you will see all of these. (*Snow Crash*, p.36)

Initially it appears that an avatar's appearance is wholly dependent on the user's taste and whim, a means of expressing oneself through visual metaphor. Stephenson later reveals, however, that there is a strict and unspoken hierarchy among avatars, heavily reliant on the user's technical proficiency:

> Most hacker types don't go in for garish avatars, because they know that it takes a lot more sophistication to render a realistic human face than a talking penis. Kind of the way people who really know clothing can appreciate the fine details that separate a cheap gray wool suit from an expensive hand-tailored gray wool suit. (*Snow Crash*, p.36)

It is here that Stephenson reveals the values upon which this hierarchy is structured. Quite simply, the most impressive avatars are those that most closely resemble a real human. In other words, an avatar is judged by its ability to disguise the technological medium through which the user is mediated. Avatars that fail to do this, and make obvious their mediation through technology, are regarded with contempt:

> ...black-and-white people—persons who are accessing the Metaverse through cheap public terminals, and who are rendered in jerky, grainy black and white.... Talking to a black-and-white on the Street is like talking to a person who has his face stuck in a xerox machine, repeatedly pounding the copy button, while you stand by the output tray pulling the sheets out one at a time and looking at them. (*Snow Crash*, p.41)

Black and white people suffer social prejudice for deeper reasons. These avatars are ostracized and disadvantaged not simply because of the way they look, but because of what they represent within the virtual world:

> As soon as she steps out into the Street, people start giving her these looks. The same kind of looks that people give her when she walks through the worsted-wool desolation of the Westlake Corporate Park in her dynamic blue-and-orange Kourier gear. She knows that the people in the Street are giving her dirty looks

because she's just coming in from a shitty public terminal. She's a trashy black-and-white person. (*Snow Crash*, p.220)

The description of black-and-white avatars as "trashy" is interesting in itself. In this context, it can be read as carrying associations with White Trash, especially since the novel is set in North America. This association has the effect of equating unsophisticated avatars with an entire tradition of socially and economically low-class white Americans, further justifying the contempt black-and-white avatars receive. The prejudice aimed at avatars that break the metaphor of the Metaverse is equated with the prejudice incurred by the economically disadvantaged and socially ostracized.

As well as appearance, an avatar's behavior also raises questions about the relationship between humans and technology. Once again realism is privileged, and the emulation of reality is paramount. Hiro, one of the hackers that helped to found the Metaverse, personally takes great pains to cover up an oversight in its design. When his avatar wins a swordfight, he is faced with the problem of concealing his opponent's "corpse," for it demonstrates—unacceptably—the unrealistic nature of avatar physiology:

> The Nipponese businessman lies cut in segments on The Black Sun's floor. Surprisingly (he looks so real when he's in one piece), no flesh, blood, or organs are visible through the new cross-sections that Hiro's sword made through his body. He is nothing more than a thin shell of epidermis, an incredibly complex inflatable doll. But the air does not rush out of him, he fails to collapse, and you can look into the aperture of a sword cut and see, instead of bones and meat, the back of the skin on the other side.
>
> It breaks the metaphor. The avatar is not acting like a real body. It reminds all The Black Sun's patrons that

> they are living in a fantasy world. People hate to be reminded of this.... Avatars are not supposed to die. Not supposed to fall apart. The creators of the Metaverse had not been morbid enough to foresee a demand for this sort of thing.... So Hiro had to kludge something together, in order that the Metaverse would not, over time, become littered with inert, dismembered avatars that never decayed.... Disposal of hacked-up avatars is taken care of by Graveyard Daemons, a new Metaverse feature that Hiro had to invent. (*Snow Crash*, p.102)

Hiro specifically created the Graveyard Daemons as a means of disguising the inauthenticity of avatar physiology. The dismembered avatar, revealed to be nothing more than "a thin shell of epidermis," needs to be disposed of as quickly as possible, lest it remind other users that their perceived experiences are computer generated.

I have used virtual reality as an illustrative example, but this anxiety about the role of humans in a technologically mediated environment is evident throughout Stephenson's novels. Since the Metaverse is a microcosm of Reality, the anxiety evident there also exists in the larger technologically-mediated environment of a futuristic society. While the example of avatars is a literal case of human mediation through technology, in most instances the interaction between humans and machines is more subtle, and the boundaries separating them more clear.

The basic concern that seems to be at work here is the idea that interaction with technology will somehow threaten what makes us essentially human. The humanist tradition defines our quintessence through the mind and through the body, and the idea that the essence of humanity could be compromised through interaction with technology is terrifying. The anxiety evident in Stephenson's work centers around the issue of the human body and mind, and the way that the increasing sophistication of technology breaches their boundaries and compromises their sanctity. It is this focus on preserving the quintessence of humanity, coupled with an underlying suspicion towards the role of technology, that marks Stephenson's novels as upholding the presuppositions of humanism.

Extrapolating upon the anxiety of technology invalidating human essence leads to an anxiety about technology completely supplanting humanity altogether. In contemporary western society technology has not yet reached a level of sophistication that justifies any such cause for alarm, but it is easy to envisage a future scenario in which this could become the case. Since Stephenson's science fiction is concerned with just such a scenario, the issue of technology threatening humanity comes into question. Realism and credibility dictate that stories set in the future concern themselves with all manner of technological innovations, but the idea of such inventions superseding and robbing us of our essential humanity is frightening. In the case of most cyberpunk stories, the future is portrayed in very pessimistic terms, as if the authors in this movement were resigned to the idea of humanity falling into the hands of its own creations. But Stephenson does not take a pessimistic approach to the future, and is therefore obliged to resolve this issue by other means.

I will be examining the means by which Stephenson resolves these issues. My analysis of the way that Stephenson's work expresses humanist ideals is divided into two parts: an examination of the relationship between technology and the human body in *Snow Crash*, identifying two contradictory ways that Stephenson addresses this issue, and a consideration of the way that technology threatens the human mind in *The Diamond Age*.

1: Technology and the Human Body in *Snow Crash*

Three theorists who have published articles on *Snow Crash* have all included the novel as part of a larger discussion, rather than taking it as their main focus. In his article "Hacking the Brainstem: Postmodern Metaphysics and Stephenson's *Snow Crash*," David Porush explores the role of irrationality as a form of transcendence in both ancient texts and postmodern science fiction, closing his discussion with *Snow Crash* as an illustrative example. Stuart Moulthrop's article "No War Machine" includes a brief critique of Stephenson's book as one of three science fiction novels, which forms part of a broader discussion on hypertextuality. In her article "The Posthumanist Body: Inscription and Incorporation in *Galatea 2.2* and *Snow Crash*," N. Katherine Hayles discusses the novel as a means of examining the posthumanist body in modern science fiction. While Hayles compares the posthumanist understanding of the body to computer systems, this is the closest any of these theorists come to discussing Stephenson's treatment of the body. None of them, in fact, pay a great deal of attention to the role of technology in the novel, nor to the attitudes Stephenson displays towards the technological through his writing. Stephenson's novels are characteristically dense with ideas worthy of exploration, resulting in a lack of specific interest in academic writing to his attitudes towards the interaction of humans and machines.

Snow Crash was Stephenson's first science fiction novel, set in North America in the very near future. While there is never any mention of date, the setting is marked by several characters' descriptions of their parents' or grandparents' experiences in the Second World War. The novel tells the story of Hiro Protagonist and his sometime business partner Y.T. ("Yours Truly") as they attempt to foil the plans of L. Bob Rife. Rife, an international telecommunications mogul, has discovered the secrets of ancient Sumerian magic, and intends to use a mimetic virus to turn the world's population into mindless drones under his control. The virus, known as Snow Crash, can infect both humans and computers. It is circulated in various ways: as a drug, a hypertext document, a bitmap of binary code comprehensible only to programmers, a surgical implant in the brain, or through infected blood. Its distribution is aided by Raven, a murderous Aleut who is hell-bent on bombing America.

These characters are emblematic of all humanity, and as such their relationship with technology in the novel is characteristic of the larger attitudes displayed towards the interaction of humans and technology in the real world. As I said earlier, humanist thought marks the body as an emblem of human essence. In its unmediated state, whole and individuated, the human body is understood to be a kind of physical manifestation of the mind, a tactile representation of the self. Whilst it is not pivotal to the humanist notion of essentialism, it certainly deserves consideration as a defining characteristic of humanity's quintessence. Hollinger identifies "the human body [as] the sacred icon of the essential self" (Hollinger, p.33). Stephenson's writing appears to adhere to this understanding of the human body, but the futuristic technology he describes poses a threat to its sanctity. This is primarily due to the ability of this technology to transgress physical boundaries and colonise the body. In cases where this has happened, the boundary separating body and machine becomes blurred, and the once clearly defined body is compromised for no longer being complete and autonomous. Humanist thought holds the view that "notions of a human nature [are] determined by a 'physical essence' of the human" (Hollinger, p.35). Since the body is thought to define the existence of the essential self, any compromising of the body's sanctity by the invasion of technology holds dire consequences for the integrity of the self.

There is an underlying sympathy for humanist principles in Stephenson's work, which is problematic when taken in the context of futuristic, technologically mediated societies. There is a tension created between the need to protect the boundaries of the body and the need to depict a credible future replete with pervasive and visceral technology. In order to extenuate this tension, the threat posed by technology needs to be in some way deflected. My reading of Stephenson's novels identifies two methods used to achieve this which, ironically, contradict one another.

Stephenson's first tactic involves a clear separation of the spheres of technology and humanity. This results in their interaction no longer being an issue, since the boundary separating machine and human remains clear and unproblematic. In contrast, the other method employed in these novels is the equation of technology with corporeality, which has the effect of diffusing the threat technology appears to pose. I will explore these methods in turn.

In Stephenson's work the sanctity of the human body is protected by an exaggeration of the distinction between humans and machines. In this context, Stephenson makes use of the word "technology" in its popular sense, taking it to mean any unfamiliar, alienating or imposing machinery. In its most literal form, this exaggerated distinction manifests as an aversion to physically invasive technology.

One example of this separation of body and machine is illustrated in Stephenson's description of the human/computer interface, especially the means by which characters access the Metaverse. In many science fiction stories, access to cyberspace requires the implanting of technology into the body, at times even directly interfacing with the brain:

> The brainworm did give you an advantage on the nets, let you use the full range of your senses, not just sight and sound, to interpret the virtual world.... The worm entailed risks: implantation and direct-to-brain wiring was always tricky.... The dollie-slots and the associated implants didn't touch the brain, ran along existing nerves.[14]

---

14. Melissa Scott, *Trouble and Her Friends* (New York: Bantam Spectra, 1994), pp.29-30.

Here, the machine is directly inserted into the user's body, so that the two are irrevocably intertwined. In scenarios such as these, where parts of a computer's hardware are directly inserted into the brain, the distinction between human and machine becomes blurred. The subject literally becomes part of the computer, problematizing ideas of human control over, and independence from, the machines we have created. In *Snow Crash*, however, Stephenson easily overcomes the problematic and highly confronting issues of human/computer interfaces by sidestepping them. Instead of requiring implants and invasive surgery, characters access the Metaverse by wholly superficial means:

> Through the use of electronic mirrors inside the computer, this beam is made to sweep back and forth across the lenses of Hiro's goggles, in much the same way as the electron beam in a television paints the inner surface of the eponymous Tube. The resulting image hangs in space in front of Hiro's view of Reality.
>
> By drawing a slightly different image in front of each eye, the image can be made three-dimensional. By changing the image seventy-two times a second, it can be made to move. By drawing the moving three-dimensional image at a resolution of 2K pixels on a side, it can be as sharp as the eye can perceive, and by pumping stereo digital sound through the little earphones, the moving 3-D pictures can have a perfectly realistic soundtrack.
>
> So Hiro's not actually here at all. He's in a computer-generated universe that his computer is drawing onto his goggles and pumping into his earphones. (*Snow Crash*, pp.32-34)

Stephenson's depiction of access to the Metaverse is no more invasive than watching television or listening to music. As Stuart Moulthrop says in "No War Machine":

> [U]nlike Gibson's "cyberspace" (which glosses over the complexities of brain-to-machine connection), Stephenson's new medium simply extends existing video technologies. Computer-generated images are projected onto the user's retina in a mild advance on current head-mounted displays.[15]

The wearing of goggles and earphones is a sight that has long been naturalized in contemporary western society, and for the most part never raises problematic issues of human identity in a technologically mediated environment. The Metaverse interface is so superficial, in fact, that it can be easily interrupted by Reality. There is certainly no danger of the boundary between human and computer being blurred in this scenario, since the human is never sufficiently enveloped by the technological for this to be a possibility. Y.T.'s experiences with the Metaverse illustrate this well, for when someone wants her attention there is very little she can do to prevent them from interrupting her activities in virtual reality:

> ...she begins to hear deep rumbling noises—Reality noises—from outside. Sounds like a cross between a machine gun and a buzz saw.... Someone is tapping her on the shoulder. Some suit who has an early morning appointment in the Metaverse, figures that whatever this Kourier is doing can't be all that important. She ignores it for a minute.
> Then Hiro's office goes out of focus, jumps up in the air like it is painted on a window shade, and she's looking into the face of a guy. (*Snow Crash*, p.420)

As this shows, the users' connections with the Metaverse are so tenuous that the link can be severed by any kind of

---

15. Stuart Moulthorp, "No War Machine," *Reading Matters*, ed. Joseph Tabbi and Michael Wutz (Ithaca and London: Cornell University Press, 1997), p. 284.

interference, even a loud noise coming in from Reality. External interruptions can, at any time, extract a user from the Metaverse and forcibly reinstate Reality, an occurrence unheard of where physically invasive interfaces are involved.

In keeping with the trend of non-invasive technology, even characters who heavily rely on computer technology wear their machines on their bodies rather than making use of implants:

> Gargoyles represent the embarrassing side of the Central Intelligence Corporation. Instead of using laptops, they wear their computers on their bodies, broken up into separate modules that hang on the waist, on the back, on the headset. They serve as human surveillance devices, recording everything around them. Nothing looks stupider; these getups are the modern-day equivalent of the slide-rule scabbard or the calculator pouch on the belt, marking the user as belonging to a class that is at once above and far below human society. They...embody the worst stereotype of the CIC stringer. They draw all of the attention. The payoff for this self-imposed ostracism is that you can be in the Metaverse all the time, and gather intelligence all the time.
>
> The CIC brass can't stand these guys because they upload staggering quantities of useless information to the database, on the off chance that some of it will eventually be useful. It's like writing down the licence number of every car you see on your way to work each morning, just in case one of them will be involved in a hit-and-run accident. Even the CIC database can only hold so much garbage. So, usually, these habitual gargoyles get kicked out of the CIC before too long. (*Snow Crash*, pp.123-124)

Stephenson's description of these compulsive "human surveillance devices" is far from flattering. Apart from being socially ostracized and detested by the very corporation that employs them, gargoyles are described as looking incredibly stupid for wearing their computers. In a genre that tends to be fascinated with the possibilities of invasive technology and cyborg bodies in general, Stephenson's gargoyles are singular for their awkwardness and inelegance. In contrast, the characters featured in cyberpunk fiction often display a characteristic flair. As Sterling remarks, "the cyberpunks...are in love with style, and are (some say) fashion-conscious to a fault" (Sterling, p.viii). A prime example of this stylishness is Molly, a character who appears in several of Gibson's stories and is clearly romanticized for having implanted technology:

> She was barely inside my fixed field of vision, a thin girl with mirrored glasses, her dark hair cut in a rough shag. She wore black leather, open over a T-shirt slashed diagonally with stripes of red and black. "Eight thou a gram weight."
> Lewis snorted his exasperation and tried to slap her out of the chair. Somehow he didn't quite connect, and her hand came up and seemed to brush his wrist as it passed. Bright blood sprayed the table. He was clutching his wrist white-knuckle tight, blood trickling from between his fingers.
> But hadn't her hand been empty?
> ...She stood. She was wearing leather jeans the color of dried blood. And I saw for the first time that the mirrored lenses were surgical inlays, the silver rising smoothly from her high cheekbones, sealing her eyes in their sockets. I saw my new face twinned there....
> And she showed me her hands, fingers slightly spread. Her fingers were slender, tapered, very white against the polished burgundy nails. Ten blades snicked

straight out from their recesses beneath her nails, each one a narrow, double-edged scalpel in pale blue steel.[16]

As is common in cyberpunk fiction, Gibson's description of his surgically-enhanced heroine imbues her with a lethal grace as alluring as it is threatening. That Stephenson should deviate from this trend so conspicuously indicates a clear rejection of the values inherent in cyberpunk's literary style. The absence of romanticized cyborg bodies is once again indicative of a strong desire to keep the body clearly separate from invasive technology.

While Stephenson's depictions of the future favor superficial interfaces, this is not to say that they contain no instances of physical invasion by technology. But in the cases when this does occur, the breaching of corporeal boundaries is depicted as a distasteful physical violation. Far from being romanticized and celebrated the way it is in Gibson's fiction, the technologically enhanced body in *Snow Crash* is regarded as freakish and disgusting:

> Where the driver's seat ought to be, there is a sort of neoprene pouch about the size of a garbage can suspended from the ceiling by a web of straps, shock cords, tubes, wires, fiber-optic cables, and hydraulic lines. It is swathed in so much stuff that it is hard to make out its actual outlines.
>
> At the top of this pouch, Y.T. can see a patch of skin with some black hair around it—the top of a balding man's head. Everything else, from the temples downward, is encased in an enormous goggle/mask/headphone/feeding-tube unit, held onto his head by smart straps that are constantly tightening and loosening themselves to keep the device comfortable and properly positioned.

---

16. Willliam Gibson, "Johnny Mnemonic," *Burning Chrome* (1986; London: Grafton Books, 1990, pp.18-21.

> Below this, on either side, where you'd sort of expect to see arms, huge bundles of wires, fiber optics, and tubes run up out of the floor and are seemingly plugged into Ng's shoulder sockets. There is a similar arrangement where his legs are supposed to be attached, and more stuff going into his groin and hooked up to various locations on his torso. The entire thing is swathed in a one-piece coverall, a pouch, larger than his torso ought to be, that is constantly bulging and throbbing as though alive.
> ..."Please excuse my appearance," he says, after a couple of awkward minutes. "My helicopter caught fire during the evacuation of Saigon in 1974." (*Snow Crash*, pp.225-26)

Ng himself is painfully aware of just how repulsive he appears, limbless and suspended in a pouch that bulges and throbs. A more unsightly means of life-support is hardly conceivable. By depicting this kind of corporeal invasion as utterly disgusting, the technologically-mediated body is kept from being romanticized. Since Stephenson does not naturalize or romanticize corporeal invasion, bodies with unbreached boundaries remain the ideal, and the belief that the human body is a marker of essential self remains unchallenged.

The anxiety surrounding technologically infiltrated bodies is further explored in Stephenson's depiction of "wireheads." Much like the victims of the Snow Crash virus, these are people who have been reduced to drone-like slaves under the control of L. Bob Rife:

> ...people with antennas coming out of their heads. The antennas look like the ones on cop walkie-talkies: short, blunt, black rubber whips. They rise up from behind the ear...he's a strange guy, stranger than all of the others, with a permanent thousand-yard stare and a bad case of the mumbles. (*Snow Crash*, p.325)

Even when active and carrying out instructions, the wireheads seem scarcely human. The impression Y.T. gets of them when they abduct her clearly illustrates the extent to which they are mindless drones:

> It's not the first time she's been thrown out of a building full of suits. This time it's a little different, though. This time, the bouncers are a couple of life-sized plastic action figures from Toys R Us.
> And it's not just that these guys probably don't speak English. They just don't act normal. She actually manages to twist one of her arms loose and the guy doesn't smack her or anything, just turns rigidly toward her and paws at her mechanically until he's got her by the arm again. No change in his face. His eyes stare like busted headlights. His mouth is open enough to let him breathe through it, but the lips never move, never change expression. (*Snow Crash*, p.421)

These wireheads are quite literally manipulated by remote control. One of the symptoms of the Snow Crash virus is the infectee's ability to communicate in the pre-Babel language of Ancient Sumer. It is this language, described as having the quasi-magical effect of mind control, that is used to instruct the wireheads. In order to receive broadcast instructions from L. Bob Rife's control tower, the wireheads are fitted with antennae, directly wired into the brain:

> A single hair-thin wire emerges from the base of the antenna and penetrates the skull. It passes straight through the brainstem and then branches and re-branches into a network of invisibly tiny wires embedded in the brain tissue. Coiled around the base of the tree.
> Which explains why this guy continues to pump out a steady stream of Raft babble even when his brain is

> missing.... It's a pentecostal radio broadcast coming through on his antenna. (*Snow Crash*, p.386)

Wireheads, having had their mental capacities and free will usurped, serve as cautionary figures. They are manifestations of the humanist anxiety that technological invasion of the body robs humanity of its essential nature. The existence of wireheads clearly equates surgical implants with the loss of self at the most fundamental level: as the example illustrates, even when a wirehead dies, their bodies remain at the service of L.Bob Rife, as though he had taken possession of their very souls.

Not all characters with technological implants are abject like Ng or cautionary like the wireheads, though. There are several others who carry similar implants with no ill effect. In cases such as these, however, there are always extenuating circumstances explaining why such an unusual favouring of implants should have taken place. The two characters to whom this applies are Hiro's love-interest Juanita, and his arch enemy Raven.

Juanita is Hiro's old flame, and another of the hackers who co-founded the Metaverse. She has traveled to L. Bob Rife's seaborne stronghold—the Raft—to study the effects of the Snow Crash virus and understand why Rife's drones speak in tongues. While there she is implanted with the same neural circuitry as the wireheads, but manages to override the programming and use the circuitry to her own advantage:

> It's Juanita. Juanita with an antenna rising out of the base of her skull.... "Don't get me wrong," Hiro says, "but aren't you one of the bad guys now?"
> ..."No. This doesn't work on me. It sort of did, for a while, but there are ways to fight it.... I've spent the last several years hanging out with Jesuits," she says. "Look. Your brain has an immune system, just like your body. The more you use it—the more viruses you get exposed to—the better your immune system becomes. And I've got a hell of an immune system.

Remember, I was an atheist for a while, and then I came back to religion the hard way."

..."Why would anyone come here voluntarily?"

"Hiro, don't you realize? This is it. This is the nerve center of a religion that is at once brand new and very ancient. Being here is like following Jesus or Mohammed around, getting to observe the birth of a new faith."

"But it's terrible. Rife is the Antichrist."

"Of course he is. But it's still interesting." (*Snow Crash*, pp.428-429)

Hiro's questioning of Juanita's motives highlights how unusual her behavior is. She is singular amongst Stephenson's characters in her desire to study and master L. Bob Rife's methods of mind control. It is for this reason that she has allowed herself to have the implants, and uses them for her own ends. But Juanita is not romanticized for this—rather it marks her as bizarre, existing outside most people's value systems. Her obsession with what she perceives as "the birth of a new faith," and her view that "the Antichrist" is more interesting than terrible, further marks her as distant from the reasoning of other characters. Juanita's acceptance of the implant does not sanction corporeal invasion, but rather illustrates how bizarre it is for someone to voluntarily choose to have their essential selves threatened in this way. And indeed, Juanita reveals to Hiro that the acceptance of the implants has changed her: "I'm a neurolinguistic hacker now, Hiro. I went through hell to obtain this knowledge. It's part of me." (*Snow Crash*, p.432.)

Stephenson's depiction of Raven works in a similar way. He, too, sports cerebral implants which mark him as existing outside the value systems of any other characters:

"...Raven's packing a torpedo warhead that he boosted from an old Soviet nuke sub. It was a torpedo that was designed to take out a carrier battle group with one shot. A nuclear torpedo. You know that funny-looking sidecar that Raven has on his Harley? Well, it's a hydrogen bomb, man. Armed and ready. The trigger's hooked up to EEG trodes embedded in his skull. If Raven dies, the bomb goes off. So when Raven comes into town, we do everything in our power to make the man feel welcome." (*Snow Crash*, pp.162-163)

That Raven uses a hydrogen bomb as a personal security measure is the first indication that this character is somewhat of an exception to the norm. Another such indication is the tattoo on his forehead which "consists of three words, written in block letters: POOR IMPULSE CONTROL." (*Snow Crash*, p.128). As it transpires, this is a disciplinary measure:

> These days, most states are franchulates or Burbclaves, much too small to have anything like a jail, or even a judicial system. So when someone does something bad, they try to find quick and dirty punishments, like flogging, confiscation of property, public humiliation, or, in the case of people who have a high potential of going on to hurt others, a warning tattoo on a prominent body part. POOR IMPULSE CONTROL. Apparently, this guy went to such a place and lost his temper real bad. (*Snow Crash*, p.128)

Raven is introduced early on in *Snow Crash* as the novel's anti-hero, an infamous and imposing character, depicted throughout as being uncontrollable and remorselessly violent. He kills legions of people as part of a larger plan to exact revenge on America for its exploitation of the Aleut people. That someone as disturbing as Raven sports cerebral implants is less of a endorsement of invasive technology than a warning of its potential misuse. While he is certainly imposing and impressive as a character, the fact that he is linked up to the nuclear torpedo is not romanticized or celebrated. Rather, it is described as an aberration, another disconcerting characteristic of an unhinged man.

All these characters are marked as unusual by their technological implants, acting as a warning of the price that must be paid for allowing one's body to be infiltrated and colonized by technology. They all stand in stark contrast to the rest of the novel's characters, who maintain a clear boundary between themselves and the machines they use. In this way, Stephenson prevents these cyborg bodies from being romanticized, maintaining the unmediated body in its position of privilege.

Having maintained the sanctity of the body in this way, Stephenson then goes on to employ a second tactic in the protection of his characters' essential selves. The way he does this, however, is highly ironic, for he takes the opposite position by merging the body with technology, describing machinery using corporeal and organic metaphors. This kind of description depicts technology not as a threat to the body, but rather as a reflection of it, which makes the technological appear less foreign and less problematic. Equating his futuristic inventions with imagery from the natural world results in a sense of familiarity and recognition which, instead of being confronting, invites us to notice how technology reflects ourselves as embodied readers:

> Whenever Hiro is using the machine, this lens emerges and clicks into place, its base flush with the surface of the computer. The neighborhood loglo is curved and foreshortened on its surface.
>
> Hiro finds it erotic. This is partly because he hasn't been properly laid in several weeks. But there's more to it. Hiro's father, who was stationed in Japan for many years, was obsessed with cameras. He kept bringing them back from his stints in the Far East, encased in many protective layers, so that when he took them out to show Hiro, it was like watching an exquisite striptease as they emerged from all that black leather

and nylon, zippers and straps. And once the lens was finally exposed, pure geometric equation made real, so powerful and vulnerable at once, Hiro could only think it was like nuzzling through skirts and lingerie and outer labia and inner labia.... It make him feel naked and weak and brave. (*Snow Crash*, pp.22-23)

The computer is clearly equated with the vulva, and as a consequence, is also blatantly eroticized. Hiro's reaction to the emerging lens is an obvious example of fetishized technophilia, which has a two-fold effect. Firstly, the machine is familiarized through its equation with female corporeality, and this provides the reader with a point of reference from which the computer can be visualized and understood. Secondly, by describing the computer in sexual terms it is relegated to being an object of desire, less a threat than a kind of sex toy in service to the subject's gratification. That Hiro feels weak just looking at the computer is more indicative of a swooning infatuation than any kind of real power it may be exerting. The overall effect of this descriptive imagery is the transformation of a potentially threatening piece of technology into a familiar device specifically designed to be in service to its user. The computer's potency is therefore not set up in competition with the human, but is rather wholly channeled into bolstering the user's capabilities.

This is again evident in Stephenson's description of Hiro's motorcycle:

> It's a beautiful bike. It draws a crowd just sitting on the parking lot—the other salesmen actually put down their coffee cups and take their feet off their desks to go outside and look at it. It looks like a black land torpedo. Two-wheel drive, natch. The wheels are so advanced they're not even wheels—they look like giant heavy-duty versions of the smartwheels that high-speed skateboards use, independently telescoping spokes with fat traction pads on the ends. Dangling

out over the front, in the nose cone of the motorcycle, is the sensor package that monitors road conditions, decides where to place each spoke as it rolls forward, how much to extend it, and how to rotate the footpad for maximum traction. It's all controlled by a bios—a Built-In Operating System—an onboard computer with a flat-panel screen built into the top of the fuel tank.

They say that this baby will do a hundred and twenty miles per hour on rubble. The bios patches itself into the CIC weather net so that it knows when it's about to run into precip. The aerodynamic cowling is totally flexible, calculates its own most efficient shape for the current speed and wind conditions, changes its curves accordingly, wraps around you like a nymphomaniacal gymnast.

...[I]t's not an easy thing for any red-blooded salesman to write out a contract to sell a sexy beast like this one at dealer invoice....

"I gotta say this," Scott says as the guy is standing on his new bike, getting his swords adjusted, doing something incredibly unauthorized to the bios, "you look like one bad motherfucker."

"Thanks, I guess." He twists the throttle up once and Scott feels, but does not hear, the power of the engine. This baby is so efficient it doesn't waste power by making noise.... The spokes flex and gather themselves and the bike springs forward out of the lot, seeming to jump off its electric paws. (*Snow Crash*, pp.269-271)

In this example the motorbike is both likened to an animal and objectified through association with female sexuality. The eroticization occurs as a function of the language used—both by Stephenson and his characters—in describing it. "This baby" draws a crowd just to admire its beauty; it is both a "nymphomaniacal gymnast" getting salesmen hot under the collar and a "sexy beast" springing off "electric paws." Yet for all its implied bestial prowess and sexual allure, the bike is never anything other than a token in an economy of power. Like any sexual object or caged beast, the value of the bike lies solely in its ability to serve. That Hiro tampers with the bike's bios is a further indication of this: not content simply to ride and possess the machine, he demonstrates his power, and his disregard for authority, by manipulating the very means by which the bike operates. It is an extravagant display of human control over technology: ownership and manipulation of an impossibly potent motorcycle, complete with an air of stylish nonchalance. That Hiro thoughtlessly abandons the bike as soon as it fails to service his needs only emphasizes its servile role. And just to drive the point home, Hiro goes on to brag about it: "I just threw away a brand-new top-of-the-line motorcycle in the middle of the street because I didn't feel like pushing it half a block to the garage" (*Snow Crash*, p.329).

As well as eroticizing potent machinery, Stephenson also repeatedly associates it with animals. As in his description of the motorcycle, this association is overt: "At the end of White Columns sits a black car, curled up like a panther, a burnished steel lens reflecting the loglo" (*Snow Crash*, p.44). The equation of machines with animals has the same effect as the eroticization of technology. In both instances the machine is relegated to an inferior position to that of the human, thereby depicted as remaining under the control of its masters. Any threat the machine might have posed to the human is in this way averted, its potency relegated to the role of service.

Interestingly, while the machines are associated with animals in a very physical sense, there are also instances when they are equated with animals behaviorally:

> The guy turns out to be fairly hip, because he just throws her plank. It lands at an odd angle on the floor between them. But the spokes have long ago seen the

floor coming, calculated all the angles, extended and flexed themselves like the legs and feet of a basketball player coming back to earth from a monster dunk. The plank lands on its feet, banks this way, then that, as it regains its balance, then steers itself right up to Y.T. and stops beside her. (*Snow Crash*, p.192)

The plank's ability to interpret its environment so successfully—calculating angles, regaining its balance, steering itself to Y.T. and stopping beside her—implies a kind of intelligence more applicable to an animal than a skateboard. Throughout the novel, Stephenson's description of the plank imbues it with the same sorts of behavioral patterns as could be expected from a loyal pet:

> She stops next to Mr. Pudgely's Acura and Mrs. Pudgely's bimbo box and steps off her plank. The spokes, noting her departure, even themselves out, plant themselves on the top of the driveway, refuse to roll backward. (*Snow Crash*, p.33)

Y.T.'s skateboard is smart enough to negotiate its way down stairs, slows down when she loses her balance, and refuses to move from where she leaves it: "a very forgiving skateboard" indeed! Curiously enough, the board's ability to anticipate and react to Y.T.'s actions does not create an impression of terrifyingly intelligent technology. Rather, because of the behavioral patterns it displays, the skateboard bears a closer resemblance to a friendly and loyal animal. The implication of this kind of relationship is that, as with a pet dog, Y.T. is the master of her plank, and need never feel it poses a threat to her identity or potency as a human. Once again, this is an example of how Stephenson's descriptions of technology work to remedy anxiety surrounding its interaction with humans.

Stephenson's means of diffusing the threat of technology are varied. I have identified the way in which the separation of machine and body is favored, as well as the way that cyborg bodies are made abject. In contrast, there are also instances in which machines are equated with corporeality, both in sexual and bestial terms, which has the effect of assuaging any threat they might pose to the human. All these tactics, I argue, are employed for the benefit of preserving the humanist understanding of the self and protecting this self from the potentially dangerous nature of futuristic technology.

My analysis so far has focused solely on the body as an emblem of the self, but this is only part of the question at hand. While the body is certainly important in the humanist understanding of what it means to be human, it does not hold as central a place in this understanding as the mind. It is the human mind, above all else, that is thought to be an indication of the existence of the essential self. Accordingly, I will next examine the attitudes Stephenson's novels display towards the mind concerning its relationship with technology. Just as technology is thought to pose a threat in its ability to invade and colonize the body, so too does it threaten the mind in its potential to display intelligence. The primary concern is that machines might attain the ability to exert intellectual control over humans. In such a scenario, the belief that humans are unique for their intellectual domination over the environment is seriously called into question, and therefore causes problems for our understanding of human nature.

2: Technology and the Human Mind in *The Diamond Age*

Whilst there is no explicit connection made between Stephenson's two science fiction novels, *The Diamond Age* can be read as following on from *Snow Crash*. The main justification for such a reading is what appears to be a character crossover: Y.T. is featured in *The Diamond Age* quite ironically in the guise of Miss Matheson, an elderly Neo-Victorian schoolmistress who dies before the close of the novel. Stephenson himself makes no direct link between the two characters, and indeed remains tight-lipped on the subject in interviews:

> *Brown:* Does Y.T. appear in *The Diamond Age*?
> *Stephenson:* I have established a strict policy against taking any stance on that.[17]

While Stephenson provides no explicit indication of his intent, the chronological relation between the novels is implied through a conspicuous passage in *The Diamond Age*:

> They went across the playing fields to the meadow where the wildflowers grew, the two girls walking and Miss Matheson's wheelchair carrying her along on its many-spoked smart wheels.
> "Chiseled Spam," Miss Matheson said, sort of mumbling to herself.
> "Pardon me, Miss Matheson?" Nell said.
> "I was just watching the smart wheels and remembering an advertisement from my youth," Miss Matheson said. "I used to be a thrasher, you know. I used to ride skateboards through the streets. Now I'm still on wheels, but a different kind. Got a few too many bumps and bruises during my earlier career, I'm afraid."[18]

The advertisement Miss Matheson refers to bears similarities to the one that Y.T. reads in *Thrasher* magazine:

---

17. Tanya Brown, "Interview with Neal Stephenson," (September 1995), p.8. http://www.avnet.co.uk/home/amaranth/Critic/ivstephs.htm

18. Neal Stephenson, *The Diamond Age* (1995; New York: Bantam Spectra, 1996) pp.320-321.

CHISELED SPAM

is what you will see in the mirror if you surf on a weak plank with dumb, fixed wheels and interface with a muffler, retread, snow turd, road kill, driveshaft, railroad tie, or unconscious pedestrian.... Buy a set of RadiKS Mark II Smartwheels—it's cheaper than a total face retread and a whole lot more fun. (*Snow Crash*, pp.27-28)

From this evidence the reader can surmise that the time elapsed between the novels is about that of the average life-expectancy of its characters. *The Diamond Age* is set in China in an era of nanotechnological ubiquity. It follows the early life of Nell, who accidentally comes to own a copy of *A Young Lady's Illustrated Primer*. Although it resembles a large, leather-bound book, the Primer is in fact a computer which supplements the education she receives from her abusive and absent parents, and raises her to adulthood. The Primer was designed by John Percival Hackworth, a Neo-Victorian nanotechnological engineer who, like Nell, unknowingly becomes embroiled in a deep-rooted plan to revolutionize and reorganize the social infrastructure of China.

Like *Snow Crash*, Stephenson's second science fiction novel initially received very little critical attention. Jan Berriend Berends' article "The Politics of Neal Stephenson's *The Diamond Age*" is, as the title suggests, a critique of the social and political climate of the novel. Her article is a pertinent and thought provoking examination of the value system at work within the novel, as well as the attitudes that Stephenson presents through his writing. Yet she does not include any discussion of how the characters interact with their technologically mediated environment, nor the importance of technology in Stephenson's understanding of what it means to be human.

Because of the existence of nanotechnology in *The Diamond Age*, the depiction of technology is different from that of *Snow*

Crash. This does not mean, however, that Stephenson's attitude towards the role of technology had changed—on the contrary, the humanist values in his writing remained evident.

I have already explored the ramifications of technology on the human body, based upon the humanist assumption that the body is a marker of essential self. Whilst the individuated body is certainly important in this regard, it holds little significance unless it is integrated with the mind. For it is the mind, above all else, which is most closely equated with the essential self as it defines the human. This understanding of the mind as an intrinsic characteristic of the human is closely adhered to in Stephenson's novels. It follows that, in the same way that Stephenson took pains to protect the sanctity of his characters' bodies, so too does he protect the integrity of their minds. As I have already shown, the threat posed by future technology is two-fold: firstly, its potency poses a direct challenge to the power and dominance of humanity; secondly, its ability to infiltrate borders results in a blurring of the boundaries between the human and the technological. Since humanism is concerned with the dominance and the integrity of humanity, both these outcomes are disturbing prospects.

The technology described in *The Diamond Age* is significantly different from that of *Snow Crash*, simply as a function of the time elapsed between the two novels. The most important development made in the later novel is the appearance of intelligent technology. The advent of intelligent machines is unsurprising considering the nanotechnological capabilities of this futuristic society: it is an age in which almost anything conceivable can be created, built one atom at a time. As Stephenson himself notes in the novel, "nanotechnology had made nearly anything possible, and so the cultural role in deciding what should be done with it had become far more important than imagining what could be done with it." (*The Diamond Age*, p.37).

As I will discuss later, Stephenson only touches on the issue of artificial or pseudo-intelligence in *The Diamond Age*. Despite this, however, the novel is littered with examples of technology that can be described as "intelligent." The potency of this technology certainly poses a threat, not physically, but mentally. Being intelligent, it calls into question the idea that humans are unique in their sentience, and therefore questions the belief that humanity is in any way superior or distinguished from any other part of our environment. Because intelligent technology has the potential to challenge and compete for human intellectual dominance it is able to undermine this understanding of what it means to be human. As a result of this threat, the more intelligent technology is described as becoming, the more important it becomes for Stephenson to reassert the illusion of human dominance in his novel. His primary means of reasserting this power relation is by undermining the apparent potency of this technology wherever it appears. Thus, the more awe-inspiring the inventions Stephenson describes, the more he subsequently belittles the very power with which he endows them. An interesting example of this is Stephenson's portrayal of chevalines, a kind of mechanical horse used for transportation:

> "Mount," he said. The chevaline rose into a crouch. Hackworth threw one leg over its saddle, which was padded with some kind of elastomeric stuff, and immediately felt it shoving him into the air. His feet left the ground and flailed around until they found the stirrups. A lumbar support pressed thoughtfully on his kidneys, and then the chevaline trotted into the street and began heading back towards the causeway.
> It wasn't supposed to do that. Hackworth was about to tell it to stop. Then he figured out why he'd gotten the chit at the last minute: Dr. X's engineers had been programming something into this mount's brain, telling it where to take him.
> ...sensing that it was reaching the edge of the business district, it started to canter. (*The Diamond Age*, p.37)

Stephenson describes the chevaline using an interesting mix of human and animal characteristics. On the one hand, it is able to understand and interpret vocal commands and carry out set instructions. It can recognize its surroundings, navigate through the city, and function appropriately within that environment. What is more, the chevaline is specifically described as having a brain with which it "senses" what is going on. But for all the potential of a machine as stunningly clever as this, the chevaline is described with very strict limitations on its capabilities. It is quite specifically described as resembling a mechanical horse, which works as a symbol of its servile role to the human rider. What is more, it is constantly under the direct command of either Dr. X's programmed instructions or Hackworth himself. My reading of Stephenson's novels suggests that the chevaline's docility is the direct result of the need to assuage any anxiety regarding its potency or potential autonomy as a machine.

This means of undermining the power with which technology is imbued is a continuation of the tactic used throughout *Snow Crash*. *The Diamond Age* also depicts the future with exemplary plausibility and internal consistency. There is great care taken in extrapolating contemporary social and political trends in order to depict societies that are pertinent and revealing outcomes of the modern condition. Yet Stephenson's dealings with the technological logistics that would be in place in a nanotechnological society at times goes curiously unexplored, particularly the conspicuous lack of artificial intelligence (A.I.) that would necessarily exist in such an environment. This is not to say that A.I. is completely absent in his rendition of the distant future, but rather that his treatment of it begs questioning. Similarly to the case of the chevaline, A.I. poses a threat to humanity through its display of intelligence, and just as the chevaline's autonomy and power are undermined and carefully controlled, so too is the artificial intelligence described in *The Diamond Age*. Although it is a technological achievement beyond anything currently conceivable, A.I. is all but ignored in Stephenson's novel. In fact, the entire subject is discussed only once, during a social conversation:

> "...Did some work on this project, as it happens."
> "What sort of work?"
> "Oh, P.I. stuff mostly," Hackworth said. Supposedly Finkle-McGraw still kept up with things and would recognize the abbreviation for pseudo-intelligence, and perhaps even appreciate that Hackworth had made this assumption.
> Finkle-McGraw brightened a bit. "You know, when I was a lad they called it A.I. Artificial Intelligence."
> Hackworth allowed himself a tight, narrow, and brief smile. "Well, there's something to be said for cheekiness, I suppose."
> "In what way was pseudo-intelligence used here?"
> "Strictly on MPS's side of the project, sir... Stereotyped behaviors were fine for the birds, dinosaurs, and so on, but for the centaurs and fauns we wanted more interactivity, something that would provide an illusion of sentience." (*The Diamond Age*, p.22).

In this conversation, there is a great deal of emphasis laid on the fact that this is pseudo, as opposed to artificial, intelligence that has been used. The distinction is a subtle but telling one. Artificiality carries implications of the intellect being non-human, but pseudo-intelligence implies that this is not true intelligence at all. As Hackworth points out, the centaurs only "provide an illusion of sentience." To anyone holding the superiority of the human mind as a central principle of their value system, this distinction is a vital one. Stephenson makes very clear the fact that these centaurs will never aspire to matching—let alone outdoing—human intellect. As Hackworth notes, the very idea of such an eventuation is cheeky.

The project that Hackworth describes is a mythical island created especially for Princess Charlotte's birthday, with the centaurs being specifically designed to interact solely with young children. It is telling that on the single occasion that P.I. is discussed, it is in reference to such a frivolous and childish event. This is once again a means of disregarding the implications of intelligent technology, for in relegating pseudo-intelligent technology to the role of children's party games, its ability to challenge human intelligence is negated.

The same point is raised in Stephenson's description of *The Young Lady's Illustrated Primer* itself—that astounding work of nanotechnological engineering around which the novel's plot revolves. Once again, the depiction of the Primer is a telling indication of the underlying attitudes Stephenson's novels display to the existence of threatening technology. Hackworth explains early on in the novel just how wondrous a creation it is:

> "It is unlikely to do anything interesting just now," Hackworth said. "It won't really activate itself until it bonds."
>
> "Bonds?"
>
> "As we discussed, it sees and hears everything in its vicinity," Hackworth said. "At the moment, it's looking for a small female. As soon as a little girl picks it up and opens the front cover for the first time, it will imprint that child's face and voice into its memory -"
>
> "Bonding with her. Yes, I see."
>
> "And thenceforth it will see all events and persons in relation to that girl, using her as a datum from which to chart a psychological terrain, as it were. Maintenance of that terrain is one of the book's primary processes. Whenever the child uses the book, then, it will perform a sort of dynamic mapping from the database onto her particular terrain." (*The Diamond Age*, p.106)

As a piece of technology, the *Primer* demonstrates amazing competence in its ability to interact with humans. It displays an understanding of human development and psychology to a level of detail unrivaled by most humans themselves. And since it was specifically designed to append the education of a Neo-Victorian child through to young womanhood, its capabilities and functions are nothing short of vast. Berends makes a pertinent observation about this:

> I have already mentioned the improbable nature of the Primer, which is a computer more intelligent and creative than any human being we encounter in the story but which is devoted entirely to the upbringing of a single girl. (Let's face it, if they could build computers like that, they'd be using them for other things!)[19]

In the same way that he handled the pseudo-intelligent centaurs, as soon as Stephenson describes a piece of technology that threatens to surpass human intelligence, he relegates it to interaction with children. As Hackworth himself explicitly mentions, "the book is engineered for girls starting around the age of four" (*The Diamond Age*, p.179). Outsmarting a toddler is a simple matter for most adults, and indeed most computers, but it is telling that the Primer is never used by an adult. Such an occurrence would bring into question the problem of who would do the outsmarting, a question that raises unpleasant implications about the intellectual supremacy of humans.

Another interesting discrepancy is evident in the Primer's functioning. Being the marvel of engineering that it is, it could be taken for granted that the Primer is a fully autonomous machine. Yet despite its multifarious abilities, there is a single, highly conspicuous failing in its design:

> "That being done, sir, there remains only for you to authorize a standing purchase order for the ractors."
> "Ah, yes, thank you for reminding me," said Finkle-McGraw, not very sincerely. "I still would have

---

19. Ian Berrien Berends, "The Politics of Neal Stephenson's *The Diamond Age*," *The New York Review of Science Fiction* 9.8 (1997), p. 18.

thought that for all the money that went into this project—"

"That we might have solved the voice-generation problem to boot, yes sir," Hackworth said. "As you know, we took some stabs at it, but none of the results were up to the level of quality you demand. After all of our technology, the pseudo-intelligence algorithms, the vast exception matrices, the portent and content monitors, and everything else, we still can't come close to generating a human voice that sounds as good as what a real, live ractor can give us."

"Can't say I'm surprised, really," said Finkle-McGraw. "I just wish it were a completely self-contained system."

"It might as well be, sir. At any given time there are tens of millions of professional ractors in their stages all over the world, in every time zone, ready to take on this kind of work at an instant's notice. We are planning to authorize payment at a relatively high rate, which should bring in only the best talent. You won't be disappointed with the results." (*The Diamond Age*, pp.108-109).

Finkle-McGraw's lack of surprise concerning the failings of the Primer marks him as a mouthpiece for the novel's underlying values. It is a charming means for Stephenson to make clear the stance his characters take on the relationship they have with technology. Even though they exist in a nanotechnological society, surrounded by technology that could conceivably slip from their tenuous control over it, these characters continue to hold a steadfast belief in their own dominance over the world. To Finkle-McGraw and his contemporaries, there seems to be no doubt whatsoever as to the supremacy of humanity, and the continued dependence technology has on them. Any fear of the potential threat this technology might pose is absent from

Finkle-McGraw's mind, for his value system does not permit any other scenario than the continued preponderance of humanity.

This discrepancy in the Primer's design is indeed conspicuous, and Stephenson appears to have anticipated the questioning of this issue by having his characters discuss the reasons behind it. Second-guessing the reader's skepticism, however, does not negate the implausibility of the scenario. Taking into account all the technological capabilities of a society that can create so complex a device as the Primer, the inability to generate sufficiently credible voice-generation seems almost absurd. Because of this, the inclusion of a ractor into the storyline of the novel can only be the result of explicit intention. Hackworth's discussion of the problem with Finkle-McGraw, then, can be read as nothing more than a superficial justification for a plot device that serves a deeper ideological function.

The requirement of human intervention in order to make the Primer functional once again places the human in a position of dominance over the technological, no matter how autonomous or intelligent that technology may be. This example of the Primer reiterates the same point illustrated by Stephenson's description of the chevaline, a point that I have been arguing throughout. In this novel, as in *Snow Crash*, the potency of technology is without exception framed in such a way as to bolster the capabilities of the user, and never to challenge them.

The significance of the ractor in the Primer's functioning highlights some important points. Not only is it indicative of failings in the machine's design, it also implies that, no matter how perfectly the Primer is tailored to an individual's "psychological terrain," this can never replace the rewards of real human interaction. The novel in fact takes great pains to make this point. Miranda, the ractor who works with the Primer in question, becomes unfalteringly dedicated to the job, almost to the point of obsession. In a move that seriously limits her blossoming career, Miranda ends up dedicating years to this one particular project:

> Miranda stumbled down from her box, fixed herself a club soda, and settled into a plastic chair. She put her shaking hands together like the cover of a book and then buried her face in them. After a few deep breaths she got tears to come, though they came silently, a temporary letting-off-steam cry, not the catharsis she was hoping for.
>
> ..."So the next question is," Miranda said after she'd steadied herself with a few gulps of the drink, "why I should get so upset over a kiddie ractive."
>
> ..."What it comes down to," she said, "is that I'm raising someone's kid for them." (*The Diamond Age*, pp.217-219)

Miranda has taken it upon herself to act as a surrogate mother to this anonymous child, obviously providing an emotional facet which the Primer, in all its capabilities as a psychological and educational tool, seems unable to provide. Beyond merely reasserting human dominance over technology, the role of the ractor in *The Diamond Age* also fulfills another important function. Miranda obviously plays an important role in Nell's growth and education over the years, and even though their interaction is anonymous, it is inevitable that a bond should form between these two women:

> "Sometimes he would burn their skin with cigarettes too," Nell whispered.
>
> The letters changed on the page of the Primer.
>
> "Princess Nell's pee-pee turned red too," Nell said, "because the Baron was a very bad man. And his real name wasn't Baron Jack. His real name was Burt."
>
> As Nell spoke the words, the story changed in the Primer.... After a long silence, the Primer began to speak again, but the lovely voice of the Vicky woman who told the story sounded thick and hoarse all of a

sudden and would stumble in the middle of sentences.
(*The Diamond Age*, p.200)

The emotional interaction obviously goes both ways in this relationship, with Miranda being as affected by what she learns from the Primer as Nell is. Stephenson takes this relationship to its logical end, so that once Nell has reached adulthood she seeks Miranda out. What is more, in the process of instigating this meeting Nell actually saves Miranda's life:

> He saw it all now...that this data had been infused into the wet Net in the course of the great orgy, and that all of it was now going to be dumped into Miranda, whose body would play host to the climax of some computation that would certainly burn her alive in the process.
> ...A lone figure, remarkable because her skin did not emit any light, was fighting her way in toward the center. She burst into the inner circle, knocking down a dancer who got in her way, and climbed up onto the central altar where Miranda lay on her back, arms outstretched as if crucified, her skin a galaxy of colored lights.
> Nell cradled Miranda's head in her arms, bent down, and kissed her, not a soft brush of the lips but a savage kiss with open mouth, and she bit down hard as she did it, biting through her own lips and Miranda's so that their blood mingled.
> The light shining from Miranda's body diminished and slowly went out as the nanosites were hunted down and destroyed by the hunter-killers that had crossed into her blood from Nell's. Miranda came awake and arose, her arms draped weakly around Nell's neck.
> (*The Diamond Age*, pp.498-499)

Miranda is found to be living among the Drummers, a mysterious phyle who inhabit underwater caverns. They recruit new members by spreading their blood-borne mites, which cause the infectee to fall into a dream-like state. The exchange of body fluids among the Drummers is a means of sharing knowledge which, through the mites' interaction, becomes part of a larger repository of information used to design new forms of technology. Hence the Drummers' orgiastic rituals, resulting in the overheating and death of those into whom vast collections of this information are deposited. Nell, who was taught nanotechnological engineering from the Primer, was at one point also exposed to these mites, and had designed an antidote to rid herself of them.

Through the course of her adventures with the Primer, Nell in fact becomes the head of her own phyle, the "Mouse Army," which earns her the title of queen. But all this clearly pales in comparison to finding the woman Nell has bonded with:

> "The woman you seek is named Miranda," he said.
> All thoughts of crowns, queens, and armies seemed to vanish from Nell's mind, and she was just another young lady again, looking for—what? Her mother? Her teacher? Her friend? (*The Diamond Age*, p.492)

That Miranda bonds with Nell so deeply has the effect of relegating the Primer—an unimaginably sophisticated educational device—to a mere mediator which facilitates an idealized example of human interaction. That an astoundingly powerful computer of this kind should be relegated to such a menial role seems aberrant. Yet it is not a singular occurrence in *The Diamond Age*. Indeed, this very scenario is played out again, as Fiona Hackworth, who also receives a Primer, has similarly exceptional experiences with it. Once again, the Primer's importance lies not in its value as an educational tool, nor in the brilliance of its design and function, but instead merely in its role as communicative device between a child and her absent parent:

> Fiona brightened up immediately, and Hackworth could not help chuckling, not for the first time, at the charming susceptibility of small people to frank bribery. "You will forgive me for ruining the surprise," he said, "by telling you that this is a book, my darling. A magic book. I made it for you, because I love you and could not think of a better way to express that love. And whenever you open its pages, no matter how far away I might be, you will find me there." (*The Diamond Age*, p.208).

Rather than leaving Hackworth's promise as a reference to the bond between parent and child, Stephenson implies that it is literally acted out. While Hackworth is serving a ten-year sentence in the caverns of the Drummers he is in fact racting, using the Primer to communicate with his daughter. When he is finally released he remembers nothing of those years, but his re-emergence into the world supplies him with clues as to how he had been spending his time away:

> "I just spoke to Fiona this morning."
> "After you left the tunnels?"
> "No. Before. Before I—woke up, or whatever."
> ..."Fiona and Gwendolyn are in Atlantis/Seattle now—half an hour from your present location by tube," he said.
> "Of course! They live—we live—in Seattle now. I knew that." He was remembering Fiona hiking around in the caldera of some snow-covered volcano.
> "If you are under the impression that you've been in contact with her recently—which is quite out of the question, I'm afraid—then it must have been mediated through the Primer. We were not able to break

the encryption on the signals passing out of the Drummers' cave, but traffic analysis suggests that you've spent a lot of time racting in the last ten years." (*The Diamond Age*, p.336)

As with Nell and Miranda, Fiona and her father use the Primer chiefly as a communicative device. Again, this is a tactic employed to diffuse the Primer's potency as a tool that could conceivably usurp the role of humans on many levels. A computer endowed with the ability to raise a child poses serious questions about the continued relevance of human interaction and parenting. But Stephenson resolves this potential crisis by repeatedly ignoring and undermining the capabilities and relevance of the Primer to its users' lives. Instead, the use of the Primer allows Stephenson's narrative to focus on the emotional interaction of his characters. The Primer's main function in this novel is not its educative capabilities, but rather its role in facilitating human relationships, especially familial ones. Both Hackworth and Miranda use the Primer to create lasting and significant relationships with their daughters, be they real or surrogate. Within the framework of *The Diamond Age*, it is this capability above all others that is celebrated in the Primer.

§

By repeatedly placing technology in service to his characters Stephenson protects their integrity and relevance, for they are emblems of all humanity as he envisages it in his futuristic scenarios. That these novels consistently and repeatedly display a concern for the preservation of human preponderance indicates a deep-rooted anxiety. It is a trepidation concerning the role that remains to humanity within a technologically developed society. That humanity needs to be protected in this way reveals a very specific understanding of what it means to be human, an understanding informed by the principles of humanist thought. What is evident in Stephenson's novels is that these principles are at times maintained even at the expense of credibility. That this should be the case implies that the anxiety surrounding the loss of self to technology is a deep one indeed.

The evidence of this anxiety is clear both in *Snow Crash* and *The Diamond Age*, where the implications of the technology described are consistently underestimated and unexplored. My discussion has examined the role of those two markers of the essential self—the mind and the body—and found that both are challenged and threatened by the existence of the technology that Stephenson envisages. That such technology should call into question these markers is a frightening eventuation for the humanist, for it brings to light the idea that there is perhaps no essential self in existence at all. If technology is allowed to breach the boundaries of the human and become inseparable from it, the very things that make us human are placed in doubt. It is for this reason that Stephenson's novels go to such lengths to protect the humanist notion of the essential self, and all the implications that follow on from that.

BIBLIOGRAPHY

Altmann, Gerry T. M. *The Ascent of Babel: An Exploration of Language, Mind, and Understanding.* Oxford, New York and Toronto: Oxford University Press, 1997.

Asaro, Catherine. "A Conversation with Neal Stephenson," *SF Site* (September 1999). http://www.sfsite.com/10b/ns67.htm

Bæcker, Ronald M. and Buxton, William A.S. eds. *Readings in Human-Computer Interaction: A Multidisciplinary Approach*, Los Altos: M. Kaufmann, 1987.

Berends, Jan Berrien. "The Politics of Neal Stephenson's *The Diamond Age*," *The New York Review of Science Fiction* 9.8 (1997), pp 15-18.

Brown, Tanya. "Interview with Neal Stephenson," (September 1995). http://www.avnet.co.uk/home/amaranth/Critic/ivstephs.htm

Bukatman, Scott. "Gibson's Typewriter," *The South Atlantic*

Quarterly, 92.4 (Fall 1993), pp 627-645.
— "Who Programs You? The Science Fiction of Spectacle." *Alien Zone: Cultural Theory and Contemporary Science Fiction Cinema*, Annette Kuhn, ed. London and New York: Verso, 1990.
Christie, John R. R. "A Tragedy for Cyborgs." *Configurations: A Journal of Literature, Science and Technology* 1.1 (1993), pp 171-196.
Crawford, Harriet. *Sumer and the Sumerians*. Cambridge: Cambridge University Press, 1991.
Dawkins, Richard. *The Selfish Gene*. New York: Oxford University Press, 1976.
Dery, Mark. *Escape Velocity: Cyberculture at the End of the Century*. London: Hodder and Stoughton, 1996.
— "Wild Nature," *21c* vol 4 (1996), pp 44-52.
Drexler, K. Eric. *Engines of Creation*. New York: Anchor Press/Doubleday, 1986.
Featherstone, Mike, and Burrows, Roger, eds. *Cyberspace/Cyberbodies/Cyberpunk: Cultures of Technological Embodiment*. London: Sage, 1995.
Foster, Thomas. "Meat Puppets or Robopaths? Cyberpunk and the Question of Embodiment," *Genders* 18 (1993), pp 11-31.
Gibson, William. *Burning Chrome*. 1986; London: Grafton Books, 1990.
— *Neuromancer*. 1984; New York: Ace Books, 1994.
— *Virtual Light*. 1993; New York: Bantam Spectra, 1994.
Goldberg, Michael. "Breaking the Code with Neal Stephenson," Addicted To Noise. http://www.addict.com/ATN/issues/1.07/Features/Neal_Stephenson/
Gozzi Jr, Raymond. "The Computer 'Virus' as Metaphor," *Et Cetera: A Review of General Semanitcs* 47.2 (Summer 1990), pp 177-180.
Gunkel, David J. "Lingua ex Machina: Computer-Mediated Communication and the Tower of Babel," *Configurations: A Journal of Literature, Science, and Technology* 7.1 (Winter 1999), pp 61-89.

Halloran, John A. "Sumerian Language Page," 1999. http://www.sumerian.org/

Harper, Mary Catherine. "Incurably Alien Other: A Case for Feminist Cyborg Writers," *Science Fiction Studies* 22.3 (1995), pp 399-420.

Harraway, Donna. *Simians, Cyborgs and Women: The Reinvention of Nature.* New York and London: Routledge, 1991.

Hayles, N. Katherine. "Boundary Disputes: Homeostasis, Reflexivity, and the Foundations of Cybernetics." *Virtual Realities and their Discontents.* Robert Markley, ed. Baltimore and London: The Johns Hopkins University Press (1996), pp 11-38.

— "The Materiality of Informatics," *Configurations: A Journal of Literature, Science, and Technology* 1.1 (Winter 1993), pp 147-170.

— "The Posthumanist Body: Inscription and Incorporation in *Galatea 2.2* and *Snow Crash*," *Configurations: A Journal of Literature, Science and Technology* 5.2 (Spring 1997), pp 241-266.

Hollinger, Veronica. "Cybernetic Deconstructions: Cyberpunk and Postmodernism," *Mosaic* 23.2 (1990), pp.29-44.

— "The Technobody and its Discontents," *Science Fiction Studies* 24.1 (1997), pp 124-132.

Jaynes, Julian. *The Origin of Consciousness in the Breakdown of the Bicameral Mind.* Boston: Houghton Mifflin Company, 1976.

Johnston, John. *Information Multiplicity: American Fiction in the Age of Media Saturation.* Baltimore: Johns Hopkins University Press, 1998.

Joy, Bill. "Why the Future Doesn't Need Us," *Wired* 8.04 (April 2000). http://www.wired.com/wired/archive/8.04/joy.html

Kay, Lily E. "Cybernetics, Information, Life: The Emergence of Scriptual Representations of Heredity," *Configurations: A Journal of Literature, Science, and Technology* 5.1 (Winter 1997), pp 23-91.

Kendrick, Michelle. "Cyberspace and the Technological Real," *Virtual Realities and their Discontents*. Robert Markley, ed. Baltimore and London: The Johns Hopkins University Press (1996), pp 143-160.

Kierkegaard, Søren. *The Concept of Anxiety: A Simple Psychologically Orienting Deliberation on the Dogmatic Issue of Hereditary Sin*. Princeton: Princeton University Press, 1980.

Kramer, Samuel Noah. *The Sumerians: Their History, Culture, and Character*. Chicago and London: University of Chicago Press, 1963.

Kunzru, Hari. "You Are Borg," *Wired* (February 1997), pp.156-159, 209-210.

Leary, Timothy. *Chaos and Cyberculture*. California: Ronin Publishing, 1994.

Markley, Robert. "Introduction: History, Theory and Virtual Reality," *Virtual Realities and their Discontents*. Robert Markley, ed. Baltimore and London: The Johns Hopkins University Press. (1996), pp 1-10.

— "Shreds and Patches: The Morphogenics of Cyberspace," *Configurations: A Journal of Literature, Science, and Technology* 2.3 (1994), pp 433-439

Moulthorp, Stuart. "No War Machine." *Reading Matters*. Joseph Tabbi and Michael Wutz, eds., Ithaca and London: Cornell University Press (1997), pp.269-309.

Nixon, Nicola. "Cyberpunk: Preparing the Ground for Revolution or Keeping the Boys Satisfied," *Science Fiction Studies* 19.2 (1992), pp 219-235.

Porush, David. "Hacking the Brainstem: Postmodern Metaphysics and Stephenson's *Snow Crash*," *Configurations: A Journal of Literature, Science and Technology* 2.3 (Autumn 1994), pp.537-571.

Ribeiro, Gustavo Lins. *Bodies and Culture in the Cyberage: A Review Essay*. Brasil: Departamento de Antropologia, Universidade de Brasília, 1997.

— *Cybercultural Politics: Political Activism at Distance in a*

Transnational World. Brasil: Departamento de Antropologia, Universidade de Brasília, 1996.

Rucker, Rudy. "On the Edge of the Pacific," *Mondo 2000: A User's Guide to the New Edge*, Rudy Rucker, R.U. Sirius and Queen Mu, eds. London: Thames and Hudson, 1993.

Salverda, Reinier. "Is Language a Virus? Reflections on the Use of Biological Metaphors in the Study of Language," *Productivity and Creativity: Sudies in General and Descriptive Linguistics in Honor of E.M. Uhlenbeck*. Mark Janse and An Verlinden, eds. Berlin and New York: Mouton de Gruyter, 1998.

Schell, Heather. "Outburst! A Chilling True Story about Emerging-Virus Narratives and Pandemic Social Change," *Configurations: A Journal of Literature, Science, and Technology* 5.1 (Winter 1997), pp 93-133.

Scott, Melissa. *Trouble and Her Friends*. New York: Bantam Spectra, 1994.

Springer, Claudia. *Electronic Eros: Bodies and Desire in the Postindustrial Age*. Austin: University of Texas Press, 1996.

Squires, Judith. "Fabulous Feminist Futures and the Lure of Cyberculture," *Fractal Dreams: New Media in Social Context*, Jon Dovey, ed. London: Lawrence and Wishart, 1996.

Star, Susan Leigh. "From Hestia to Homepage: Feminism and the Concept of Home in Cyberspace," *Between Monsters, Goddesses and Cyborgs: Feminist Confrontations with Science, Medicine and Cyberspace*, Nine Lykke and Rosi Braidotti, eds. London and New Jersey: Zed Books, 1996, pp 30-46.

Stephenson, Neal. *The Diamond Age*. 1995; New York: Bantam Spectra, 1996.

— *Snow Crash*. 1992; New York: Bantam Spectra, 1993.

Sterling, Bruce. "Preface," *Burning Chrome*, William Gibson. 1990; London: Victor Gollancz, 1986.

— *Mirrorshades: The Cyberpunk Anthology*. 1986; London: HarperCollins, 1994.

"The Unabomber's Manifesto: Industrial Society and Its Future," http://www.panix.com/~clays/Una/

SCIENCE FICTION, PARAFICTION, AND PETER CAREY
BY GEORGE TURNER

In need of a word for books whose authors showed obvious familiarity with the idiom and techniques of science fiction but used them for unexpected purposes, I came up with the clumsy and inadequate "parafiction"—a neologism for works whose content was fictional but whose mode and meaning fell at a crossroad where mainstream, fantasy, and science fiction combined with an author's personal approach to produce a work which partook of all of these things but could not be adequately described in terms of any of them.

I had in mind such novels as Alastair Gray's *Lanark*, Rodney Hall's *Just Relations*, Anthony Burgess's *End of the World News*, Christopher Priest's *The Affirmation*, and some short stories of Frank Moorhouse and Peter Carey. Since then I have been able to add, among others, Priest's *The Glamour*, John Calvin Batchelor's *The Further Adventures of Halley's Comet*. Not all of these are successful in their exploitation of the strange in harness with the familiar (*The Glamour* seems to me a notable failure and the Burgess novel unwieldy) but, in general, these highly individual works make use of science fictional ideas and attitudes to produce commentary of a kind that science fiction rarely aims for and, when it does, usually misses.

If "the proper study of Mankind is Man" (and it had better

be if we are to survive) conventional sf has contributed little since Orwell's *Nineteen Eighty-Four*; Ursula Le Guin and Thomas M. Disch stand almost alone in displaying any interest in people, and even their interest seems fairly narrow and exclusive. The mainstream of fiction still carries the only current of meaningful commentary in depth—or so I would have said until these strange parafictional works began to edge their way out of the commercial woodwork.

Note that three of the practitioners named above are Australian; all of them are important in the local canon as well as known and published overseas. Hall and Moorhouse are only fringe parafictionists, but Carey is not afraid to take sf clichés by the scruffs of their aging necks and toss them into the muddy humanitarian waters where their more trendy propagators don't dare paddle. His stories are worth thinking about, not only for their merits as vigorous literary expressions but because they demonstrate, with a high degree of virtuosity, what the trivial conventions of sf can be forced to disgorge when shaken by an angry writer who loves his fellow man but cannot forever condone him.

§

What Carey thinks of science fiction I do not know; I am told that he has refused invitations to write for sf anthologies. It is plain, however, that he is aware of its major preoccupations and can make casual use of them when they fit his purpose—just as it is plain that his purpose involves probing more deeply than those preoccupations commonly allow.

His two volumes of short stories, *The Fat Man in History* (1974) and *War Crimes* (1979), contain ten tales (less than half the total) which in my opinion can be considered parafictional in their form. Five of them, while by no means trivial, need not detain us very long. "Crabs" is a neat little tale of the nightmarish future of technological collapse and the equally nightmarish capacity of the human animal to adapt to what it had thought would be disaster. (For a full treatment of this forbidding theme, see J.G. Ballard's novel, *Empire of the Sun*, and wonder if your conception of "normality" may not need reconsideration.)

"Windmill in the West" is a fairly conventional treatment of the theme of uncertainty as to where one's responsibilities lie and how far they must be pursued. A lonely sentry, his world defined by a fence, a road, and some sparse orders, exists in a Kafka universe where no final understanding is possible. Though the metaphor is familiar, the treatment is not; what could have been a forgettable vignette achieves the immediacy of powerful visualization.

"Conversations With Unicorns," which Damien Broderick included in his anthology *The Zeitgeist Machine* (1977), is a parable about the unholiness of innocence, effective in its way though not the best Carey tale he could have selected at that date. (But anthologists cannot always get what they want; the professional complications can be dismaying.) "The Puzzling Nature of Blue" and "Exotic Pleasures" come as close to magazine fiction as Carey allows himself to approach, a joke and a horror story respectively, fully professional but ephemeral.

All five display Carey's pointed selection of detail and incident allied to spareness of presentation—nothing wasted, nothing blunted, nothing merely decorative—but are shallow by comparison with the five remaining. The main matter for note is that the first three are what I have called "parafiction"; they merely gesture towards the sf genre, using its props to shore up private purposes, to make statements far from the science fictional norm.

The nature of these statements can be better observed in the other five tales.

"Report on the Shadow Industry" uses the *new invention* theme in a thoroughly cavalier way, giving no more than the bare minimum of information. (This is a Carey characteristic.) Factories are producing boxes of manufactured shadows; the nature of the shadows is unknown and you buy "on spec." The shadow fad is pandemic; everybody wants them, be they good or bad, because the next one may be the perfect possession. In what way? We are not told, nor does it matter; what we are shown is mankind in the grip of wish and illusion. Think of films, TV, video, the great twentieth century shadow-dreams; think then of horse racing, poker machines, lotto, those metaphors for impossible wealth which strain credibility but must be followed because the impossible just might happen.... That is the portrait of mankind entangled in its dreams.

Take a step further. You can buy private dreams, ready packaged, in the supermarket, with the possibility that in the next packet may be the shadow life that matches yourself as you see yourself. There can be few more destructive illusions than this; Carey's packets contain just enough promise to keep you buying because the next one.... People paw through their purchase in private and emerge with silent, fallen faces; a man sees something in his package that causes him to walk at once out of his family's life....

Here Carey is meditating—for there is no plot in this story—on the human need/greed for something more. More than what? Just more, other, different.... What kind of—Any kind! Most of all, to hold a mirror to oneself and see one's ideal self image. Which may turn out to be the illusion one would have done better without.

This simple metaphor for desperation will lead to greater complexities in other stories as Carey wrestles with his concerned vision of humanity.

§

Cartographers have mapped the world. Today they are mapping it from space with finer detail than ever before, but is this enough? Hidden in the fine detail are features the satellite cameras can locate, the rising and falling, emerging and vanishing structures raised and demolished. They, too, are environment, needing mapping. (More immediately so than the shrinking forests, polluted rivers and slaughtered species? Possibly so, because in real life we appeal to the shadow industry of desperate dreams.)

The cartographers of "Do You Love Me?" map every surface feature. They must. Features continually disappear and are lost. Buildings, no longer wanted, are torn down. In the final evolution of unwanting, they fade from sight as curious passersby watch. Unwanted, they are deserted by love, and so non-existent in real terms. For Carey, the terms of the spirit are the real terms.

People fade and vanish because only love (not sexual love but the love which binds beyond sex) can support them in reality. A cartographer begins to fade from view as his family watches. A guilty son cries, "I love you, Dad," but it is too late and anyway it is only a shamed lie. He vanishes and Mother cries in fear to the son who has failed one parent, "Do you love me?"

Does he answer? Does she live? Carey does not tell us. We children of the shadow industries have retired within ourselves and forgotten the deeper love which makes of humans, Humanity. We watch each other die.

It is a nasty little story, blandly told with little overt verbal forcefulness. It ends in mid-air, leaving you to contemplate your own mind and wonder where you stand. If you have the courage for such honesty.

The story's power lies in Carey's ability to make you believe his thesis. Such belief is too easily classified as the familiar "suspension of disbelief" from which you'll wake up, untouched, when it's all over. You will, won't you? With Carey it is best not to be too sure of this; his unasked questions reverberate long after the source is forgotten.

Should I probe technique and word-use to discover how the effect is achieved? The probing is not difficult, but any writer seeking to obtain the same power in the same way will fail because every technique requires a personal "something more" that analysis will not reveal, a sort of literary McGuffin which keeps the work safe from imitation. All Carey does, in technical terms, is write straightforwardly in simple language as though it is all perfectly true; he makes little effort to convince, simply assumes that you believe him. And so you do, because you find no literary subtleties of the kind you can leap on with *Ha! Caught him at it!* and so expose him as a trickster in words. When nothing disturbs your belief, you believe.

This is one more reason why I think of Carey's work as parafiction rather than science fiction. Science fiction is forever explaining itself in order to achieve credibility, and forever falling short. Carey never explains; he merely states. And when he's done stating you are left with the uneasy feeling that he is very possibly right.

§

If it begins to appear that love and self-doubt are at the heart of Carey's fiction (they may be but don't lay your bets yet) turn to the very science fictionish "The Chance"—science fictionish, that is, until you realize that he has used a conventional magazine idea only as a supporting frame—then pushed it out of the way to get on with the real business.

The Fastalogians have come to Earth. Where from? Are they human or not? Who cares? They are a background gimmick and Carey saves several thousand unnecessary words by not bothering with what any sf fan can fill in for himself, which is another reason for calling his work "para" rather than "science" fiction. What matters is that they have brought with them the Genetic Lottery, the chance to change your body for another. Who knows but that you may, as with the shadow industry, find one that reflects what you feel yourself to be?

Expensive, of course, but how magnetic to the soul! No wonder the Fastalogians are cornering the money supply. But there are Earthly dissidents, grouping for uprising against what they see as eventual Fastalogian hegemony; they flaunt their hate by opting for ugly bodies; their reasoning is muddled, but perhaps they feel that with ugliness they exalt the common, less than perfect human. Their uprising fails—or perhaps it succeeds. It doesn't matter to the story, because, either way, the Genetic Lottery is here to stay. Mankind can chase forever the dream that forever recedes.

That is the outer tale. The inner tale is a love story. A beautiful girl dissident determines to assert herself in an ugly body; her non-dissident lover tries to dissuade her but she is adamant. As the change day draws near, he exerts all his love against it but she believes that in love the physical form does not count. She is wrong. Her lover wakes in the night to see a fat slob sitting by his bed and in cowardice pretends to be asleep. But she knows, and in the morning is gone. The love that she believed in has shown its true face.

The last paragraph of this long tale is one of Carey's rare adventures into emotional evocation, a hundred words or so from the weeping heart of the lover who could not face the moment of truth and has fled for the rest of his life through one body after another. But there is none that will fit his failure.

§

With "The Fat Man In History" Carey leaves love behind, be it sexual or pan-humanitarian, except as an incidental. He moves to another area of the human scene—the presence of the eternal scapegoat in history.

We have always found scapegoats on whom to unload our self-hate; today we lighten the psychological load with bland phrases like "second class citizen." So Hitler had his Jews, Stalin had the kulaks, the Japanese have the Ainu, the Spartans had the helots, the Americans have Chicanos, Polacks and blacks while Australians have Aborigines, aesthetes, women's libbers and greens. Not all second class? Of course not; we merely behave as though they are.

All these, if they care to work at it, can become acceptably human, but nobody really loves a fat man. He doesn't much love himself. The comic finger has been pointed at him throughout history, and from sniggering to persecution is a small step. Carey presents a collapsing world of poverty in which the fat man, whether his obesity springs from greed or hormonal malfunction, is the target of distrust, resentment and abuse.

Carey's fat men do what scapegoat populations always do; they form a ghetto in a rundown part of the city. The story focuses on a single household, a male enclave of lodgers whose only bond is their ostracism; they form a small society with its rules and its miniature approximations to the forms of the larger world. They share because sharing is necessary to survival but they do not form a commune of equals. Social stratification appears, with varying degrees of accommodation and patronage, presided over by Fantoni. The man at the top has no title but he is always "Fantoni"; they have invented ritual, power, and continuity.

With growing consciousness of apartheid solidarity, they become "Fat Men Against the Revolution." (The Revolution is an activity of the outer world which, typically, the reader must flesh out for himself; Carey is a superbly unwasteful writer.) They, accused by the world of loving food, and therefore themselves, too much, will externalize this love in "a total and literal act of consummation" by "bodily consuming a senior member of the revolution."

But which revolution? It is Fantoni they kill and eat, unwittingly confirming the adage that revolution eats its own children. Ghettoized, cut off, they have re-invented the world that denies them. There is a final twist which is open to a variety of interpretations: the fat men have a girl friend—their rent collector, who is not fat—whom they call Florence Nightingale in honor of her looking after them by not being too insistent upon unpaid dues. They do not know that she is a sociology student preparing her thesis by nudging them into situations of crisis for observing and recording. The outer world, through her, can study itself in microcosm. The fat men have become a laboratory hive over which, as an outcast group, society need shed no tears. Whether the world knows that what it sees is itself we are not told; Carey never stresses his conclusions.

Here love has become self-love, the same love that powers the shadow factories, disperses the cartographer, denies the idealism of the dissident body-changer, and coolly observes its own detritus from behind a mask of caring.

There is a step still to be taken, consideration of the man dead to all love.

"War Crimes" is not science fiction, indeed only parafiction in the minimal sense of being set in a vague near future wherein little has changed technologically but an air of despairing decrepitude hangs over the scene. It must be included here because it says a final word on the themes of the more overtly parafictional stories. It is a longish tale, about 11,000 words, which can be summarized fairly briefly.

A brilliant man on the make in a collapsing civilization takes over a rundown factory and, by ruthless exploitation, turns it into a super-profitable business. His ruthlessness becomes total when he misunderstands an accounting ploy by his chief clerk, who is in fact honest; he has the man killed and his head exposed on the wire fence.

Wholly in control of the local economy and the local population, he is king of his paranoid vision of power. But, outside the factory, the poor are massing because this is a food factory and they are starving. The king, responsible, must deal with them. He does, with flame-throwers.

He watches the operation and tells his thoughts, struck about half sane at the end:

> ...thousands of men had stood on hills and roofs and watched such scenes of terrible destruction, the result of nothing more than their fear and their intelligence.... I wished I had been born a great painter. I would have worn fine clothes and celebrated the glories of man... rather than wearily kept vigil on this hill, hunchbacked, crippled, one more guilty fool with blood on his hands.

Hunchbacked? Crippled? He had withheld that until these last lines of confession. He is another fat man of history, unloved and finally unloving in a ghetto of one, but powerful enough to take revenge on the helpless mob. And needing love badly enough to finally cave in to the knowledge of deadly power and deadly inadequacy.

This is raw exposure of the theme underlying most of Carey's short fiction: the need for racial, communal love if we are not to destroy ourselves in the savagery of spiritual alienation and solitude.

I repeat that Carey is a user of science fiction, not a genre writer. He is the best user of it in Australia, not only a better writer in every sense than the rest of us but unafraid to turn his usage to themes closer to basic love and despair than the rest of us have courage for. We are those he writes about.

CAREY GOES CYBERSURFING
BY MARIE MACLEAN

Peter Carey's *The Unusual Life of Tristan Smith* is a dazzling book. A sprawling, sensual, rambunctious marvel of a novel, it drives its readers out of their everyday world and every comfortable preconception. It takes enormous risks, not at least that of demanding our understanding for the monstrous.

The first striking achievement of *The Unusual Life of Tristan Smith* is in creating two wholly imaginary countries on some alternative Earth, countries with their customs, their governments, their literatures, their languages, their entangled histories. It is a feat I have rarely seen equaled, except perhaps in Ursula Le Guin's *The Dispossessed*. Yet these lands, like hers, are based at the same time on a study of actual human history. In the case of *Tristan Smith* this history is particularly that of colonization. These living pages say more about the colonial, the post-colonial and the way they shape minds for generations than many an academic text.

As with so many stories of virtual worlds, there is a strong ideological climate constructed. But Carey's brilliant way of avoiding the didacticism which always threatens books of this sort is that the ideological warfare takes place not so much between two political systems, though they are adumbrated, as between the theatrical life of two countries. This permits ideologies to speak through the body. In one country, the island state of Efrica, these are sexual bodies, acrobatic bodies, contorting bodies. In the other, the master state of Voorstand, falling bodies dicing with death contend with pseudo-physical images in the shimmering world of simulacra.

The relationship between the two countries is similar to that between South Africa (the Boer experience is explicitly acknowledged by Peter Carey as a model) and a neighboring area of influence - the suggestion conveyed by language and customs is somewhere like Mauritius. But there is no direct correlation: indeed, every time one is tempted to establish an allegory or even a coherent virtuality, the text neatly sidesteps in a move rather akin to cybersurfing.

One could say that the closest equivalent to the dominant culture, that of Voorstand and its capital, Saarlim, is the grotesquely dichotomized world of the future conjured up by Philip K. Dick in *Do Androids Dream of Electric Sheep*, the novel which became *Blade Runner*, or by William Gibson in stories like *Virtual Light*. One finds the same contrast of the wealthy technological masters in their marble towers, and the groveling, mutant, kill-you-for-a-buck, horde of illegal immigrants and beggars who populate the streets. In *Tristan Smith*, however, one culture and one architectural icon dominate: the Sirkus and its ubiquitous domes.

The Sirkus, once established as a theater to enshrine the strongly moral folk tales of the original Voortrekkers, has become what the Games were in Rome. The thrill for the elite, the pabulum of the masses, it combines the vast screens and acoustic and visual magic of the latest technology with primitive blood lust, as ever more death defying human acts combine with real blood and brains in your front row seat. The performers will do anything for the money, and you can buy anything with yours.

Set against this is the other world, that of Efrica. Though still attractive by comparison with Voorstand, its culture is being gradually invaded by the Sirkus just as its politics are controlled through stealth - or through murder if need be—by the machinations of the Voorstand secret police.

The ideological opposition and earlier popular culture of Efrica are represented by yet another circus/theater. This is the Feu Follet where the book and Tristan's life begin, and where much of the first (Efrican) half of the story takes place. This theater is centered on the body and on immense bodily control. It has its roots in the true circus, and even its obligatory performances of the classics, like the "Scottish play" of the book's opening, are transformed by circus techniques. But here the actors are not expendable...when they dive from the high wire they have a safety net. They don't become mega-stars or earn mega-bucks, their financial and emotional safety net is their collective.

None of this is sentimentalized. Carey knows the world of alternative theater intimately. It's all there in a series of unforgettable scenes, the idealism, the bitchiness, the energy, the wild flashes of actor and audience rapport, the shoe-string budgets, the adrenalin and the envy; and all heightened to the point of hysteria by the sudden birth of a monstrous, misbegotten scrap of genius to Felicity Smith. the actor manager of the Feu Follet.

The account of the birth is a *tour de force* in itself, told from the point of view of the fetus. The time I have spent researching stories of naming and multiple parenting makes me appreciate the more the wonderful immediacy of literature. Nothing I might write could ever have the impact of the scene after Tristan's birth when the nurse confronts his three fathers, who love his mother, live with her sometimes, have sex with her, perhaps; each therefore having a different social or biological claim on the mewling scrap of life she has produced. Which, the nurse asks, is Mr. Smith?

But there is no Mr. Smith. Tristan bears no father's name, indeed Smith is only his mother's pseudonym, and on his birth certificate the whole question of genealogy is resolved when he is registered as Tristan Actor-Manager.

One of Carey's immense qualities is the way he forces you to rethink conventional gendering. All his characters are highly sexed and freely sexually active, but as for the conventions of feminine and masculine behavior, forget it. These people make their own lives, and the women are as likely to be fathering as the men to be mothering. The wonderful freedom of his female protagonists has always been one of Carey's strengths. There are reminiscences in Tristan's theater director mother of the women in *Illywhacker*: Phoebe flying off to another life, Leah doing her emu dance, Emma fiercely nurturing her monster brood.

For Felicity Smith too gives birth to a monster, the clawing screaming figure of that other, the artist, whom most of us, eventually, strangle before it can take over our bodies and our lives. But in this case, generated from a performance of *Macbeth*, the "birth strangled babe, ditch delivered by a drab" is saved to be raised as the new messiah of the grotesque. His mother snatched him from kindly euthanasia and staggers back to her theater and her part. Displaying him to her stunned audience, she says: "Thou shalt get kings, though thou be none."

Like all oracles this is true in its own way. Fierce determination and that complete disregard for the wishes or comfort of others, which characterizes genius, finally enable the deformed scrap of humanity to become an actor. On the stage, behind the make-up, My God what make-up, and in an ever progressive series of masks and disguises, he does in the end generate royalty, the absolute power of the successful actor.

The first half of the book ends up with Felicity dangling grotesquely from the flies of the Feu Follet, murdered by the secret police. In the second half of the book, set in Voorstand, Tristan takes his revenge. He subverts the whole culture by removing the electronics from a simulacrum of the country's most revered icon, Bruder Mouse, and re-humanizing or re-demonizing the creature. In the end our hero escapes; the book refuses closure. I hope this is not just a fashionable gesture but that Tristan and his ambiguous entourage of father-mothers will be back with another volume of his unusual life.

Peter Carey has the chutzpah to set up his masterly work as the latter-day equivalent of the greatest pre-post-modern novel of them all, *The Life and Opinions of Tristram Shandy*. Like Sterne, he entertains, he shocks and he makes enormous demands on the readers. We jump from mind to mind and from the seemingly real to the frankly incredible. At the same time, like Sterne's readers, we are led into endless fascinating byways where we can lose ourselves for hours.

There is, for example, the taste of other languages, a playing with the relations of one dialect to another and of English to Afrikaans, French and Spanish. If you're a language junkie like me you can explore the glossary to your heart's content. Carey's research is remarkable. His use of folklore alone reveals profound knowledge, and yet it is all so lightly handled that the work involved may not be apparent to a casual reader. On the other hand, you may be hooked on history, on oral literature, on cooking, or geography. Then you are led away into the multiple possibilities of the footnotes, chuckling at each simulacrum of scholarship and enticed into even further Sternian speculation. Mind you, you can ignore all these fascinating byways and resolutely follow the main adventures of the protagonist. The choice is yours.

There are three main lines characteristic of Carey's work which are triumphantly carried through in *The Unusual Life of Tristan Smith*. The first is the construction of alternative worlds and virtual realities, which has so startled us from *The Fat Man in History* and *Bliss* onwards. This is coupled with the demand on readers that they embark on the same magical *tour de force* as "making the dragon" (*Illywhacker*). One more effort, one moment of perfect concentration, and you too can suddenly be transported into a different plane of being.

The second is his subordination of the conventions of society to the demands of the artist, the genius and the loner, so characteristic of *Oscar and Lucinda* and *Tristan Smith*. This overthrow of convention goes hand in hand with the liberation of the body. No other Australian writer is such a virtuoso of the sensual, of touch, of taste, of color and texture.

The third is the way he boldly tears the monstrous and

grotesques from their comfortable repression, confronting us, as he has done all the way from *The Fat Man* to *The Tax Inspector*, with the knowledge that, until we can inspect, accept, love or detest the monstrous in ourselves, we can never be truly human.

POSTMODERNISM VS POSTCOLONIALISM
BY ELIZABETH HARDY

The earth holds an infinite profusion of seeds. Seeds contain forms and worlds yet to germinate, the roots, leaves, and flowers of the entire plant are invisibly enclosed in the seed. Paradoxically, the unborn potential of future life is fused, within a seed, to primordial patterns that were laid down in the very beginning. The seed's capacity to engender new life seems to derive from the imprint of patterns carried through the ages.

Robert Lawlor,
*Voices of the First Day:
Awakening in the Aboriginal Dreamtime*[20]

The myriad and kaleidoscopic worlds that comprise Peter Carey's *The Unusual Life of Tristan Smith* are a key source of the disorientation that frequently threatens to dominate this book. As I see it, though, these disparate sources of confusion and contradiction are countered by a narrative exploration of causality that recalls the organic lifecycle of a seed. Carey's preoccupation with the interrelationship of past, present and

---

20. Robert Lawlor, *Voices of the First Day: Awakening in the Aboriginal Dreamtime* (Rochester, Vermont: Inner Traditions, 1991), p.1.

future creates a cyclical continuity that echoes the eternally renewable patterns of nature.

What are some of the sources of disorder and disunity in this text? There are many, but I want to focus on two: the ambiguous and shifting relationships that exist between Australia and the imaginary country Efica, and between the United States and imaginary Voorstand, and the generically eclectic bricks with which Carey has "built" this text.

This is a novel that demands, on several levels, to be termed "postmodern": from its sustained delight in language games and signification and overt "sampling" of a range of genres (such as science fiction, magic realism, detective fiction and farce), to the explorations of visual evidence of the postmodern presence, in the appearance of the simulacrum, and a range of examples of postmodern architecture and interior design.[21] Added to this generic melting pot—and in stark contrast to the "apolitical" stance of postmodernism[22]—is postcolonialism, and its overtly political agenda. Although the logical effect of such stylistic mutability would be intensified confusion, in fact the addition of a strong postcolonial element returns the focus to the interrelationship of past, present and future and "anchors"

---

21. For example, when the characters are driving towards Saarlim they see a life-size robotic simulacrum of Bruder Mouse, a key protagonist of the Saarlim Sirkus, running through the landscape and knock it down with the car in order to keep it as a "souvenir." Tristan relates his first sighting of the creature: "I looked out the window...there, on the right, on a cutting, a three-foot high Mouse was running beside the car" (p.286).

The most striking example of postmodern architecture can be seen in the Feu Follet building, which combines different architectural styles and periods: "Between the striking black and white posters was a rusty roller door. Above the roller door was a second floor with six high, gracefully arched windows. The building was topped by the tower in which I had been conceived...the rest of the company lived in little monks' cells scattered through the building." (p.19).

22. See Diana Brydon's discussion of postmodernism as "politically ambivalent" in "The White Inuit Speaks: Contamination as Literary Strategy" in *The Postcolonial Studies Reader*, edited by Bill Ashcroft, Gareth Griffiths and Helen Tiffin (London: Routledge, 1995), pp.136.

the text in an exploration of the enduring presence of the past in this imaginary universe. The postcolonial presence in the text modifies the postmodern tendency to internationalization, maintaining instead a local perspective and a sustained emphasis on the continuing relevance of the past. The focus on temporal cycles facilitates the text's examination of some of the enduring problems experienced by a postcolonial society that cannot divorce itself from its historical exploitation, but continues to define itself negatively in relation to a dominant cultural center. In both the imaginary worlds of Voorstand and Efica, the past does not exist as a static, long-forgotten series of events that are irrelevant to the contemporary world; instead, history is perceived as an incomplete record of past events that demands to be augmented and reinterpreted by those living in the present. The many historical references and commentaries in Tristan's footnotes, for example, create a parallel text that insists that there is always another point of view which exists outside the authoritative textual body. The footnotes allow Tristan to include an overtly subversive perspective on Efican history that is clearly missing from official accounts, and so take the first steps towards a future of cultural autonomy for Efica, through the rewriting of that country's past.

Similarly, it is clear that the decisions made in the present will profoundly affect the nature and quality of life in the future. Descriptions of the countryside on the outskirts of Saarlim City, Voorstand's capital, reveal that the poisonous postmodern culture of the Saarlim Sirkus is inexorably encroaching across the entire country, and beyond: "As we came closer and closer to Voorstand...color crept into the soil, first in pinks which became more and more bilious, then in acid greens. We stopped to rest beneath butts as gorgeous and sickly as melted ice-cream" (p.263).

The Unusual Life of Tristan Smith is a perpetual tussle between the postmodern and postcolonial, chaos and order. Although many recognizable components and themes of postmodern literature feature in this text, several postcolonial issues repeatedly arise: the center/periphery division, Efica's negative self-definition based on its differences from the dominant Voorstand culture, the complete eradication of an indigenous people and culture, and the feeling in Efica of being culturally abandoned by rapacious colonizing figures.[23] In this novel, however, the postmodern and the postcolonial are not always discrete presences, but frequently come together in a fusion that develops the postcolonial project. This phenomenon can be seen, for example, in the novel's ending. Having offended an influential member of the Saarlim Sirkus culture, and dodging assassins from Efica and Voorstand's equivalents of the CIA, the characters disguise themselves and escape from Voorstand, into yet another imaginary country. Unlike the imaginary Efica and Voorstand, this place is not mapped for the reader, but Tristan offers a detailed description of this new landscape, seeing it as a pastoral paradise where new beginnings are possible: "We drove five days across some of the most beautiful country I have ever seen.... As we went higher, the cornfields were silver, gold, brown.... Raw eggs we ate, by streams in sunlight, mung beans by the handful, hard corn intended for cattle" (pp.412-13). As the characters escape from the pages of the novel into another adventure, refusing to accept textual closure, they participate simultaneously in the end of the novel, and the beginning of a new adventure. And, although it seems that the ending is distinctively postmodern, it is also postcolonial: in the same moment of textual escape, the characters enter a new world of intense purity and natural beauty that is untouched by any colonizing force. While enacting elements of postmodern theory, the characters have simultaneously achieved a viable alternative to the postcolonial ideal of decolonization, by changing worlds to discover an "uncontaminated"[24] environment free from the

---

23. See the introduction to *The Empire Writes Back: Theory and Practice in Postcolonial Literatures*, edited by Bill Ashcroft et al (London: Routledge, 1989) for a comprehensive discussion of the components of postcolonialism.

24. This is, of course, a relative description of the unnamed imaginary world to which the characters escape. To quote Kwame Anthony Appiah in

cultural oppression they have endured in contemporary postcolonial Efica and Voorstand, the cultural center.

The interconnection of past, present and future is also significantly developed in the confusing and contradictory parallels that exist between Efica and Australia, and Voorstand and the United States. Although Efica shares Australia's open spaces and harsh light, its history of indigenous oppression, its laconic speech patterns and a severe case of "cultural cringe," Efica is not simply an imagined or futuristic version of Australia. Similarly, although Voorstand's Sirkus culture is a parodic exaggeration of the colonizing potential of the United States' Disneyland culture, and the increasingly violent nature of everyday life on its city streets, Voorstand cannot simply be seen as the US of the future. The imaginary and real countries share a more ephemeral relationship that is difficult to categorize. The reader is invited to fit together this shifting jigsaw, and find the similarities between the real and imaginary cultures, and the concomitant implications about the nature and direction of Australian and American society.

The ambiguous relationship between real and imaginary nations is developed in the text's geographical paradox. References to real-world countries, such as Britain and France, and their cultures make it clear that Efica and Voorstand are part of a world that is shaped very much like the real world of the reader. Several clues in the text indicate that Efica and Voorstand may be geographically proximate to the positions of Australia and the United States respectively, in the real world.[25]

"The Postcolonial and the Postmodern" in *The Postcolonial Studies Reader*: "If there is a lesson in the broad shape of this circulation of cultures, it is surely that we are all already contaminated by each other." (p. 124).

25. One of these clues appears on the novel's first page, where it is stated that Efica is situated "between the tropic of Capricorn and the 30th parallel" (p.5) and the second is contained in the map of Voorstand which appears at the beginning of Book Two, indicating that this country intersects the Arctic Circle and shares some topographical features with the USA. It seems that these geographical indicators are deliberately vague to further prevent a direct parallel from being drawn between the two sets of real and

However, in the imaginary universe of the text Australia and the United States do not seem to exist. Have Australia and the United States simply been chopped out of the world map, with Efica and Voorstand pasted across the resulting gaps? I would argue that the US and Australia have not been "removed" from the fictional universe but have been covered over by Voorstand and Efica, both of which display many traces of the "original" cultures as a part of their everyday reality. For example, the scene which describes the entry point to Saarlim City is comprised of images instantly associated with large American cities; a large, shifting population of many different cultures, all of whom have come in search of The American/Voorstandish dream, hoping to find freedom and unlimited entertainment. The would-be immigrants stand in line to become official POWS:

> The crowds which had scared me now parted before me. And even the queue of would-be POWs—Chinese, Malays, Afghans, Indians (no one Flemish, no one white like the crowds in the vids and zines)—whilst remaining locked fearfully in its proper order, flexed and shifted like a tail threatened with a red-hot poker. (p.296)

Similarly, when Roxanna, buoyed by her fleeting economic independence, insists on buying tickets for a Sirkus playing in Efica, she uses a well-known Australian slang term:

> "Come on." She spoke loudly, so the boy in the foyer could hear. "I'm going to shout you all the Sirkus. Not a vid. The real thing." (p. 159)

The American and Australian "essences" are undeniably present in the imaginary countries, and contribute significantly to Voorstandish and Efican realities. Voorstand and Efica are

---

imaginary countries.

composite nations, comprised partly from fictional material and partly from aspects of real world culture. Carey's creation of a subtle and playfully enigmatic relationship between the real and the imaginary thus avoids being directly representational, and instead, the imaginary countries sustain an allegorical relationship with the countries of the real world. This strong, yet shifting relationship between the real and imaginary countries allows the novel to comment obliquely on the current and future states of Australian and American society, telling us that the future is at least partly under the control of the present generation and will be molded by a combination of the lessons of the past and the actions of the present. Just as the choices and actions in the past have unavoidably affected the present, so irresponsible, violent or weak decisions taken in the present moment will shape the expectations and daily reality of life in the future.

A further link between Efica and Australia is discernible in the structure of this novel. Tristan, as Efican narrator, is at times guided through the contemporary maze of postmodernism towards the postcolonial goal of decolonization by calculated flashes of inspiration that he cannot quite recognize. These flashes emanate from the pre-colonial time that was rich in spiritual meaning in the real country that lies beneath Efica: the Australian Aboriginal Dreaming. Although the indigenous Efican presence has been systematically removed by the colonizers, Tristan indirectly has access to the primal power of a native culture that is inseparable from the land he inhabits. This form of guidance does not become a sustained subtextual presence, but rather offers itself as inspiration when the gaps between worlds allow it to become visible.

Cultural theory has suggested that an Aboriginal person must move through two states (the inner and outer Dream Journeys) to commune with the Dreaming.[26] Tristan has embarked on

---

26, See James Cowan's discussion of inner and outer Dream Journeys and their relationship to the Dreaming, in *Mysteries of the Dreaming: The Spiritual Life of Australian Aborigines* (Dorset: Prism Press, 1989), especially pp.57-70.

a quest for meaningfulness and a sense of stability, and his journey follows the same structure as a Dream Journey, moving through an inner landscape in Book One, and leaving his home to embark on an external journey in Book Two. Tristan is by no means a modern day "Efican Aborigine," but is, rather, adapting a form of buried knowledge from the past to structure the quest for meaning in his present. In this way, a contemporary reinterpretation of some of the guiding principles of the Dreaming are occasionally used by the Efican travelers as they journey towards the possibility of a world imbued with personal meaningfulness. As Tristan continues his search for personal meaning by travelling through new lands beyond the pages of the text, it may be the traces of traditional Aboriginal culture that lead him on his nomadic quest, and indicate that his search will be a life-long cyclical journey, marked by births and deaths, beginnings and endings. The seeds of the Aboriginal past have been blown far into the future to take root in the imaginary soil of Efica.

It is initially surprising to discover that an organic world-view based on cyclical unity underlies a text which overtly embraces contradiction and disorder. However, even as it embraces many of the key tenets of postmodern literature, the text simultaneously rejects the associated cynical postmodern aesthetic of chaos and meaninglessness. Instead, it celebrates and develops the postmodern assertion that the reader has a vital role in bringing a text to life: if coherence can be discerned in the most confusing literary universe, it may also be present in the real world, which is often more bewildering and difficult to "read" than any work of literature. The spirit of optimism that survives through all the book's temporal periods and physical settings suggests that hope, and life itself, are potentially eternally renewable. This belief in the triumph of personal regeneration is evident on the novel's last page, as Tristan asserts "my unusual life was really just beginning" (p.414)—the narrative circle is both completed and opened again to begin another cycle that has not yet been recorded in the pages of a book.

THE ART OF XENOGRAPHY: JACK VANCE'S "GENERAL CULTURE" NOVELS
BY TERRY DOWLING

> I told of force and time and space,
> I told of hence and yonder;
> I asked if she would come with me
> To know my worlds of wonder.
>
> Navarth/
> *The Palace of Love*

> "After all, it's just another planet with strange customs. There are millions of them."
>
> Rosenbaum,
> "A Dusk of Idols"[27]

> "Give 'em the old human angle—glamor, mystery, thrills."
>
> Howard Freyburg/
> "Sjambak"

In the early part of his novel *Emphyrio* (1969), Jack Vance has his fifteen-year-old hero, Ghyl Tarvoke, make the remark:

---

27. James Blish, "A Dusk of Idols." *Amazing*, March 1961, p.28.

> "As I see it, the cosmos is probably infinite.... So there are local situations—a tremendous number of them. Indeed in a situation of infinity, there are an indefinite set of local conditions, so that somewhere there is bound to be anything, if this anything is even remotely possible." (Em/l/54)

Vance's abiding concern is with such "local situations." His is the art of xenography—of devising and exploring exotic and alien societies in a very distant future period when mankind has spread far from our own planetary system.[28]

Vance is not alone in this xenological enterprise. As Poul Anderson says: "Planet-building is a lot of fun,"[29] and the art of the worldsmith—of the xenographical "travelogue"—has always been firmly established. Larry Niven contrived a most wonderful universe in his Known Space stories; Frank Herbert put together his ConSentiency (probably in a completely different universe to his famous *Dune* series); and Poul Anderson had his own "future history," incorporating as it does countless xenographical adventures and xenological mysteries set in the years of the Polesotechnic League, the Terran Empire, and the subsequent Breakup with the inevitable "lost colonies" and "genetic drift." Others like Hal Clement, Isaac Asimov, Keith Laumer, Cordwainer Smith, Harry Harrison, Ursula Le Guin, James Schmitz, Andre Norton, E. C. Tubb, Sydney Van Scyoc and Lloyd Biggle Jr., to name a few, have all turned their hands to it.

In spite of an impressive checklist of authors and works, there still exists for many people a difficulty in accepting and

---

28. The Vance editions cited in this survey are coded as shown in the list at the end of this chapter. While *Wyst: Alastor 1716* (DAW, 1978), and "Frietzke's Turn," in *Triax*, edited by Robert Silverberg (Pinnacle, 1977), were not available for consideration when this article was first written, several minor amendments have been made in this 2013 reprinted version to allow for aspects of their content.

29. Poul Anderson, "Introduction," *Question and Answer* (Ace, 1978).

assessing sf works concerned with the "soft" sciences and humanities, perhaps because the creation and exploitation of alien cultures and technologies was one of the main areas of abuse in the formative days of the genre. The Barsooms, Pellucidars and Mongos were needed as contexts for the scientific adventure romances; the more "hard"-science/technology oriented readers were quickly disenchanted with those who raged pell-mell along the road pioneered by Wells and neglected the more sober approach of Verne and his successors. The point seemed to be missed (or more probably obscured) that Wells—himself the recipient of a scientific education from T.H. Huxley that was in some ways superior to that of Verne—chose to be primarily concerned with sociological and ideological matters.

For some, the contemporary position is hardly different. It is as if sciences like social anthropology, archaeology, comparative ethnology, semiology, philology, etc., do not qualify for the genre because they overlook technological extrapolations for the business of noting how humans function. When Vance writes merely that the space-pirates fleeing Welgen failed to "go into whisk" (T:A/12) or star-drive, it is because he has other things to attend to. The hyperdrive is merely hardware, just as a Cessna aircraft or a Land-Rover are utility items serving their users. Those who take exception to this "oversimplification" and pseudo-science are guilty of pettifoggery. In *Dune* (1965) Frank Herbert does not bother to explain how his Heighliners or ornithopters function. They are furniture for the complex sociological-ecological stage he has set.

For our purposes, we shall make one important distinction. *Xenology* (also called Exobiology) is alien "anthropology"—the study of the stranger, *Xenography* is the portrayal of that life-form within the physical and demographical environment that is its natural and/or chosen habitat. *Xenological* stories are those dealing with First Contacts, initial pioneering confrontations, extraterrestrial visitations and so on, and are most frequently puzzle stories relying on some sort of cultural analysis. We recall James Blish's excellent short story, "And

Some Were Savages" (1960), Stanley Weinbaum's classic "A Martian Odyssey" (1934), P.F. Woods' unforgettable "Fishing Trip" (1962), Brian Aldiss' "Tyrant's Territory" (1962), or Poul Anderson's "Hiding Place" (1961), as well as novels like James White's *All Judgment Fled* (1968), Lem's *Solaris* (1961), and even Clarke's *Rendezvous with Rama* (1973)—though here we have the xenographical treatment of the artifact rather than the resolution of the puzzle of Rama's ultimate purpose or the fate of its occupants.

The *xenographical* story, on the other hand, attempts to put together the alien world and lifestyle in all their "mundane" detail, to create the alien and exotic as commonplace. We could describe it as conceptual, extrapolative or speculative ethnography, but whatever term we use, it is the portrayal of alien worlds in sufficient detail for that portrayal to have been one of the main reasons for the writing of the book.

Inevitably, the two strands can become inseparable, although few novels are long enough or written cohesively enough to build on and develop the initial First Contact/xenological mystery premise and still give a truly substantial and convincing xenographical picture as well.

But there are exceptions. A perfect example of the successful blending of xenological themes with things xenographical, one that is an exception to the usual rule of superficial and over-ambitious works, is Niven and Pournelle's *The Mote in God's Eye* (1975). To field its central xenological mystery and create the proper First Contact "tension," this novel uses the full range of "teasers" presented in a mounting sequence. We are first given the alien artifact and its technological and phenomenal implications; then a non-human alien life-form—conveniently dead so as to sustain the mystery surrounding origins and attitudes; sufficient hints to amplify the possibilities of anything, leaving readers to capitalize on clues and make their own attempts at preliminary cultural analyses.

What natural selection could produce such an asymmetrical somatic type? What were the "statues of gods" discarded into space before the probe was intercepted?

So the careful pattern goes on, both revealing and withholding. Finally, when all the classic First Contact potentialities have been realized, we are given an idea of the alien ethos of the Moties, and the xenological mystery has a xenographical denouement rather akin to Van Scyoc's final revelations in *Assignment: Nor'Dyren* (1973).

A MILLION ECCENTRIC LITTLE CIVILIZATIONS

If we could speak of such a thing as a typical xenographical novel, we would probably end up with something like this: It is set in the reasonably distant future of the human race, when our species has spread beyond the Solar System to other star systems. The continued homogeneity of this human stock would depend entirely upon the sophistication of communication and transportation links, and on whether or not there are extraterrestrial cultures to encourage racial cohesion or contribute to its breakdown due to cultural exchange and/or exploitation. Either way, local loyalties prevail, and there is invariably some sort of "federation" of these human (and possibly extraterrestrial) ally worlds, often co-ordinated from Earth.

Generally speaking, however, the resulting picture is founded on a fundamental premise ably summed up by one of Poul Anderson's characters:

> "Before long, the scale of human society will become so big as to be forever beyond human control. The idea of a unified Galaxy is nonsense, if you stop to think about it; there isn't that much trade or intercourse of any sort. A million eccentric little civilizations will spring up and go their own ways."[30]

---

30. Poul Anderson, *Question and Answer*, p.142.

Sometimes these civilizations remain regionally cohesive, so that in Bayley's *The Garments of Caean* (1978), for example, we hear of how "nearly a hundred inhabited planets made up the Ziode nation"—a single vast interstellar "country."[31] But most often we have the solitary "lost colonies" of so many xenographical works.

Because of wars (interstellar, interplanetary, international and civil, arising for whatever ideological, economic or xenophobic reasons); and because of communication problems (arising from the resulting cycles of expansion and abandonment or from sheer logistical limitations—e.g., Niven's slowboats, Le Guin's NAFAL ships, Cordwainer Smith's huge slower-than-light sailships, Kornbluth and Pohl's longliners, etc.), we have either a human-derived planetary culture that is somehow isolated and given time in which to become a distinct racial and cultural subtype, a parallel-evolution anthrotype culture, or a non-human culture, being discovered/re-discovered and examined with an eye to incorporating that culture into the federation.

This contact can be anything from a formal survey team to shipwrecked spacefarers, rescue missions, individual soldiers-of-fortune, etc. For example, an expedition of Ziode cultural anthropologists—

> ...had begun outside Caeanic civilization proper, on that part of the Tzist Arm along which it was presumed mankind had emigrated. They hoped to find early settlements, by-passed outposts, which might give them some clues as to how the peculiarities of Caeanic culture had developed.[32]

Usually such agencies (especially at the level of the formal survey team) are bound to observe a non-interference code of some kind (e.g., Biggle Jr.'s IPR regulation preventing "outside

---

31. Barrington J. Bayley, *The Garments of Caean* (Fontana, 1978), p.42.

32. Barrington J. Bayley, *The Garments of Caean*, p.27.

intervention" on Branoff IV in *The World Menders* (1971) or de Camp's "technological blockade" on Krishna in *The Tower of Zanid* [1958]).[33] It is through the adventures, wanderings and discoveries of such a representative body or troubleshooter that the xenographical picture develops, the plot of the novel is enacted, and usually some sort of xenological mystery solved. Inevitably, such a context makes for a collision of values, mores and prejudices, and at this point a novel might identify itself as being predominantly homiletic, polemical, satirical or designed as exotic adventure entertainment and "wondermongering." Quite often the nature of the sub-genre means the development of all of these aspects to some extent. And whether a xenographical novel's fundamental concerns be sociological and ideological (*The Dispossessed* [1974]) or simple xenological mystery (*Assignment: Nor'Dyren*), there is always the basic idea of cultural analysis.

To take three examples not written by Vance to illustrate the type of work we are considering, we have Ursula K. Le Guin's Hugo and Nebula winning *The Left Hand of Darkness* (1969), Poul Anderson's *The Night Face* (1963) and Kornbluth and Pohl's *Search the Sky* (1954).

In *The Left Hand of Darkness*, an envoy is sent to the cold world of Gethen or Winter in an effort to encourage its various planetary societies and a most uniquely adapted "human" racial type to renew dealings with the other human worlds. Genly Ai, the envoy, wants them to join an eighty-three planet Ekumen of Known Worlds (reminiscent of Vance's Oikumene and so many other "federations"—Herbert's ConSentiency, Biggle Jr.'s Federation of Independent Worlds, Van Scyoc's Civilized Unity, etc.), but is limited in how he can induce the locals to do this by Ekumen policy—what is essentially a form of noninterference code—the Law of Cultural Embargo.

While Gethen is by no means a technologically primitive world (as so many often are in the xenographer's index), it still

---

33. Lloyd Biggle Jr, *The World Menders* (Arrow, 1975), p.22; L. Sprague de Camp, *The Tower of Zanid* (Airmont, 1963), p.8.

possesses an almost characteristic medieval aspect—or rather, one of what we shall call "enlightened medievalism": more of a sociological and ideological than technological kind. We are made to feel that this is all a part of local climatic factors and Gethen's isolation. The keynote is isolation.

> It is a marginal world, on the edge. Out beyond it towards the South Orion Arm no world has been found where men live. And it is a long way back from Winter to the prime worlds of the Ekumen, the hearth-worlds of our race: fifty years to Hain-Davenant, a man's lifetime to Earth.[34]

The cultural, philosophical and psychological "collisions" that occur on Gethen stem mainly from the fact that the Gethen anthrotype has developed for itself a unique sexual condition—an androgynous estrus cycle known as "kemmer." For a majority of the time a Gethenian is a hermaphroditic neuter, polarizing to one sex or the other according to a partner's emerging role for only a few days in each month. Genly Ai only comes to appreciate what this means and how it colors the differing worldviews through a personal telepathic union with Estraven. Cultural analysis has shown him the intricate cultural profile of Gethen, but only in a detached, analytical way. Genly Ai must achieve some measure of empathy to grasp what this new "humanity" and "normal" really mean.

One final factor that is a frequent staple of xenographical works is the inclusion of some added paranormal dimension within the culture being examined. The members of such an alien society are often presented as having some well-developed psionic skills; an indication not only of their alienness but also a reminder that there are mysteries to the universe that different groups of sentients under different circumstances may have solved. This has always been one of the basic ploys for making

---

34. Ursula K. Le Guin, *The Left Hand of Darkness* (Panther, 1973), p.200.

extraterrestrials as "alien" as possible—to give them qualities we as a race generally don't have. Typically, we hear that:

> Martian civilization had developed in a quite different direction from that of Earth. It had developed no important knowledge of the physical sciences, no technology. But it had developed the social sciences.... And it had developed fully the parapsychological sciences of the mind, which Earth was just beginning to discover.[35]

On Gethen this dimension is represented by the Foretellers, intricate groups of gifted individuals dwelling in their Fastnesses and capable of predicting the future.

The Night Face features many of the characteristics of Le Guin's novel. It concerns the re-establishment of contact with a "lost colony" isolated from the mainstream of human civilization for twelve hundred years.[36] During this time there has occurred the same inevitable "genetic drift" (p. 22), and the Gwydiona anthrotype too has undergone "no degeneracy: rather, a refinement" (p. 15). It is the full nature and significance of this "modification" that the members of the Namerican/Lochlann expedition to Gwydion must understand. A mutation has drastically altered the metabolism of the local anthrotype, and for a period of ten days known as Bale at the beginning of every Gwydiona springtime, the unusually peaceful and anarchistic natives go insane and show the "Night Face."

ALONG THE SCENIC ROUTE

> "It is good to have an end to journey towards; but it is the journey that matters, in the end."
> Genly Ai / *The Left Hand of Darkness*

---

35. Fredric Brown, "Earthmen Bearing Gifts," *Galaxy*. June, 1960, p.149.
36. Poul Anderson, *The Night Face* (Ace, 1978), Reference edition.

It should be mentioned right away, before coming to Vance's stories, that they are first and foremost exotic adventures. They are not meant to be ethnographical treatises (though in the course of presenting the adventure this becomes one of Vance's richest gifts to the reader) but rather belong to the tradition of the peripatetic novel—tales of journeys and quests (and hence travelogues) with occasional touches of the picaresque and the satirical.

Once again, all this is in accord with firm sf traditions. The peripatetic format ideally suits the genre, for what better way to give a protagonist encounters with the unusual than to send him on a journey, to give him a goal or an objective which requires a series of such confrontations. Whether this is to win a kingdom that is rightfully his, rescue a princess, or nullify a terrible secret weapon, the hero must get "out on the road." Thus we have something like Stanley Weinbaum's "A Martian Odyssey," William F. Temple's *The Three Suns of Amara* (aka *A Trek to Na-Abiza*) (1961) or Cordwainer Smith's *Quest of the Three Worlds* (1966); and inevitably we have xenological quest-adventure novels like Eric Frank Russell's *Men, Martians and Machines* (1955) and van Vogt's *The Voyage of the Space Beagle* (1951) (in which the members of an exploratory expedition are brought into contact with one alien life-form after another: Coeurl, Ixtl and the Anabis), or xenographical adventures like Niven's *Ringworld* (1970) and Kornbluth and Pohl's *Search the Sky*.[37]

In this last novel we have the same breakdown of links between civilizations and the same isolation of colonies found in *The Night Face* or in Asimov's *Foundation* trilogy, though here it is due to what might be termed "gene loss." We are back in an Asimov-like "humans-only" universe, and the story opens on the colony world of Halsey's Planet fourteen hundred years after it has been settled. One man, Ross, is eager to discover why he is surrounded by regression and decay, acres of aban-

---

37. C. M. Kornbluth and Frederik Pohl, *Search the Sky* (Digit, 1960), Reference edition.

doned urban development known as Ghost Towns, declining population numbers, and a sinister lassitude that ignores such factors, pretending that they are a part of natural progress.

Here, as well, we are in a universe that has been settled centuries ago by human colonists travelling in closed-system, multigeneration starships called longliners, without which "the inhabited solar systems would have no means of contact or commerce" (p. 12). On Halsey's Planet, rival trading factions eagerly await the rare arrival of such vessels, hoping they will contain valuable trade commodities and new technological ideas—the benefits of cross-culturalization with the other, older human worlds.

When such a ship does arrive, its crew blissfully ignorant of their true origins, Ross learns that his world was its seventh alternative choice as an intended destination, that six other planets did not activate the huge ship's programmed landing pattern. From a trader named Haarland he then learns that the previous starship arrival from Sirius IV fifteen years before had also bypassed its first three potential destinations. The ominous conclusion: at least nine planets—theoretically flourishing human civilizations—have either been vacated or have deteriorated below the technological level needed to monitor starship approaches and initiate their automatic landing programs.

Haarland then reveals to Ross yet another surprise. Orbiting Halsey's Planet is a scout-ship from the dismantled longliner that originally colonized the world fourteen hundred years before, and it provides Ross with a further mystery. For this ship is a marvelous faster-than-light (F-T-L) vessel, possessing the nucleophoretic or Wesley drive and capable of reaching other star-systems in weeks instead of centuries. Haarland, it turns out, belongs to what is known as a Wesley Family; he is one of a group of people on every human settled world who are aware of the secret of such F-T-L ships, and he explains how longliners were used for colonization deliberately to isolate the settled worlds and forestall interstellar war. He goes on to tell Ross that the recently arrived longliner travelled two centuries to convey to the Wesley representative on Halsey's Planet a warning about genetic impoverishment; something having happened to their own F-T-L ship.

Ross' task is made clear. Haarland wants him to go out in the scoutship and discover why it is that nine worlds have dropped from human ken, ceasing to be in communication with the rest of humanity. He is to locate any other Wesley enclaves possessing the secret of the F-T-L drive and warn them of what is happening: the human race is in danger. As Haarland says: "Maybe the time has come to get the ships out of hiding,"

With the xenological puzzle of the colonies' fates to solve, Ross sets off, and now the novel becomes a xenographical satirical adventure. His first destination, Ragansworld, he finds reduced to dust by war; the second, Gemser, is a regressed gerontocracy, and we are given a harrowing glimpse of its workings as Ross endeavors to escape from its sterile, hidebound social order. On the next world, Azor, he finds a thriving matriarchy, a society in which men are completely subservient to women; and then there is Jones, a world whose population belongs to a rigidly uniform society, its members sharing the identical genetically-selected somatype of their god-figure, Jones. When Ross finally reaches Earth he finds it a planet of naive child-like individuals constantly watched over by a minority of kindly human custodians—all this the result of the Earth having lost its more dynamic genetic strains in the centuries-long colonization programs.

Talking with the custodians, Ross is left to work out the puzzle: to assemble a composite picture of humanity's fate among the stars. He comes to understand full well the significance of the decision to spare humankind the awesome curse of interstellar war, the reason for choosing generation ships and giving them small F-T-L scout-ships to range ahead and seek out suitable worlds for settlement. As Ross realizes: "The F-T-L families have kept their secret too well. No wars between the planets—but stagnation worse than wars" (p. 157). And for such a plight there can only be one remedy:

> "Humanity, then, imprisoned in a thousand sterile tubes, cut off from each other, dying. We feared war, and so we isolated the members with a wall of time.... What if the walls are cracked?... We'll bridge the galaxy with F-T-L transports; and we'll pack the ships with a galaxy of crews! New genes for old; hybrid vigor for dreary decay.... Smash the smooth, declining curve. Cross the strains and then breed them back. Let mankind become genetically wild again...."

Search the Sky admirably illustrates the most common of the two forms of the journey in sf: a "grand tour" approach used by everyone from "Doc" Smith to Isaac Asimov. The second kind may be called the "planetary trek," and it permits an "anthology" of settings and encounters on a single world (e.g., Edgar Rice Burroughs' Martian and Venusian novels, Temple's *The Three Suns of Amara*, etc.).

Vance, of course, makes use of both forms to yield the same end. *The Five Gold Bands* (1950) is of the "grand tour" sort, extending Paddy Blackthorn's quest through a sequence of planetary cultures. The four Tschai novels, on the other hand, utilize the planetary trek. But for Vance, as for so many other authors, no general rule applies. Magnus Ridolph is an epicure-cum-effectuator (rather like the latterday Miro Hetzel in the "general culture" stories), called upon to investigate all manner of xenological mysteries in exotic extraterrestrial settings. Those potentially open-ended series-foundation works like "The Man from Zodiac" (1967) and "Sjambak" (1953) give us Milton Hack, a field representative for a company engaged in selling cultural-development contracts to backward human-derived alien communities, and Wilbur Murphy, a roving "reporter" for a media program, "Know Your Universe!" All three approaches serve to keep a troubleshooter figure "out on the road," combining both forms of the journey and making available a potentially endless variety of exotic settings.

Likewise, the Demon Princes novels combine both forms to

excellent advantage—giving the "grand tour" spectacle of the Oikumene and the Beyond as well as Gersen's overland trek to Aglabat, his ramblings on Sogdian, Sarkovy and Moudervelt.

Through these overland journeyings or sea-voyages Vance does something more than merely "showcase" his chosen exotica. The journey also permits a consolidation of known factors in the face of the otherworldly. It provides a relaxation from excessive "wondermongering"; it is a vital delaying tactic. Many pages of Vance's books are spent in transit from one point to another, and his works can be said to illustrate the truism that it is better to travel hopefully than to arrive, as well as Ruskin's contention that a journey is boring in direct proportion to its swiftness. In Vance's novels there are days when nothing happens, and we must traverse these as well, with the consequent expectation and disappointment.

With Vance the xenographical art is at its most refined, and the purpose of this study is an examination of what he has achieved within the sub-genre. Vance came to his present prominent position as worldsmith and xenographer par excellence through publications like *Startling Stories* (which featured works like *The Five Gold Bands* and *Big Planet* [1952] among many others) and *Thrilling Wonder Stories* (including titles like "The World Thinker" [1945] and *Son of the Tree* [1951]), emerging out of the general mass of writers as an author who brought to the usual exotic alien adventure story a greater sensitivity to background detail, a finer grasp of what it means to be "alien" and therefore a different kind of "normal."[38]

Such an energetic and effective "pulp" apprenticeship also produced an early cohesive-universe anthology series like the Magnus Ridolph stories, anticipating the more ambitious later works. Perhaps we could speak of a noticeable shift and refinement of themes during the sixties with novels like *The Dragon Masters* (1962), *The Last Castle* (1966) and *The Blue World* (1966), but suffice it to say that Vance simply grew better at his

---

38. P. Schuyler Miller, "The Reference Library." *Analog*, January 1965, p.89.

craft, and without the pressures of serving a pulp market was able to tailor his work more strictly according to his own preferences.

We should note, though, what these preferences are. It is not possible to speak of "space opera" simply giving way to works of cultural analysis. For Vance the two modes are inseparable: the one making possible and then benefiting from the other. *The Five Gold Bands*, *Son of the Tree*, *Big Planet*, *The Languages of Pao* (1958), and the Magnus Ridolph stories are all early works demonstrating this blend, and the "space opera" strand continues, whether in the starmenters who raid Trullion and the other Alastrid worlds or in the various activities of, say, Kirth Gersen in the *Demon Princes* series.

To recall Howard Frayberg in "Sjambak," Vance is continually giving his reader "the old human angle—glamor, mystery, thrills," though he is doing this intelligently and with more inspired perceptiveness than is customary among adventure writers. If one is to project cultural extrapolations, then it should be done in an "accessible" fashion.

Like many of the other authors already mentioned, Vance also enjoys developing his universe horizontally as well as chronologically—that is, expanding it at single points in a long time-span, usually through a single character (as Tubb has done with Dumarest, Anderson with Flandry and Nicholas Van Rijn, or Laumer with Retief). Consequently, he has produced a number of series, some of them generously fleshed out, others apparently abandoned mid-stride after one or two episodes. We have stories built around key characters like Magnus Ridolph, Kirth Gersen (in the Demon Princes quintalogy), Adam Reith (in the Tschai tetralogy), Gastel Etzwane (the Durdane trilogy), Cugel the Clever, Milton Hack, and Miro Hetzel.

The problem with such a series approach—the single character approach—is that much of a work's individual appeal, its impact and integrity, comes to rest on the success of any given central character as the author's creation. The novels especially are somehow never truly autonomous, and they can be the unfortunate victims of an author's growing disenchantment with his central figure. Perhaps it is for this reason that a writer like Larry Niven forestalls such a crisis by confining a Known Space character like Louis Wu to a very small chronological and quantitative niche.

Vance has had far more successes than failures in this regard, however. His most successful novels (both unrelated works and those belonging to a series) avoid these possible structural weaknesses by taking a selected planetary focus—like Tschai, Durdane, Big Planet, etc.—and featuring a character who is involved with it, rather than the other way around, with the planet as one more exotic whistlestop for our hero.

It is a significant difference. By limiting the action almost exclusively to that chosen focus, a series then tends to establish its own uppermost limit of development and structuring. The planet Tschai, for example, is host to (at least) four non-human races! It follows then that the adventures of the central character—an errant Earthman named Adam Reith—should cover four books, each dealing significantly with one of these four races and their particular geographical concentration. On the other hand, events in the Durdane trilogy (all involving Gastel Etzwane, a native of the planet) describe an expanding spiral: domestic to local to international to interplanetary and interstellar.

But these are both limited or closed sequences, unlike those open-ended series developed (or to be developed) around a Magnus Ridolph or a Milton Hack. They are cohesive and autonomous units rather than unlimited anthology affairs.

As a general rule then, Vance's autonomous selected focus works (both "unrelated" novels and closed series) are far more successful than those using the anthology/central-character format. But since 1973 Vance has been adding to a "new series" in which he seems to have solved the problem of the open-ended sequence completely. The series so far includes such novels as *Alastor 2262* (1973), *The Gray Prince* (1974), *Showboat World* (1975), *Marune: Alastor 933* (1975), *The Dogtown Tourist*

Agency (1975) and *Maske: Thaery* (1976)—all self-contained works dealing with separate world-situations, but all set in a related spatial framework.

In placing these various world cultures in the same universe, Vance has taken pains to make this process a somewhat retrospective one, and through a number of carefully developed clues we can add to the above list *Emphyrio* and the earlier novels of the Durdane trilogy (*The Anome* (1971), *The Brave Free Men* (1972), *The Asutra* (1973). Even the four Tschai novels (*City of the Chasch* (1968), *Servants of the Wankh* (1969), *The Dirdir* (1969), *The Pnume* (1970) and other less recent works are amenable to its framework, although one must take care to place checks upon such an inclusive tendency.

While many of the name duplications that occur (and they are inevitable considering the great number used) are mutually compatible—the world of Alode known to the people of Ambroy on Halma may have some "cosmopolitan" connection with Alode the Cliff on Marune—it is bootless to press for too many connections. One might argue that the quarti-quartino of Blue Ruin sipped by Magnus Ridolph on the Glass Jetty at Providencia connects his interstellar adventures to the new series under discussion via the tub of Blue Ruin offered in an inn at Lanteen on Big Planet, but such correspondences do not automatically justify claims for compatibility. One is an expensive liqueur, the other very much a local home-brew. So too Detwiler, the Phrone noble from Ethelrinda Cordas in "The Man from Zodiac," has no kinship whatever with Zarfo Detwiler, the Lokhar mechanic from Central Kislovan on Tschai.

The fact remains that Vance's universe has been largely an organic development, augmented and consciously developed only belatedly. The slender threads that can be seen as holding it together provide as many problems as useful connection points—one need only consider the difficulties of reconciling a Commonwealth of worlds with an Oikumene or a Gaean Reach; or ponder the chances of the world Alpheratz VI visited by Miro Hetzel in his boyhood being the same Alpheratz visited by Milton Hack or being the Langtry world of that name in *The Five Gold Bands*.

But elsewhere these connections are unmistakably intentional, and the clues that link up the "general culture" stories are quite deliberately placed. A showboat plying the Lower Vissel on Big Planet bears the name "Miraldra's Enchantment" after Miraldra the Enchantress, a constellation visible from the planet Koryphon depicted in *The Gray Prince*. The same showboat performs the play "Emphyrio"—a legend central to the adventures of Ghyl Tarvoke on the planet Halma in the novel *Emphyrio*. Similarly, the dexax that explodes the torcs worn by the citizens of Shant on Durdane is used to tip the harpoons of the Uldra sky-sharks of Koryphon. The Historical Institute of Earth is common to Emphyrio, the Durdane trilogy, and the universe of the Oikumene and the Demon Princes, while Alastor Cluster and many of its cultural appurtenances (the Connatic, the Whelm, starmenters, the sport of hussade, and common forms of address, etc.) link *Trullion: Alastor 2262* and *Marune: Alastor 933* to *The Gray Prince* and *The Dogtown Tourist Agency*. *Big Planet* automatically qualifies through its sequel, *Showboat World*, and one is readily tempted to accomodate those other outposts of forsaken humanity such as Aerlith (*The Dragon Masters*), Pangborn ("The Miracle Workers") and the eponymous planet presented in *The Blue World*. By extending the process in time as well as space, we can even assimilate *The Five Gold Bands* and the Earth of *To Live Forever* (1956) and *The Last Castle* into the pattern, though here caution must finally get the better of our enthusiasm.

A CYCLE OF DIFFERENTIATION

The basic premise of this more recent interstellar canvas is the "general culture" of the Gaean Reach: more a racial than a political, economic, or imperialistic phenomenon, but a little of all four. Its background is outlined in the Prologue to *The Gray Prince*:

The space age is thirty thousand years old. Men have moved from star to star in search of wealth and glory; the Gaean Reach encompasses a perceptible fraction of the galaxy. Trade routes thread space like capillaries in living tissue; thousands of worlds have been colonized, each different from every other, each working its specific change upon those men who live there. Never has the human race been less homogeneous. The outward surge has been anything but regular or even. Men have come and gone in waves and fluctuations, responding to wars, to religious impetus, to compulsions totally mysterious. (GP/l)

Hence we learn of "exiles from Earth" including "twenty thousand Chama Reya, a cult of aestheticians" (An/131) coming to Durdane and deliberately marooning themselves by sinking their spaceships in the Purple Ocean; and a penal ship on its way to New Ossining being commandeered by the two hundred felons on board and used to make an heroic "Escape" down to Blue World, their twenty thousand descendants twelve generations later (when the novel is set) forming a most astonishing caste structure from the forgotten criminal categories of their forebears. Pangborn is also typical of these fluctuations:

> Sixteen hundred years before, with war raging through space, a group of space captains, their home bases destroyed, had taken refuge on Pangborn. To protect themselves against vengeful enemies, they built great forts armed with weapons from the dismantled spaceships.
> The wars receded, Pangborn was forgotten. The newcomers drove the First Folk into the forests, planted and harvested the river valleys. (MW/17)

And again, humans come to Aerlith "as exiles during the War of the Ten Stars. The Nightmare Coalition apparently had defeated the Old Rule..." (DM/33)

This situation is no less a constant in the "general culture" stories. We have Koryphon's most recent imposition, for example:

> Two hundred years ago a group of off-planet freebooters dropped down upon Uaia, surprised and captured a conclave of Uldra chieftains, and compelled cession of title to certain tribal lands: the notorious Submission Treaties.... In due course these tracts became the great "domains" of the Alouan, upon which the "land barons" and their descendants live.... (GP/6)

So too has humankind come to Maske:

> No one knows how many waves of human migration have crossed the Great Hole to Mora; perhaps no more than two. The most recent arrivals, a fourteen ship contingent of Credential Renunciators from the world Diosophede, discovered upon Maske and Skay a population of great antiquity, human but considerably diverged from *Home gaea*: the Saidanese, of a species which became known as *Homo mora*. (M:T/l)

Such "divergences" (caused, in this case, by thirty centuries of "waves and fluctuations") are a crucial factor in Vance's xenographical method. Like Pangborn, countless other worlds have been touched by human settlers, only to be forgotten and left to develop on their own, isolated from the main stream of Gaean culture. As with the colonial expansion of the ancient Greek city-states, this divergence is accentuated as the first-generation colonies go forth to establish colonies of their own, and so on. One outcome of such expansion and inevitable isolation is the loss of a precise knowledge of origins, and across

Vance's stories—even in works that lie well outside the "general culture" format—there is the recurring motif of Earth as legend, exactly the situation encountered by Tubb's wandering Earthman in the Dumarest stories. For example, Joe Smith must defend the existence of his homeworld to a diverse group of human types in *Son of the Tree*:

> "I can assure you that Earth is no legend," said Joe. "Somehow in the outward migrations, among the wars and the planetary programs of propaganda, the real existence of Earth has been called to question. And we travel very rarely into this outer swirl of the galaxy." (ST/53)

Gersen confronts a similar ignorance in *The Killing Machine* (1964):

> "He spoke of Thamber and the legend that it had become, to which the Baron replied that the remainder of humanity was no less a myth to the folk of Thamber. (KM/144).

This situation remains a constant throughout the "general culture" framework:

> All his life Ghyl had heard speculation as to the provenance of man. Some declared Earth to be the source of the human migration; another group inclined towards Triptolemus; others pointed to Amenaro, the lone planet of Deneb Kaitos; a few argued spontaneous generation from a universal float of spores. (Em/2/64)

But this is one concomitant feature of a more total and far more important situation. Because of the distances involved, because of the unique conditions distinguishing one planet from another, the end result is a divergent and diluted Gaean culture, with regional off-shoots each with its own parochial cultural profile, its own unique bias. As P. Schuyler Miller has said:

> ...the Balkanization of space that Vance has used...is far more logical than the close-knit empires of space that we find in other stories. The great breeder of races and cultures has been isolation, and isolation is the keynote of space. Given times and strange enough worlds, who knows what may become of Earth men?[39]

Consequently, in the universe containing Vance's "general culture" there are two kinds of aliens:

1) the extraterrestrial in origin, made up of:

a) sophisticated, completely non-human sentients such as the Liss and the Olefract, the asutra and the Ka; the Basics (or grephs), the Chasch, Wankh, Dirdir and Pnume, the Damarans, and potentially the Meks and Star Kings, etc.;
b) technologically unsophisticated, partially sophisticated or technologically impoverished indigenes (whether completely autochthonous or adapted) like the Fwai-chi, the Gomaz, the First Folk, the degenerated erjins and morphotes, the oels, merlings and ahulphs, the dekabrachs of Sabria, etc); and:

2) the terrestrial-derived.

---

39. P. Schuyler Miller, "The Reference Library." *Analog*, January 1965, p.89.

THE "JENNY HANIVER" SCHOOL OF ET'S;
SEVEN BLIND MEN AND AN ELEPHANT

"...as a non-human, he would have no points of engagement...A leopard does not attack a tree; they are different orders of beings."

Magnus Ridolph / "Coup de Grace" (MR/200)

One of the difficulties that has always faced the writer of the xenological/xenographical story is how to avoid anthropomorphizing the alien—how to refrain from "humanizing" its drives, motives; and thought processes. As Peter Nicholls says of Hal Clement's Mesklinites in *Mission of Gravity* (1954):

> They are so different from us in appearance and environment as to be awe-inspiring until they open their mouths, whereupon they sound exactly like Calvin Coolidge.[40]

This is a rather ungenerous return for the worldsmith who has given us *Cycle of Fire* (1957) and *Close to Critical* (1958) as well as the Mesklinite society of his 1954 novel, but it does draw our attention to the important dilemma of how to present the alien adequately. The inherent limitation facing such a rendering is that the unknown can only be apprehended in terms of the known. To quote one of Clifford Simak's characters, the situation is along the lines of: "There were seven blind men and they chanced to come upon an elephant."[41] In other words, they had an encounter with the totally inexplicable—with something they lacked the referents for understanding, except by analogy (the trunk becoming a snake-like grasping appendage, the ears seen as "wing-like," and so on). While the xenological writer

---

40. Peter Nicholls, *Explorations of the Marvellous* (Fontana, 1978), p.174.

41, Clifford Simak, "Limiting Factor," *Contact*, ed., Noel Keyes (Paperback Library, 1963), p.87.

can sometimes proceed without analogizing (as in Lem's *Solaris*), he cannot continue doing so if he also means to be xenographical. It is one thing to create a truly alien entity—such as the sentient ocean in Lem's intriguing xenological novel, or the machine-alien pyramids in *Wolfbane* (1959)—but to reveal the alien in the workaday, humdrum society that is normal for it, the writer must be allowed certain liberties. Not even Lem could "normalize" the world of his Solaris entity without such compromising referents, such human-based perceptual clues. It is a contradiction that cannot be avoided.

The xenographical writer's task is entirely different from that of his xenological colleague, for his task requires that the alien be revealed to the point of its being commonplace. He must see his "elephant," or at least dress his alien up in sufficiently elephantine terms, so that our imaginations can meet the author's conception of it as an elephant *plus*. Which invariably leads to the art of the "Jenny Haniver."

A practice especially well documented in the seventeenth, eighteenth and nineteenth centuries but common enough throughout recorded human history was for skilled artisans to manufacture fake monsters for the thriving market in things teratological. Dragons were produced on short order from dried lizards, bats' wings, birds' claws and parts of fish, and then sold to eager clients. Such amazing creations were referred to as "Jenny Hanivers," and it is a term that neatly accounts for the most common approach to describing the alien—assembling it as a composite in terms of known referents. Thus we have such blatant throwaways as de Camp's Isidian—"an eight-legged nightmare of elephant and dachshund,"[42] or Ixtl, van Vogt's monster from ancient Glor, a "regular blood-red devil spewed out of a nightmare."[43] We have Frank Herbert telling us that "Taprisiots came in odd shapes like sawed-off lengths of burned conifers, with stub limbs jutting every which way, needlelike

---

42. L. Sprague de Camp, *The Tower of Zanid*, p.22.

43. A. E. van Vogt, *The Voyage of the Space Beagle* (Panther, 1973), p.99.

speech appendages fluttering,"⁴⁴ and Poul Anderson's rather self-conscious description of the Azkashi ("There is an old game in which you show a picture of a nonhuman to your friends and ask them to describe the being. No xenological co-ordinates allowed; they must use words alone."⁴⁵), as creatures resembling "web-footed kangaroos, a bit shorter than men, with hands and hairless grey skins, bulldog muzzles, mule ears, and eyes as big as the Round Tower,"⁴⁶ Any writer, whether he learned the ET/BEM trade in pulp-school or not, will know the grim necessities of the "Jenny Haniver" approach.

Most often, Vance too creates his non-human aliens by this classic and time-honored pulp technique, juxtaposing unexpected commonplaces, directing the reader back to familiar referents suddenly displaced and made grotesque. In this way a constant anthropomorphic tension (not of things that are necessarily human themselves, but things that belong to the human universe of experience) is kept in play, rather as Niven has used for establishing his Monks in "The Fourth Profession" (1971):

> He showed nothing of himself but one hand. That hand looked like a chicken's foot, but bigger, with lumpy-looking, very flexible joints, and with five toes instead of four.⁴⁷

Out of context, divorced from the stark economy of Niven's narrative style, this is a description straight from the pages of *Weird Tales*. But the keynote is understatement. In context, it is a mere hint, thrown away with no sensationalism whatsoever as one more fact in an "ordinary" world.

The same "controlled" anthropomorphism/composite

---

44. Frank Herbert, *Whipping Star* (New English Library, 1972), p,8.

45. Poul Anderson, *World Without Stars* (Ace, 1978), p.54.

46. Poul Anderson, *World Without Stars*, p.54.

47. Larry Niven, "The Fourth Profession." *A Hole in Space* (Del Rey, 1974), p.149.

approach—the "Jenny Haniver" technique—is used by Vance to describe the mysterious Pnume, a blending of commonplaces from our own phenomenal world re-arranged and inverted:

> Reith studied the oddly jointed creature: the first Pnume he had seen, except for a darkling glimpse in the dungeons of Pera. It stood about the height of a man and within its voluminous black cloak seemed slight, even frail. A black hat shaded its eye-sockets; its visage, the cast and color of a horse's skull, was expressionless; under the lower edge a complicated set of rasping and chewing parts surrounded a near-invisible mouth. The articulation of the creature's legs worked in reverse to that of the human: it moved forward with the motion of a man walking backward. The narrow feet were bare and mottled, dark red and black; three arched toes tapped the ground as a nervous man might tap his fingers. (Pn/22)

We find another such composite in the rendering of the ahulphs of Durdane as "hairy goblin-dogs" (An/79) with "hairy dog-spider" heads (p.83) and "foot-noses" (p.80) for tracking the prey they will tie into parcels and take home.

But Vance operates along a full range of techniques for accomplishing this task of rendering the alien. While he will often opt for the "Jenny Haniver" composites, he will sometimes totally avoid the blatancies of contrasted elements thrown together and describe his creatures in non-analogous terms—giving posture, gesture, skeletal structure, colors, etc.; using substances like fur and cartilage, or vocabulary (deliberately avoiding "Jenny Haniver" terms like "elephantine" and "dog-like" for neutral references like "ruff," "crest," etc.), thus producing such marvelously vague creations as "a twelve-spine devil-chaser with triple fans and a purple lattice" (GP/14), the word "devil" being exploited but at the same time avoided.

Another way in which Vance avoids the usual pitfalls involved in rendering the alien is, of course, by carefully restricting himself to examining the cultures of divergent human subtypes (the Waels, the Rhunes, the Trill, etc.), or those non-human species which have acquired for themselves (for liaison purposes) specialized human "bridge" races that have some deeper insight into their alien psyches, usually through some form of genetic engineering and/or something as fundamental as language skills. The Wankhmen are able to make some sense of the Wankh chimes; the Basics have their interpreters—the human-derived Weaponeers; the Ka have certain humans taught their Great Song, and so on. This way, Vance can keep his non-humans at a distance for much of the time, while still creating a solid sense of their presence.

Sometimes the ethos of a non-human race can be broadly measured by what emerge as analogous human social imperatives and institutions, or by the way its members pursue their lifestyles in relation to human neighbors. This is anthropomorphizing, of course, but it is empirically based, relying on observable behavior traits, and we are carefully reminded that such observations are always of the most superficial kind. For instance, before their uprising the erjins of Koryphon in *The Gray Prince* conform neatly to the human classification of a quasi-intelligent "servile" race. After their abortive coup they become recognized as sentient beings—a devious and resurgent warrior people whose motives for "world conquest" are still amenable to our own interpretations of such imperatives ("This world is ours and we are now resuming control" [GP/161]). On the other hand, we have the Gomaz of Maz, a race of sentient autochthones who seem to have devised for themselves a recognizably feudalistic society, but whose sexual imperatives are largely incomprehensible to human observers. We can reduce the Gomaz ethos "mechanistically" and by analogy into roughly human terms, but we cannot fathom the spirit and force of their psychological impetus.

The totally non-human sentients without human-derived "bridge" races are rarely approached by Vance, and it is the exception in *The Dogtown Tourist Agency* to see him bringing into the "general culture" universe of the Gaean Reach and Alastor Cluster two totally outré and xenophobic spacefaring peoples—the Liss and the Olefract—defined almost by what they are not rather than by what they are. They are characterized mainly by their artifacts ("The Liss and the Olefract vessels drifted above and to the side, and all the passengers craned their necks to study the artifacts of these exotic transgalactic intelligences" [p.473]), by anonymity ("entering areas in which the Liss and the Olefract exerted at least theoretical control, and certainly a psychological influence" [p.477]), selected hints ("He passed a Liss on its way to the Triskelion—a lithe dark creature in a scarlet robe—and a moment later he saw an Olefract at a somewhat greater distance" [p.477]), and a general aloof indifference.

This sort of alien-by-implication-and-artifact (rather what Niven has done with his Slaver Empire, Clarke with his Ramans, etc.) represents one extreme. It is the evocative evasion, the exotic vacuum, and it can only work when the reader's attention is deservedly focused elsewhere. If one has an alien culture being developed (namely the Gomaz or the human-derived Trill), it is generally one way of giving perspective and "density" to the xenographical canvas to include additional sentients (the Liss and the Olefract) or mysterious indigenes like the merlings.

So, while Vance will virtually "throw away" an alien race like the Chasch and the Dirdir, or the erjins and the Gomaz, exposing them to the full light of day so as to counter the sensational and the bizarre with the exotic as mundane, as a hardened xenographer he knows too well the blessings of a "less is more" approach, and there will always be the deliberately uncompleted conception—the "exotic vacuum" aliens like the Pnume, the merlings and the morphotes—created to a far greater extent in the reader's own imagination by carefully selected hints.

Vance does devise purely extraterrestrial races, making a virtue of necessity and confronting the very dilemma of anthropomorphization that could compromise, if not doom, the xenographical adventure. But in most of his works he features that other kind of alien: the terrestrial-derived.

THE BALKANIZATION OF SPACE

This latter type stems from our important thematic idea that each planet's environment will work its own "natural" selection on the Gaean stock who colonize that particular world. Our humanity is to be seen as a fragile (and quite relative) condition, determined by all manner of interrelated factors: gravity, climate, radiation, diet, etc., and once these fundamentals are altered and replaced with others, so too will there be fundamental changes in that humanity. Consider Fay Bursill's remarks to Paddy Blackthorn in *The Five Gold Bands*:

> "Isn't it a marvel, Paddy? When man first landed here he was man. In two generations the tall skinny ones predominated, in four the skull formation had begun. And now look at them. And to think that in spite of their appearance they're men. They can breed with true men and the same goes for the Asmasians, the Canopes, the Shauls,...the Loristanese, the Creepers, the Green-bags—and all the rest of the in-bred overmen. It's truly wonderful how the planetary influence acts.... Today we're the root-stock, and all these splits and changes brought about by the differences in light, food, atmosphere, gravity—they produce a race as much better than man as men were to the proto-simians.... Human history has always been a series—a cycle of differentiation." (pp.47-48)

While in more recent works Vance has limited the procreative capability of these "differentiated" human types considerably, the options are kept open, so that an unresolved situation exists. As with the Men-men of Arcady Major on Moritaba in an earlier Magnus Ridolph story (allegedly a hybrid race out of the mingling of a group of freebooters with the autochthones of the area "despite the protests of orthodox biologists that such a union is impossible" (MR/83)), we are told in *Maske: Thaery* that:

> The Saidanese of Skay and the Djan of Maske comprise the species *Homo mora*, which cannot fruitfully interbreed with *Homo gaea*—though the Waels of Wellas and certain Dohobay tribes are reputedly hybrid races. (p. 209)

Whatever the circumstances, the cycle of differentiation outlined by Fay Bursill provides the general and fundamental framework for Vance's universe. It is a premise constantly enacted in Vance's novels, whether *The Gray Prince*, *The Five Gold Bands* or *The Killing Machine*:

> Human evolution...has never gone in a smooth flow, but always in a cyclical pulse, which, as history is scanned, seems almost convulsive. The tribes mingle and merge to form a race, then comes a time of expulsion, of migration, isolation, differentiation into new tribes.
> For more than a thousand years, this latter process has been on the ascendant, as the human race has swept across space. Isolation, special conditions, inbreeding have created dozens of new racial subtypes. But now there is stasis in the Oikumene, with many comings and goings, and it seems that perhaps the pendulum is about to swing back.
> But only in the Oikumene! Folk still fare beyond, ever outward. Never has isolation been more easy, never has personal freedom been so cheap!
> The eventualities? Anyone's guess is good. The Oikumene may be forced to expand. Other Oikumenes may come into existence. Conceivably men may

collide with the realm of another race, for there is abundant evidence that other space-travelling peoples have gone before us, how and why to disappear no-one can say. (KM/72)

Ideally, the Oikumene should be seen as simply one stage in the development of the Gaean Reach, one momentary glimpse into one part of the chain of pulses producing that vast interstellar demographical phenomenon—that truly "general culture" with its scattered and deviant offspring—that stands at the end of thirty-thousand years of such cyclic expansion.

But regardless of how tempting such an arrangement might be, it may ultimately be denied us. For while the Oikumene novels anticipate so much of what is to become the Gaean Reach—the isolation and diversification of human types (the Sarkoy, the Krokinole Imps, etc.), the workings of an organization called the Institute, in fact Vance's whole xenographical method—the one thing that it does not anticipate is humanity's collision with a completely alien, *sophisticated* non-human species.

In the "general culture" series this momentous encounter is presented in the pre-Gaean Reach Durdane trilogy, the Asutra being "the first technologically competent non-human creatures" (As/32) of which Earth's Historical Institute is aware. In the Oikumene/Demon Princes novels this contact has already taken place. There are already the non-human Star Kings of Lambda Grus III, as well as mention of everything from other major non-human starfaring races (more or less akin to Niven's Outsiders or Andre Norton's Forerunners) to "non-human nursemaids" (PL/182). And if we lose the Demon Princes novels, we also lose *The Blue World* (the New Ossining given as the destination of the shipload of criminals is presumably the New Ossining that is one of the three major cities on Olliphane, nineteenth planet of the Rigel Concourse), and *Son of the Tree* (Druids who visit the Palace of Love, while from Vale or Virgo VII, are presumably related ideologically to those of Kyril, since they too revere an all-powerful Tree), not to mention Sirene and "The Moon Moth" (1961). (Note *Star King* [1964], pp. 108-9.)

Without wishing to force a case for a compatibility that may simply not exist, there is nevertheless one answer. The working date for the Oikumene stories is 3524 AD (Kirth Gersen being born in 3490 AD). We are told that by 3500 AD (1500 in the New System dating of the Oikumene):

> ...As men have travelled from star to star they have encountered many forms of life, intelligent and non-intelligent (to emphasize a perfectly arbitrary and possibly anthropomorphic parameter). (SK/131)

Conceivably, the Durdane stories could belong to an even earlier period in humanity's history, one preceding even Ridolph's Commonwealth of Worlds (if and whenever that can be placed), but certainly preceding the Oikumene. Our earlier inclusion of the Durdane novels in the "general culture" series almost 2700 years later rests entirely on its proximity in time of publication to *Emphyrio*, the Tschai novels, and the Gaean Reach/Alastor stories, which may mean nothing, and on the fact of the explosive dexax being found on both pre-Gaean Reach Durdane and Gaean Reach contemporary, Koryphon, a connection which may be invalidated altogether simply by allowing that dexax is as fundamental and enduring a discovery as gunpowder—or, more appropriately, the eventual result of a centuries-long process of technological dissemination that has finally reached Koryphon,

So, where to place the Durdane books? Should Durdane have a more recent pre-Gaean Reach kinship, we can postulate a relatively short period of accelerating inter-racial contact in which human explorers discover the Chasch, Wankh, Dirdir and Pnume, a period culminating in *The Dogtown Tourist Agency* with a much-expanded cosmopolitan Gaean culture sharing its immediate frontiers with the Liss and Olefract Empires. But this way the Oikumene stories are lost to us, and must be seen as a completely autonomous series. By making Durdane a pre-Oikumene planetary setting, we preserve a reasonable compatibility, with only dexax providing the temptation of a much later classification. Then again, the whole Durdane problem could perhaps be solved by allowing Durdane its pre-Gaean Reach connection and simply reconsidering Ifness' remarks. The Asutra are the first extant "technologically competent" non-human race that mankind has encountered—not necessarily the first race of sentient non-humans. In *The Killing Machine* we are told that man has not yet collided with "the *realm* of another race" (p. 72—my italics). Perhaps the Asutra's realm, in its post-Oikumene, pre-Gaean Reach setting, is the first of these, followed by an endless array of others.

But this is academic, and the ultimate value in considering the earlier works here is simply to show the uniformity of Vance's xenographical method. After all, we do not even know what relationship in time the "general culture" stories have to one another. For this reason, the novels that exist outside the "general culture" stories should be seen as points along the way in this history of humanity in space, stories forever elusively open-ended in their relationships, an informal collation with occasional pockets of formality where a series expands a particular point.

Whatever the degree of compatibility, whatever the stage reached in this progression towards contact with non-humans, the human-settled worlds have already provided their own vast array of alien peoples as the cycle of differentiation continues unabated. On Durdane, for instance, Ifness, Fellow of the Historical Institute, points out to Etzwane how "the Aesthetes are a distinctive group—a race, in fact, in the process of differentiating" (An/1/78),

By the time of the Gaean Reach, who knows what they may have become? We see the beginnings of this same specialization and hybridization on Cirgamesk—the Javanese, Arab, Malay settled world in "Sjambak"—at a reasonably early period in our human expansion: a mere five thousand years after we have made space our domain. Elsewhere, we hear of:

> ...three round Monagi commercial travelers, Earth stock, but after a hundred and fifty years, already modified by the environment of Monago or Taurus 61 III, to a characteristic somatic type. (HI/60)

Or the Sarkoy venefice, Sivij Suthiro, with "a face shaped by more than a thousand years of specialization and in-breeding" (SL/59). Another of Vance's heroes, Joe Smith, tells the young Druidess Elfane:

> "No two planets are alike. Ours is an old stable culture—mellowed, kindly. Our races have merged—I am the result of their mingling. In these outer regions men have blocked off and separated and have specialized once again." (ST/57)

In this way are the local situations, the local cultures, produced: the Waels, the Rhunes, the Wind-runners, the Alpheratz Eagles, the sacerdotes of Aerlith, and the like, and Vance is always careful to emphasize a twofold viewpoint regarding them—both the relative and totally unique, absolute nature of these peoples' various "local" points of view. It is as the Minie tells Jubal Droad:

> "The cosmos is various; many environments occupy the same area. The 'whats' and 'hows' and 'whys' are different from each. All you could learn in Wellas are our local insights. Our realities are our neighbors' superstitions." (MT/181)

Similarly, on Koryphon, it is the differences and not the similarities between the various strands of humanity that matter:

Schaine retorted: "Why shouldn't Uldras be invited to parties? They're human."

"Approximately human. Their *weldewiste* is alien to ours. They've drifted quite a distance on the evolutionary flow." (GP/20)

So too can Adam Reith see himself from the Dirdirman viewpoint as "an irresponsible iconoclast" (Pn/11), and watching the Peran driver, Emmink, can reflect:

A man like Anacho, like Traz, like himself, ultimately derived from the soil of Earth.... How dilute now, how tenuous, was the terrestrial essence? Emmink had become a man of Tschai, his soul conditioned by the Tschai landscape, the amber sunlight, the gunmetal sky, the quiet rich colors. (CC/126-7)

THE SELECTIVE FOCUS

No matter how weird, wild, wonderful and outrageously improbable something is, if it's familiar it will seem to be normal, natural...and by no means mysterious or supernatural.
John W. Campbell[48]

It should be remembered that Vance's approach to the examination of an alien culture is a most thoughtful and all-embracing one, mindful of such crucial basics as self-image, language, symbology, morality, and the notion of the social contract basic to any society. Vance proceeds by regarding the great diversity of existing and extinct terrestrial cultures and customs as objectively as possible, so that they are seen as conglomerations of traits and distinctive behavior patterns,

---

48. J. W. Campbell. *Analog.* April 1965, p.4.

determined by environment and the degree to which a people are able to master or be mastered by it.

Observed this way, many commonplace practices seem random and regional. Uniquely interesting social mores and collective taboos exist even in the most technologically advanced contemporary cultures. Vance objectifies the elements of our own social humanity, and extrapolates from trends and tendencies that he has thus distilled to create alien communities which are ultimately no more exotic, no more bizarre and random, than those which any travelog or history will show to comprise our own Earth.

Once we see equivalents objectified in an alien context—whether it be apartheid, vestigial Christian procedures of baptism and marriage, the Mexican "Day of the Dead" festival or the sexual practices of Bedouin tribesmen—we are seeing our own multifaceted species with its countless regional variations and racial subtypes (and parochial absolutes) projected and re-arranged on a different canvas.

This may seem a simple task, but ironically (considering our own variegated present-day terrestrial canvas) once cultures and mores have been "reduced" and reproduced with all their dazzling and ingenious variations, it is the real test of a writer's skill to animate them once again, to produce cultures that not only ring true but which can generate a sense of the commonplace about themselves, an ordinariness of its "humanity" and life-patterns. Just as Vance is faced with the difficulties of bringing his "Jenny Haniver" aliens to life, so too must he animate planetary societies that are very much "Jenny Haniver" composites. He must show that a given society is exotic and "divergent," yet he must also allow us to see that it is normal and matter-of-fact to a hero who is a member of that society.

To realize his setting, Vance must proceed like an archeologist, reconstructing a society in terms of its architecture, diet, art forms, fashions, legal and religious codes, etc., according to a whole complex and interacting ecological, anthropological, and demographical profile. To quote Jon Noble:

...if there has been a dearth of good non-human societies in sf then to some extent this has been redeemed by the human ones. Only Jack Vance has succeeded in book after book at achieving this, but other authors have been able to do it in individual works.... Yet no author has been so consistently able to create viable human societies that are so enchantingly different from our own.... In his novella "The Moon Moth" for instance, [Vance] has the masks and the music of the people, both described in considerable detail. But there is more to a Vancean society than art; there are often several new occupations, a political system and an administration system complete with factions and malcontents, strange crimes and stranger punishments... in short, the whole richness of any extinct culture, but found in some new one.[49]

And as for the method used to achieve this end, Joanna Russ has noted (in connection with *Emphyrio*) how:

Science fiction, like all literature, usually tries to make the strange familiar, but Mr. Vance makes the familiar strange. One would swear he had read Bert Brecht and decided to produce a novel that would be one extended *Verfremdungseffekt* (usually translated as "alienation effect." It might be better rendered (as Brecht has done) as distancing, or the framing effect...).[50]

In actual fact, this "framing effect" makes use of the two-fold approach. The strange is made familiar (sunset from Dunkum Heights on Halma; the view across the Thaumaturge Ocean

---

49. Jon Noble, "How Green Was My Martian," *Scytale* 2. August 1978, pp. 36-37.

50. Joanna Russ, "Books," *The Magazine of Fantasy and Science Fiction*. January 1970, p.41.

from the Avente Esplanade on Alphanor; avness descending upon the Merlank Fens on Trullion, the sea-voices heard just before sunset on Zeck: *Alastor 503*, etc.) and the familiar is made strange (through the re-location of known words like "Druid" or "Hoodwink," concepts, etc.). In order to consider Vance's xenographical method we should note both of these strands at work simultaneously, handled through what we might call the "close and selective focus" on a particular landscape—the setting that is to be developed in detail.

Whether this is the fictitious San Rodrigo County in conventional Vance mysteries like *The Pleasant Grove Murders* (UK, 1968) or *The Fox Valley Murders* (1966) or his most exotic planetary setting, one of the reader's most vivid recollections will be a sense of landscape—the feeling of having personally experienced a setting through one's own senses.

In creating his chosen loci, Vance will often use maps to help achieve this detail of locality, as in *The Fox Valley Murders* with its two maps to establish the hypothetical Fox Valley/Marblestone environs, or the magazine version of *The Dragon Masters* (*Galaxy*, 1962) with its location of Banbeck Vale and Happy Valley and the harsh topography that intervenes. In the "general culture" series, *Trullion: Alastor 2262* has a map of the Fens district of Merlank; *Emphyrio* a map of the various precincts of Ambroy, and we are given a cartographer's rendering of the Vissel River/Lune XXIII South region of Big Planet in *Showboat World*. Two maps are given to create Maske for us—one showing the districts of Thaery, another locating them in a Mercator's projection of the world. Extending the compass of the series, we have the Tschai novels providing a Mercator's projection to trace the course of Adam Reith's planetary trek.

Such a tactic has always been well-used in the science fiction and fantasy genre (by everyone from Tolkien and Robert E. Howard to Lin Carter and Ursula Le Guin), and it is a valuable consolidating aid for the worldsmith—lending verisimilitude to a setting and prying us loose at the outset from our own rigid preconceptions about continental and known planetographical configurations.

Alternatively, the xenographer might use some other kind of schematic device, such as Vance provides with his classification chart for the solar phases of Marune's four suns; or the "heraldic" list of the aristocratic Castle families of Earth in *The Last Castle*; or appendices and glossaries (e.g., Eisel Musicology and the amazingly intricate Djan behavioral schedule in *Maske: Thaery*); footnotes (a device common to every "general culture" work) and quotes from texts as prefatory notes to chapters (e.g., the Demon Princes novels, "Rumfuddle" [1973], etc.).

Central to every xenographical novel is the local culture and the inevitable parochialism (and hence crisis potential) that goes with it. Vance defines the problem:

> Should Alastor Cluster be considered a segment of the Gaean Reach? The folk of the Cluster, some four or five trillion of them on more than three thousand worlds, seldom reflected upon the matter, and indeed considered themselves neither Gaean nor Alastrid. The typical inhabitant, when asked as to his origin, might perhaps cite his native world or, more usually, his local district, as if this place were so extraordinary, so special and widely famed that its reputation hung on every tongue of the galaxy. (M:A/l)

And so it has been with almost all of his world cultures. The Druids of Kyril in that earlier work *Son of the Tree* "are completely provincial, completely assured of Kyril's place as the center of all space, all time" (ST/10); and on Ethelrinda Cordas, Milton Hack is surrounded by curious children, and reflects on how "Seprissa was the center of their universe...with Earth the planet remote and bizarre" (MZ/16).

In each "general culture" novel we are given such a local cultural "entry-point." On Maske it is Wysrod or Duskerl Bay, "a small town in the center of the Great Hole—but for Thariots the focus of sentient life" (M:T/41), with its eccentric hacks, the Marine Parade and the Cham. On Trullion it is Welgen and the surrounding fens; on Big Planet the port of Coble on Surmise Bay, and so the pattern goes—whether it be Olanje, Garwiy or Ambroy. Even if we approach these foci from without, entering from the "general culture" first—as is the case with Axistil on Maz, Port Mar on Marune and Arrabus on Wyst—these centers remain the nodes whose distinctive cultural "flavors" permeate the works in which they are set.

Having established these astonishingly divergent modes, Vance then engineers the confrontation that is the basis of most of his xenographical adventures. To borrow from the glossary to *Maske: Thaery*: "when a general culture such as that of the Gaean Reach suffuses a local culture, there will be a mingling..." (p.214), and Vance's fundamental technique is to have an enactment of this mingling—to have a member of either the local culture or the general culture brought into collision with the other. Glinnes Hulden returns home to Trullion after broadening his *Weltanschauung* by a stint in the Alastor space-navy; Ghyl Tarvoke comes to question the very basis of the Ambroy welfare-state and then to challenge the Damaran economic control of Halma by his growing awareness of conditions beyond his own previous life-style, Jubal Droad and Gastel Etzwane are both led to a similar overview, liberating themselves out of personal necessity from parochial confines; the wandering amnesiac, Efraim, returns home to his beloved Scharrode on Marune "tainted" with all manner of off-world heresies. So too does Schaine Madduc return to Koryphon from school on Tanquil having developed sufficiently for her to finally accept Gerd Jemasze's "general culture"-oriented views on the grim necessities of land tenure on their Alouan estates.

To create world-cultures that are at the same time familiar and unfamiliar, and that create the regional basis for the collision that qualifies the local outlook, Vance uses his "selective focus"—a deliberate concentration on certain details of landscape, architecture, food, clothing, custom, etc., while overlooking others. Whatever the "feature" culture, there are never supermarkets, plastics, or high-technology consumer corporations. We never hear of neon signs or advertising at any level beyond that of guilds and hucksters and local tourist organizations. The exceptions to this—Kyash on Eiselbar, Daillie on Maastricht, etc.—are rarely the main settings. And when cities do take a feature role, as with Clarges, Hant and Arrabus (this last a thriving city state of three billion souls), they *feel* curiously unmodern, in spite of having space travel facilities and the kind of rapid-transit man-ways we find on Wyst.

Just as Vance in 1953 resolved to build his house "using as little chrome, plastic and plywood as possible," so too with the folk in his novels.[51] Vance's universe is very much a homespun, rusticated affair, filled with village industries, handicrafts, folk-dances and wandering minstrels.

In developing it, Vance emerges as something of a confirmed "medievalist." In Ambroy on Halma the Welfare Agency maintains a guild system producing goods for off-world trade. The hallmark of these Ambroy products is that there is no mass-production and no duplication at all; they are all hand-made originals. Shops never reach department-store size. They are most often "booths," to be found in bazaars and market-places and down streets with "quaint" high-gabled houses. Typically, we hear of Etzwane eating "a meat bun and a cake of cheese at a late-hour booth" (An/193), and of Efraim stopping "at a booth devoted to the sale of off-world periodicals" (M:A/55). Anacho the Dirdirman reminds Adam Reith that "spaceships are not wart-scissors, to be picked up at any bazaar booth" (D/12).

Rarely are we given urban commercial districts anything like those to be found in contemporary Western cities. When we are given an industrial area, it invariably has that quaint old-world charm about it, and the distinctively modern elements are somehow distanced. Typically:

---

51. Jack Vance, *Vandals of the Void* (Winston, 1953).

> Ferristoun was a dismal district of industrial structures, warehouses, an occasional tavern: these latter cheerful little nooks, lavish with ornament, colored glass, carved wood, in emulation of the grand pleasure arcades along the lake shore.
>
> The time was middle morning; rain had darkened the black cobblestone pavement. Six-wheeled drays lumbered along the streets.... (SK/65)

Street names themselves are distinctively medieval in flavor: Avenue of the Agency, Street of Brass Boxes, Avenue of Strangers, Street of the Clever Flea—to draw from Port Mar alone.

So the trend continues. On Tschai, when a hapless victim of the Priestesses of the Female Mystery is suffocated, he has "a bag of transparent membrane" (CC/91) pulled over his head, not a plastic bag. One tower of Akadie's manse on Trullion is roofed with "the artificial material spandex" (T:A/87), hinting at synthetics, but the transport terminal of the Port Maheul spaceport on that planet is "a tall structure of black iron and glass crusted pale green and violet with age" (p.224). At least the lockers are of "sound sheet metal" (p.224) and are opened with magnetic keys.

Even Axistil on Maz, that juncture where three interstellar races meet (Gaean, Liss, and Olefract) is a technological "vacuum." Only in such areas as weapons, communications and transportation do we find the hardware and trappings of the high-level technologies implicitly involved. But sometimes even in these areas we find an unexpected antiquity. Efraim and Lorcas fly to the Rhune Realms in an air car whose engine has not failed "in a hundred and two years" (M:A/66).

Of course, this is "the golden afternoon of the human race" (T:A/161), and in almost all the "general culture" novels we are dealing with frontier situations: the colonies, fringes and outposts of human empire. But nevertheless, these "locals" and "cosmopolitans" alike live very much in a selectively delineated cosmos. The Outkers of Koryphon attend all manner of parties, fetes, discussion groups; they sit in inns and attend morphote-viewings. They do not sit at home and watch television.

In accommodating this taste for medievalism, this intermingling of the anachronistic with the sophisticated, Vance is employing a variation on the sword-and-sorcery format favored by writers like Moorcock, Tolkien, Howard, Carter and Jakes, and partly pioneered by himself; producing an essentially medieval context in which there exists: (a) a forgotten science, and/or (b) magic. Vance has used this staple fantasy basis himself in *The Dying Earth* (1950), *The Eyes of the Overworld* (1966) and the other Cugel stories, positing a time in the final days of Earth's existence when science is unrecognizable to its users as anything but magic. One cannot blame P. Schuyler Miller for setting *Emphyrio* aside for a while because he thought it was "a fantasy along the lines of Vance's 'Dying Earth' series." As he says, "it has much of the same mood, but not the overlapping into sorcery and the supernatural."[52]

But contrary to those publishers who would classify the Tschai novels as "science fantasy" rather than science fiction (presumably because they are too far in the future, too demanding in their scope, too much preoccupied with none of the familiar "hard" sciences), Vance is building his universe upon sound extrapolative analysis. As mentioned earlier, given interstellar colonization and the circumstances under which it takes place (war, the conflict of ideologies, economic exploitation, etc.), the level of civilization enjoyed by the colonies depends entirely on the sophistication and efficiency of the channels of communication that are available. Should these break down, then we have precisely that potential for degeneration and differentiation fundamental to Vance's novels. We need only consider the dark ages following the fall of the Roman Empire to see this phenomenon of fragmentation and cultural impoverishment at work. Prior to the Renaissance, artisans could not duplicate the techniques used by the Romans to manufacture torsion-powered

---

52. P. Schuyler Miller, "The Reference Library." *Analog*, October 1970, p.165.

siege-engines, provide plumbing and sewerage, or build roads and aqueducts.

One of the unquestioned *données* of the "general culture" stories is that such efficient channels of communication are commonplace, even if somewhat intermittent—so routine as to warrant no further mention than the appurtenances of present-day air and sea travel. Hence:

> Glinnes visited the spaceport. A ship of the Andrujukha Line had departed Port Maheul on the day following Sodergang's visit to the Fens.... (T:A/200)

> "I thereupon made inquiries at the Ultimo spaceport, which is served by the Krugh Line, the Red Griffin Line, and occasionally the Osiris Line." (DTA/-469)

> The *Ectobant* of the Prydania Line took Pardero to Baruilla, on Deulle, Alastor 2121, where he transferred to the *Lusimar* of the Gaean Trunk Line, and so was conveyed to Calypso Junction on Imber, and thence by the *Wispen Argent* to Numenes. (M:A/14)

While such adequate communication links *are* now available, we are reminded that this has not always been the case, and Vance has no trouble in obtaining his "medieval-modern," "cosmopolitan-provincial" settings. Initially he does this, as we have seen, by locating his worlds in remote backwaters, on frontiers or on half-forgotten fringes of expansion (Marune is out "along the Fontinella Wisp" [M:A/43], Halma is "back of the Mirabilis Cluster" [BFM/4/*F&SF*], and so on), so that we find planets like Marune, Maske, Koryphon and Big Planet that have known many waves of human migration and numerous "degenerations" and "differentiations" (the Wind-runners and Uldras of Koryphon, the Djan and Waels of Maske, etc.), only to have the most recent wave of "cosmopolitan" Gaean colonization superimposing its control over its own divergent forerunners.

This idea of an "enforced medievalism" is not new in the xenographical field (especially considering the various non-interference codes). Laumer's Jame Retief, in one typical instance, warns a Groaci minister that:

> "...a Peace Force will come out here and reduce Groac to a sub-technical cultural level and set up a monitor system to insure she doesn't get any more expansionist ideas."[53]

So it is not unusual to have the Connatic's Second Edict and an embargo on energy weapons enforcing a state of "medievalism" on the Rhunes; a similar injunction is in force against the Gomaz.

Another factor contributing to this enforced "rustication" of the race is the working of the Institute itself. Funian Lubby complains to Kirth Gersen:

> "I am by no means uninformed in these matters. I am an accredited Scientific Academician of Boomaraw College on Lorgan, and in fact have done research on the flatfish of the Neuster Ocean, until my appointment was cancelled—another regressive trick of the Institute, of that I am sure."
>
> "Yes, a sad situation," Gersen agreed. "A person wonders where it will end. Do they want to make cavemen of us all?"
>
> "Who knows what the wretched malcontents hope for? I have heard that they are slowly acquiring control of the Jarnel Corporation, that when they finally secure their fifty-one percent—then *pfui!* no more spaceships, no more travel." (KM/100)

---

53. Keith Laumer, "Policy," *Envoy to New Worlds* (Ace, 1963), p.107.

Given the trivial overspecialization of Lubby's study in the face of a more pragmatic cosmos, filled with such grim realities as Interchange and the Demon Princes, the Institute's policy of preserving a *status-quo* in mankind's development, in making humanity work for its rewards, in allegedly maintaining the more vital qualities of the race, seems a benevolent one in the long term. Their reasons for this stance:

> "Humanity is old, civilization new: the mesh of cogs is by no means smooth—and this is as it should be. Never should a man enter a building of glass or metal, or a spaceship, or a submarine, without a small shock of astonishment; never should he avoid an act of passion without a small sense of effort.... We of the Institute receive an intensive historical inculcation; we know the men of the past, and we have projected dozens of possible future variations, which, without exceptions, are repulsive. Man as he exists now, with all his faults and vices, a thousand gloriously irrational compromises between two thousand sterile absolutes—is optimal. Or so it seems to us who are men." (KM/38)

So it is, in terms of this overall view, that the Institute leaves the civilization of Shant on Durdane to face seeming extermination at the hands of the Rogushkoi (interfering only when it is demonstrated that non-human enemies are involved), and can philosophically accept a pirate and murderer like Kokor Hekkus because of his role as catalyst within the societal organism, finding "certain by-products of his evil" rewarding (KM/43), or as the Connatic would say, providing one of those "exemplars against which virtue can measure itself" (T:A/216). It is, of course, a detachment that benefits the race, and not the individual, directly.

This Institute policy of non-interference, of deliberately withholding cultural/technological assistance, appears in the "general culture" series with *Emphyrio* and the Durdane books, but we should realize that the recurring medievalism of worlds here is due only in part to the Institute's program. Those other factors of ideological and economic conflict, the movements of migrant populations, inadequate communication links, minority group reactions against a technological way of life, etc.—all these complete what a conscious cultural-technological embargo has already begun. Thus can a world like the legendary Thamber be readily accounted for:

> This world had been settled in ancient days, then lost and forgotten until Kokor Hekkus rediscovered it. (KM/28).

Similarly, the settlement profile of a world like Aloysius can reflect the variety of "anachronizing" factors. The origins in this instance:

> Aloysius with its sister planets, Boniface and Cuthbert, were the first worlds to be intensively colonized from Earth. Aloysius, hence, presents aspects of considerable antiquity, the more so that the first settlers, a dynamic group of Conservationists, refused to build structures not in harmony with the landscape. (PL/28)

The result:

> New Wexford lay twenty miles north, a city of crooked streets, steep hills and old buildings of almost medieval aspect. (PL/29)

Alternatively, then, this condition of medievalism might be circumstantial rather than enforced. On the metal-poor worlds of Big Planet and Durdane, metallurgy (and the concomitant technological advances that such a science assists) is virtually nonexistent. But even where the technological trappings do exist, there is invariably some process of degeneration at work that severely limits their full development and application, an impoverishment that allows the cultural "anachronisms" to proceed apace. On Durdane, for instance, we learn of how the patricians of Shant:

> ...drew their income from country estates, from shipping, from the laboratories and workshops where torcs, radios, glow-bulbs, a few other electronic devices, were assembled, using components produced elsewhere in Shant: mono-molecular conductor strands, semi-organic electron-control devices, magnetic cores of sintered ironweb, a few trifles of copper, gold, silver, lead, for connections and switches. No technician comprehended the circuits he used; whatever the original degree of theoretical knowledge, it would now have become lore: a mastery of techniques rather than of principles. (An/134)

And so we get that peculiar situation where the descendants of space-colonists (exiles who sank their own spaceships) come to lament the languishing of much-needed skills:

> "If we had engines to move the balloons, there's a different story, but you can't build engines from withe and glass, even if someone remembered the ancient crafts." (BFM/48)

And yet, in spite of this regression, the human inhabitants of worlds like Durdane and Tschai speak a largely homogeneous language and evince no incredulity at talk of spaceships and alien invaders. They are "cosmopolitan" provincials indeed. When Etzwane, Ifness, and their guide Fabrache plead for assistance against slavers from the Alula tribe of Caraz, and Fabrache describes the non-human Ka who is their companion as "the sole survivor of a wrecked spaceship" (As/83), the

Alul warrior merely replies: "In that case, kill it as well. Why should we nurture off-world enemies?" (As/83). He does not bat an eyelid at the reference to the fact or means of its origin. Similarly, the technist Doneis can matter-of-factly make a comment that shows the most remarkable self-awareness of their deprived state: "The workmanship is beyond our capabilities. I doubt if we could learn more than the fact of our own deterioration" (BFM/123).

The most extreme example of this sort of "enlightened medievalism" is perhaps on Pangborn. "The Miracle Workers" is not a fantasy adventure; it is merely presenting an intricate and sophisticated society that has rationalized away its ignorance of ancient technological skills and has devised a "scientific" methodology of its own, one that superficially resembles the magics and sorceries of the sword-and-sorcery sub-genre. We are simply to be reminded that one person's science is another's magic, as with Ifness and Etzwane landing their sky-boat among a tribe of clam-diggers and posing as magicians. Ifness says: "We have made memorable at least one day of their lives" (As/36-37). Or again, Gersen and Alusz Iphigenia realize that in their air-boat they would appear to the local barbarians as "a magic bird" (KM/121). The trivial and the commonplace of our own age would be marvels to the village communities of tenth-century Europe, very much the "magic bird" situation.

Thus on Pangborn we find such ironical inversions as:

> Conditions had changed; there had been enormous advances since the dark ages sixteen hundred years ago. For instance, the ancients had used intricate fetishes of metal and glass to communicate with each other. Lord Faide need merely voice his needs: Hein Huss could project his mind a hundred miles, to see, to hear, to relay Lord Faide's words. The ancients had contrived dozens of such objects, but the old magic had worn away and they never seemed to function. Lord Ballant's side-arm had melted, after merely stinging Lord

Faide. Imagine a troop armed thus trying to cope with a platoon of demon-possessed warriors!... Again Lord Faide wondered skeptically about the ancients. Clever, of course, but to look at the hard facts, they were little more advanced than the First Folk: neither had facility with telepathy or voyance or demon-command. And the magic of the ancients: might there not be a great deal of exaggeration in legends? (MW/23).

According to different circumstances, different imperatives, terms like "sophisticated," "science," and "civilized" come to be severely qualified, always to be measured in local as well as general terms. Ifness reinforces the need for an attitude of open-minded objectivity:

> "Bah," growled Etzwane. "Iron is iron, glass is glass, and this is the same here or at the other end of the universe."
>
> "True once more. The gross elementals are known to all. But there is no finite limit to knowledge. Each set of apparent ultimates is susceptible to examination and must be analyzed in new terms. These succeeding layers of knowledge are numberless. Those familiar to us are each derived from the level above, or below. Conceivably entire disassociated phases of knowledge exist; the field of parapsychology comes to mind. The basic law of the cosmos is this: in a situation of infinity, whatever is possible exists in fact. To particularize, the technology which propels an alien spaceship may be different from that of Earth, and such a technology must be a matter of intense interest, if only philosophically." (As/69)

Consequently, we have the ship-building Waels of Wellas on Maske who can project their images, turn men into trees or dissolve the corking of their ships from vast distances; the Uldras of Koryphon with their crazy-boxes and emotions of *aurau* and *xheng*; the sacerdotes of Aerlith with their various paranormal skills: pockets of transformed humanity, conditioned—not to the standard devices of fantasy—but to a different alien science.

Nor is Earth the vast high-level technological planet one would have expected having launched this great wave of interstellar expansion. It is very much a "softened" world bathing in the afterglow of its enterprise, with the sort of self-consciousness one would think fitting for the Home sought after by the Yearning Refluxives on Tschai. It is a world of antiquarians, scholars and tourists, of the Historical Institute, painstakingly chronicling the various fates of its scattered offspring, a world that never fails to work its sad magical attraction on any terrestrial-derived visitor who should go there.

Across the full range of Vance's work we are given assorted impressions of humanity's original home, but by distinguishing carefully, a true picture emerges. First, there are the extremes, given, for instance, by the mad poet Navarth:

> "We are stagnant, slowly decaying! Where is our vitality? Drained to the outworlds! We have bled our life away! On Earth remain the sickly, the depraved, the cryptic thinkers, the sunset wanderers on the mud flats, the paranoids and involutes, the great epicures, the timid dreamers, the medievalists." (PL/74)

Or by the ersatz human, Warweave:

> "Out here...we think of Earthmen in terms of stereotypes: cultists, mystics, hyper-civilized epicenes, sinister old men in Institute black, decadent aristocrats.... (SK/94-5)

But it is a Vance-surrogate/protagonist who provides us with the more balanced view, that of a revitalized and replenished world:

> In many ways the reality of Earth was at odds with Ghyl's preconceptions. He had thought to find a dismal world, the horizon spiked with rotting ruins, the sun a flaming red eye, the seas oily and stagnant from the seepage of years.
>
> But the sun was warm and yellow-white...and the sea seemed considerably more fresh than Deep Ocean to the west of Fortinone.
>
> The people of Earth were another surprise. Ghyl had been ready for weary cynicism, a jaded autumnal lassitude, inversions, eccentricities, subtle sophistications; and in this expectation he was not completely wide of the mark. Certain of the people he met displayed these qualities, but others were as easy and uncomplicated as children. Still others perplexed Ghyl by their fervor, the intensity of their conduct, as if the day were too short for the transaction of all their business. (Em/2/64-65)

And as Maastricht mercantilist, Jodel Heurisx, tells Ghyl:

> "...there are enormous variations. Some devote their energies to visionary schemes. Others turn inward to become sybarites, voluptuaries, connoisseurs, collectors, aesthetes; or they concentrate upon the study of some arcane speciality. To be sure, there are numerous ordinary folk, but somehow they are never noticed, and only serve to heighten the contrast." (Em/2/65)

Above all else, however, it is important to note the distinct "antiquarian cast" Earth has assumed, that same refined and enlightened medievalism of form and tenor that characterizes all of Vance's central "local focus" settings. If robots exist in the Earth cities of Gersen's age, which we are told they do, then they are relegated to that secondary role beyond Vance's selective focus, and they do not alter the prevailing picture of an ancient, almost backwater world. As we have seen, the truly modern cities that do exist in Vance's universe are also secondary, almost neutral settings like Daillie on Maastricht, planned and spacious, but made of synthetics and somehow lacking in a unique character all its own.

This same medievalism pervades characterization and dialog as well. Most of Vance's human characters, high-born and low-life alike, speak as mannered philosophers—whether Fellow of the Institute, space-pirate, village hetman or inn-keeper. Even his rogues are eloquent. Rarely are they at a loss for words, and even when they are, it is a failing itself couched in urbane and self-aware expression, rather than slang or obscenity. For example:

> "Bah," muttered Sul. "I am unable to chop logic with you; you have the superior sleight with words." (As/164)

They speak repeated formulae of conversation, and so there emerges a recognizable and stylized old-world charm that contributes to the metamorphosis of alien locales into the commonplace, the ordinary-extraordinary. Highly conventional forms are used to trigger the nostalgia, the poignancy, and the vital rapport that animates the local situation for the reader. Lop Loiqua, doomed warlord of the Whants, can say: "Otherwise it is all one" (ShW/45), grimly accepting his fate; a dock master can utter the same expression: "It is all one, since you evidently arrived" (ShW/167). "It's all one, so long as I have my berries" (An/13) says the young girl, Azouk, on Durdane, and Anacho the Dirdirman can make a similar remark (SW/21), as can disguised Wankhman, Helsse (SW/91). Such an expression can be traced back to the character Peter Quince in *A Midsummer Night's Dream*: "That's all one" (I;2:142).[54]

So too do we find ample models for Lop Loiqua's recal-

---

54. William Shakespeare. *A Midsummer Night's Dream* (Nelson, 1970).

citrance or starmenter Sagmondo Bandolio's stoic acceptance of his fate in a character like Barnadine in *Measure for Measure* with his jocular defiance, showing an association with Shakespeare's characters that becomes very tempting indeed. We have the pompous Poloniuses, the sad introspective Hamlets, the loyal Gonzales, the opportunists like Angelo and Macbeth, jesters like Trinculo and Touchstone, the unsuspected Iagos, the Prosperos and so on. We have Elbows, Pompeys and Falstaffs to spare, their dialog and interrelationships constantly measured by the numerous stylisms ("Just as you say" [Em/2/63], "All this is undoubtedly correct" [M:T/148], "This may well be" [DTA/471]).

But rather than obtruding, these patterns push forward a sense of formal elegance, out of place on its own but effective in "humanizing" the exotic settings—producing a conventional (if conventionalized) framework against which the variations are made to stand out even more. Elsewhere we learn of Frolitz, leader of a Shant musical troupe, calling for "The Merrydown" (An/170), or the Lokhar mechanic, Zarfo, calling a companion a "poltroon" (SW/148). We encounter the same archaistic flavor in Helsse saying: "He would as soon don a buffoon's cap and cut capers in Merrymakers' Round" (SW/100), or in the proprietor of a squalid inn in the wildlands of Caraz addressing Etzwane as "my cockscomb" (As/174).

The medievalism of Vance's selective focus is an important counterweight to the more outlandish factors that are supplied. It maintains the important tension between things that are dear and familiar, and those that are extraordinary but which our recognizably human "locals" treat as commonplace. The same circumstances that allow Vance to opt for manor houses and rural communities in general show this balance at work. Etzwane rides the balloon-way on Durdane and observes that:

> In the dank lower valleys stood redwoods, hoary giants five hundred feet tall, half as old as the coming of the human race. Lower still, along the piedmont, were

hangman trees, black oaks and green elms, the unique syndic trees whose seeds sprouted legs and poisonous pincers. After walking to a satisfactory location, each seed roved within a ten-foot circle, poisoning all competing vegetation, then dug a hole and buried itself. (An/76)

With incredible ease does the familiar merge with the unfamiliar:

> Glinnes brought a flask of green wine from the cupboard and poured full a goblet. He went to the verandah and looked up and down the water. It lay calm and dreaming, broken only by the ripple of a merling who somewhere had surfaced. (T:A/176)

This is a scene of peace and tranquility. Of no great moment are the harsh realities of coexistence with the merlings. They are as much a normal part of Trill life as the flask of wine and the goblet. Similarly, after a cross-country trek involving all manner of alien exotica—erjins, Blues and sky-sharks—Schaine Madduc comes home:

> And there ahead: Morningswake, serene among tall frail green-gums and lordly transtellar oaks, with the brimming Chip-chap flowing to the side: the landscape of a dear reverie; a place forever precious.... (GP/59)

With Schaine, we too have come home. This elegant manorhouse is something out of our own strong traditions—reinforced in the novels of Austen, Bronte, and George Eliot. What matter that it is made of Fairy Forest gadroon and Szintarre teak and that the roof sports "a line of black iron ghost-chasers in the shape of trefoils" (GP/60). We have already identified the dormers and wainscotings from our own experience. The furniture and chandeliers may have come from "one of the far

Old Worlds" (p.60), but they are recognizably what they are, and provide us with a cultural haven—a reference point—from which to regard the unsettling contrasts in the outer world of kachembas, karoos and crazy-boxes.

Here Vance is following the same advice that Dame Isabel Grayce gives her company in *Space Opera* (1965). He must give his readers "the largest possible number of contacts with the audience's own milieu, the largest possible number of situations with which they can identify their own existences" (p.41).

Having "primed" us with such familiar things, there then occurs the confrontation with the otherworldly. Efraim can travel by air car over forest valleys filled with "interstellar yew" (M:A/70), but overhead there are four dwarf suns "sliding in different directions across the sky" (p.43), an almost unimaginable reality for us to envisage. So too we must employ our mind's-eye in a most exacting way to make real for ourselves that "commonplace" on Maske when "awesome Skay trundles down the sky" (p.209). Failing in this task, we are thrown back on commonplaces closer to a home—the hacks, the feluccas of the Sea-Nationals and so on, the far more accessible exotica.

But rarely does Vance demand more than the reader can easily provide. True to Dame Isabel's advice, he taps an association with traditions and the names and places of personal experience, carefully using language to achieve a verisimilitude that a statement of the more essential planetographical realities cannot readily evoke. So we get places: Grigglesby Corners, Hyalis Park, Vashmont, Riverside Park—precincts of Ambroy; Prairie View, Funk's Grove, Massacre Bend—towns of the Lower Vissel; Ascalon, Morningshore, Wild Rose—cantons of Shant; or vegetation: sad-apple trees, pipwillows, barchnuts and other hauntingly familiar growths like catafalque trees and hangman trees, which work on our sense of the known by tapping words like "catafalque" and our ability to imagine a gallows. The names of people likewise receive this careful blending. Alongside Finnerack and Ishiel at Angwin Junction on Durdane, there works a Dickon—a good medieval name.

To extend this process still further, we may remind ourselves that Vance often conceives his local situations in terms of known cultural antecedents and actual historical analogues. He will often plainly acknowledge these "derivations." Part of that spectacular expansion of terrestrial peoples into space that eventually led to the Gaean Reach and the richly diverse human-settled universe of Vance's work, also led to world-cultures that reflect an amalgamation of recognizable Earthly cultural and national groups transplanted onto new soil. Ethelrinda Cordas in "The Man from Zodiac" is a planet with a cultural profile distinctly reflecting its ancient Iberian origins. In "Sjambak" one character asks another: "Sirgamesk is a Javanese planet, isn't it?" and is answered: "Javanese, Arab, Malay" (p.6); and much of the xenographical travelogue which follows is Vance relocating his own knowledge of the cultural forms of those peoples, devising his own hybrid culture and one unfortunate consequence—the sjambaks—resulting from this blending.

On other occasions, these "derivations" are by no means as clear. The central idea for the intricate human castle societies in *The Last Castle* came from an article on Japanese social interactions; and after the first part of *Marune: Alastor 933* (dealing with Pardero's privations and his return home as Efraim), we have in the second part what is almost a mid-European Renaissance court intrigue, involving disputes over succession and inheritance, alliances of advantage, the nuances of diplomacy, maneuverings to gain territory, feudalistic warfare, etc. This picture emerges as much from the names of places as from events themselves. A pronounced Germanic flavor, for example, surrounds the entire Rhune culture, with numerous associations in names like Rhune (Rhine), Kaiark (Kaiser), Strang (Stuhl), a mountain called the Tassenberg, as well as the rigid, militaristic nature of the Rhunes themselves. No significant correspondence is intended by this, it must be added; it is simply a device for obtaining resonance from a setting, for animating it. For this reason, we are given an equally distinctive flavor of the Italian (Gosso of Gorgetto, a chamber known as the Sacarlatto, and countless structural debts to Machiavelli), and the French (the chamberlain Agnois, the title Lissolet, places like Disbague and Eccord). Added to this is a land-agreement dispute straight out of the American West. When Efraim goes to Whispering Ridge to locate some tangible proof of an ancient agreement, the words spoken by the Fwai-chi are those of the perennial noble savage of the television western:

> "I am the Kaiark."
> "Then you must know the treaty is real."
> "The treaty won't mean much if the land is transferred to Eccord."
> "That may not be done. We repeated to each other the word 'forever'."
> "I would like to see this treaty myself," said Efraim. "I will carefully check my records."
> "The treaty is not among your records," said the Fwai-chi, and the group shuffled back to the forest. (M:A/123)

In this, Vance, like Poul Anderson and so many other xenographers, is "interpreting the past of mankind by projecting his future."[55] This is not so central and intentional as to warrant charges of producing allegory and satire, but it is one inevitable outcome. When Anderson writes about Van Rijn and the trading companies of his age, he is, as P. Schuyler Miller suggests, devising a useful analogy for those nineteenth-century fur traders of the American north-west who knew the Indians they traded with far better than the urban-dwellers they ultimately served. When Vance brings his fourteen-ship contingent of Credential Renunciators to Thaery on the world Maske, he is giving us just one more variation on that other group of dissidents who reached the New World in the *Mayflower*.

But whether it be a *mélange* of terrestrial historical and

---

55. P. Schuyler Miller, "The Reference Library." *Analog*, January 1965, p.86.

cultural precedents, or merely the suffix "willow" or the word "Park" after a tree or a place, the effect is of a half-known, half-remembered thing, of places and objects one feels one should know; and so the locales, spread out beneath their sun or suns' light become dear to us, sufficiently removed to be both alien and quaint, exotic enough to provoke our sense of wonder, familiar enough to generate nostalgia.

MYSTERYMONGERING

On an even par with Vance the xenographer and Vance the traveler-adventurer, we have Vance the mystery writer. Under the name of John Holbrook Vance he has produced a number of conventional mystery stories: *The Man in the Cage* (1960), *The Fox Valley Murders* (1966), *The Pleasant Grove Murders* (1968), *The Deadly Isles* (1969), *Bad Ronald* (1973), etc.

Like his science fiction works, these novels are also exotic travelogs built around a central mystery—the classic "Whodunnit" format. The solving of the mystery takes the protagonist through all manner of social and ethnic groups. In *The Man in the Cage* this involves a journey to Morocco; in *The Deadly Isles* we have the land- and sea-scapes of Tahiti and the Marquesas.

With barely any effort at all, these stories might be as easily transferred to another planet—in fact, these same environs (involving rural, desert or island communities) recur as off-world settings. The cross-country trek and the sea-voyage are staples in these mysteries as well; they permit the tensions to develop and allow the necessary ferment of an individual's normally atrophied sense of experience.

Vance clearly enjoys his mystery-mongering, and we can safely suggest that the xenographical science fiction sub-genre ideally suits his needs, providing endless varieties and permutations of the standard themes, and permitting full use of an imaginative span somewhat vitiated by an Earth-bound focus. The xenological mystery simply makes possible the sort of "cultural analysis" (MR/187) that is used by Magnus Ridolph to solve the dilemma in "Coup de Grace" (1966), or that Kirth Gersen uses to track down his five Demon Princes.

This does not diminish the importance of the central mystery—it remains integral. But whether we consider short stories like "Coup de Grace" or "The Gift of Gab" (1955) or almost any of the novels, the mystery is the springboard into this "cultural analysis"—the mystery invariably operating as a "teaser" or structural framework that makes such an analysis possible.

Sometimes this integration of mystery story with xenographical travelogue is not successful. The reader is left with the feeling that the mystery and its solution are not up to the standard promised by the richness of the cultural setting and the "teaser." Vance is adept at providing both of these and using them to good advantage. But we have been spoiled by his own best offerings, such as the two stories just mentioned and a work like "The Moon Moth," and we quickly recognize stories that deliver less than is promised, that seem to offer an average (and somewhat anticlimactic) denouement for what looked to be a fulsome "cultural analysis" mystery. In "Sjambak," for example, Wilbur Murphy has been sent to the Javanese, Arab, Malay world of Cirgamesc to investigate the wild claim that there is a "Horseman of Space" who rides up to meet approaching spaceships. The "teaser" is there, and the exotic "lid-city" sultanate of Singhalût provides a satisfying foundation for Murphy's adventures. When the Horseman is explained, the story ends somewhat perfunctorily (as many of Vance's pieces appear to do), leaving the reader with the nagging feeling that he has been deprived, that far more could have been made of the sjambaks, that this whole story should have been a full length novel.

Similarly, in "The Man from Zodiac," we have Milton Hack faced with the task of implementing a contract to help the Phrones of the world Ethelrinda Cordas achieve a higher standard of living; although it turns out that the Phrones are only interested in obtaining off-world military assistance to help overthrow their neighbors, the Sabols. This story begins with all the fullness of background detail to which we are accustomed, but then ends like the average Retief story.

To an extent, this problem is an inevitable result of the nature of the sub-genre. Just as the amazing artifact of that Dyson civilization in Niven's *Ringworld* dominates the subsequent xenographical action, creating a sense of anticlimax before the sheer immensity of the initial premise of the ringworld itself, so too are many of Vance's exotic adventure-mysteries upstaged by the richness of their settings. If works like *Emphyrio*, the Durdane novels, and *Marune: Alastor 933* seem to end abruptly, even when the central mystery has been resolved satisfactorily, it is because Vance cannot "switch off" his worlds. A certain "momentum" has been created, and any resolution of the action is a curiously perfunctory cue for terminating the reader's involvement with the setting.

But more often than not, Vance assimilates his various elements with success; the cultural analysis being relevant and integral and carefully balanced. For instance, "The Gift of Gab" opens with the disappearance of a crew-member from a nine-man minerals-recovery craft operating on the ocean world Sabria. It is the classic disappearance situation, and suspense is immediately created by Fletcher's unsuccessful search of the raft and its environs. But within minutes Carl Raight's fate is known, and the focus shifts onto a mystery of the purely xenological kind—why have the aquatic autochthones of Sabria suddenly launched full-scale hostilities against the humans? Once again, this mystery is dissolved quite early in the story as rival operator Ted Chrystal's exploitation of the native dekabrachs is made apparent, and the story becomes a xenographical "communication" mystery—requiring cultural analysis to resolve the dilemma of how to converse with the intelligent but non-human dekabrachs.

Similarly, in "The Moon Moth" an Earth official must locate a dangerous criminal in an alien society whose members are continually masked in public, and who communicate with the aid of musical instruments. The criminal's identity is discovered and the official's life saved through his ingenious application of this same cultural analysis.

The study of local situations, cultural analysis and the central mystery therefore go hand in hand. It is by spending two hours in the library researching the cultural backgrounds of the various suspects to be questioned in a murder case that Magnus Ridolph discovers that no crime was committed: it being shown that what is to one race an act of pre-meditated murder is to another an act of the utmost charity and kindness. As a deliberate counterpoint to such a crucial approach, we have the parochial, over-zealous Pan Pascoglu who cannot help but see the situation from his own cultural bias.

THE OLD HUMAN ANGLE

"You have only one life; you must make the best of it."
—Kirth Gersen / *The Palace of Love*

"It's just a world, neither good nor evil."
—Darrell Hutson / *The Man in the Cage*

Although the Tschai novels are not explicitly works of the "general culture" group, they do not contradict its precepts, and as an autonomous unit they do provide an excellent focus for many of Vance's prime concerns. The planetary-trek of Adam Reith described in the tetralogy permits a host of ethnological and xenographical miniatures, not the least being the three alien races occupying Tschai, and those sentient indigenes, the Pnume.

Although a novel is assigned to each of these four peoples in turn—the Chasch, the Wankh, the Dirdir and the Pnume—the true focus is always on the humanity that attends them: those "bridge" races—the Chaschmen, the Wankhmen, the Dirdirmen, and the Pnumekin. It is not possible to delineate the extraterrestrial races with anything more than hints of exotica, suggestions of inscrutable purpose, and implication. The best method is to measure their alienness by observing the ways in which their attendant sub-men seek to vary themselves from any familiar human form:

> Reith thought of the other man-composites of Tschai, all more or less mutated toward their host-race: the Dirdirmen—sinister absurdities; the stupid and brutish Chaschmen; the venal overcivilized Wankhmen. The essential humanity of all these, except perhaps in the case of the Dirdirmen Immaculates, remained intact. (Pn/21)

It is this "essential humanity" that is central to every one of Vance's xenographical adventures, and reflected in his creation of extreme, random and disparate human types is a double stance: an encompassing, often cynical overview concerning any expression of the human condition, and a compassion sometimes bordering on the sentimental. In this, Vance is very close to his anonymous and world-wandering ruler of the Alastor Cluster: the Connatic. That ruler's words to one of his ministers could be said to sum up Vance's whole technique and personal philosophy as writer:

> "I enjoy the comradeship of the public house, the country inn, the dockside tavern, I travel the worlds of Alastor and everywhere I find people whom I love. Each individual of the five trillion is a cosmos in himself; each is irreplaceable, unique.... Sometimes I find a man or a woman to hate. I look into their faces and I see malice, cruelty, corruption. Then I think, these folk are equally useful in the total scheme of things; they act as exemplars against which virtue can measure itself. Life without contrast is food without salt... As Connatic I must think in terms of policy; then I only see the aggregate man, whose face is a blur of five

trillion faces. Towards this man I feel no emotion."
(T:A/216)

Vance loves his humanity, but he is never deceived by it. The greatest crimes in Vance's world-views and worlds-view are on the one hand to be dull and stolid, with no sensitivity to the finer nuances of existence, and on the other to be "over-subtle, over-civilized" (D/12), as with the Yao civilization on Tschai, burdened and stifled with ritual and decorum as ends in themselves. Most often, Vance's heroes—the protagonist-adventurers who are such tempting Vance-surrogates—are men of action: able pragmatists, close to their own vital forces, sensitive to their humanity and its framing landscapes.

Having noted the various facets of Vance's method, this brings us to the one area of questioning that yet remains. Where does Vance himself stand in relation to all of this? For as well as giving a series of xenographical adventure-mysteries, planetary-treks and cultural travelogues, there are those "collisions" we have mentioned.

The "general culture" stories involve social revolution and the clash of ideologies and interests—showing societies in states of flux and ferment, whether this is the growth of Fanscherade on Trullion and its subsequent demise due to the Trevanyi; the introduction of the virility hormone *chir*, cheaply synthesized to induce the autochthones of Maz to toil at the production of electrical components; the contravention of Thaery's Alien Influence Act and Mandate of Isolation by a local noble intent upon opening up the planet Maske to off-world tourism; the outrageous violations of rigid Rhune custom by supposedly its strongest adherents; a vicious land-rights debate over sequestered territories which uncovers an embarrassing truth for the human populations of Koryphon—this coupled with an uprising of both the human-derived Blues and the non-human erjins, and so on. The two Big Planet novels, because of the sheer size of the world on which they are set, give us a series of even more localized social upheavals—the defeat of Earthman renegade and opportunist, Charley Lysidder; the death of an all-powerful local warlord, Lop Loiqua; the legal overthrow of the royal House of Soyvanesse and the resulting social scandal, etc. To include *Emphyrio* and the Durdane books, we have the complete re-organization of whole planetary societies, the overthrow of an aristocracy of Lords and a welfare system on the one hand, the replacement of a cantonal-autocracy with the rudiments of a parliamentary system on the other.

Furthermore, these are merely the main social crises at work. Caught up in the larger conflicts are those others involving religions (the worship of Finuka, Galexis, the Female Mystery, etc.); succession and inheritance; economic programs; and a whole "panorama" of intricate human intercourse.

We have already noted an important connection with the men of action who are the protagonists of the novels, and we have suggested an equally strong connection with the Connatic, roving ruler of Alastor Cluster. Repeatedly, other characters are given the viewpoints, reflections and longings that make up a picture of Vance as "ethical pragmatist" (to borrow from his own dearly-loved "mouthpiece" character, Magnus Ridolph), as existentialist, as the traveler, musician, and craftsman, collating his own experiences-of-the-road into an overview of humanity and human culture, cherishing the vistas, the ebb and flow of thoughts and emotions, the public houses, the niceties of custom and cuisine, the trivia and idiosyncrasies which distinguish one place from another. It is as Ryl Shermatz (probably the disguised Connatic) says:

> "Each world...projects a mood of its own, and the sensitive traveler quickly learns to identify and savor this individuality." (T:A/193)

Out of continual exposure to local conditions (both real and imagined), Vance has synthesized an important ethical and philosophical stance. Firstly, there are no absolutes, particularly in those areas where humankind has institutionalized its appetites and yearnings: religion and morality, a code of justice, political forms, and so on. When Alusz Iphigenia criticizes the grim habits of the Sarkoy, Gersen replies: "That isn't a fair statement. The people live by a system different from ours" (PL/23). And again, Magnus Ridolph reminds us:

> "In all the many-colored worlds of the universe no single ethical code shows a universal force. The good citizen on Almanatz would be executed on Judith IV. Commonplace conduct on Medellin excites the wildest revulsion on Earth and on Moritaba a deft thief commands the highest respect. I am convinced that virtue is but a reflection of good intent." (MR/161)

Throughout the whole local focus framework (and because it is contained in a larger and more general framework) there emerges the fact that ethics and metaphysics are to be seen as local and relative expressions of yearnings fundamental to our humanity. There is no absolute right and wrong, no one political ideology, no single formalization of the god-perception. There are only variations on themes, permutations and regionalisms—all unassailably right to the cultures holding them, all determined by such easily quantified factors as environment, level of technological expertise, threats to survival, etc. Thus we have Magnus Ridolph holding forth with his caution to Pan Pascoglu: "Justice, after all, has no absolute values'" (MR/127) (a truism which the story "Coup de Grace" then goes on to demonstrate), or his being forced to confess:

> "I have fallen into the common fault of wishing to impose my personal tenor of living upon creatures constitutionally disposed to another." (MR/137)

Another cosmopolitan observer, Matho Lorcas, can describe the Rhunes as "walking bundles of neuroses" and "smothered in convention" (M:A/159), and in being reminded of relative norms, we learn too of socially-sanctioned incestuous marriages on Ys, or that few people on Trullion would spare a second thought for a girl losing her virginity at the age of nine.

To deal with a humanity rife with such local absolutes, Vance has taken the broadest perspective possible—that afforded by history, comparative social anthropology and ontology. Humankind is a beloved phenomenon, to be scrutinized as rigorously and as dispassionately as possible when it comes to the realm of its ideas about itself. Such a broad perspective produces pragmatist- philosophers like the Connatic or Mialambre, High Arbiter of Wale on Durdane. Mialambre writes:

> If the study of human interactions could become a science, I suspect that an inviolate axiom might be discovered to this effect: *Every social disposition creates a disparity of advantages.* Further: *Every innovation designed to correct the disparities, no matter how altruistic in concept, works only to create a new and different set of disparities.* (BFM/100-101)

This is a grim message indeed, and a novel like *The Gray Prince*, for instance, can be said to illustrate one point, however regrettable, that is fully in keeping with life in a pragmatic cosmos. As Walt Hobius says in *The Fox Valley Murders*: "'One man's gain is another man's loss: that's the way life goes" (p.218). Rather than seeing this as a cynical and resigned point of view on Vance's part, we should see it as he has Mialambre see it, as a lamentable but recurring fact of human social behavior. To say that Vance endorses such a viewpoint is an ungenerous and facile statement. Part of his specialization as xenographer (an interesting synthesis of disciplines anyway) has been to note how humanity's best intentions, noblest dreams and most laudable aspirations are continually being "sabotaged" by their application and expression within any given society. Where an ideal exists, it stands to be abused; compromised quite often by those who are, ironically, its most fervent adherents.

Consequently, we have "spokesman" figures like Magnus Ridolph, Mialambre or the Connatic, Oman Ursht:

> To the casual observer, Alastor Cluster is a system placid and peaceful. The Connatic knows differently. He recognizes that wherever human beings strive for advantage, disequilibrium exists; lacking easement, the social fabric becomes taut and sometimes rips asunder. The Connatic conceives his function to be the identification and relief of social stresses. Sometimes he ameliorates, sometimes he employs techniques of distraction. When harshness becomes unavoidable he deploys his military agency, the Whelm. Oman Ursht winces to see an insect injured; the Connatic without compunction orders a million persons to their doom. In many cases, believing that each condition generates its own counter-condition, he stands aloof, fearing to introduce a confusing third factor. *When in doubt, do nothing*: this is one of the Connatic's favorite credos. (T:A/2)

Nor is this philosophical stance a recent one. It has always been an integral part of Vance's xenographical overview—evident in earlier novels like *The Houses of Iszm* (1954):

> The Szecr sub-commandant twirled his viewer. "The universe is eight billion years old, the last two million of which had produced intelligent life. During this time not one hour of absolute equity has prevailed. It should be no surprise to find this basic condition applying to your personal affairs." (HIY67)

It is evident also in *The Palace of Love*, where Gersen ponders the relative merits of justice:

> The same question, in different terms, had been troubling Gersen himself. With his wealth, he might have bought the whole of Qualag and Juniper and every other factory in Sabra, and brought each of the wretched women to their homes.... What then? he asked himself. Sabra tapestries were in demand. New factories would be established, new slaves imported. A year later all would be as before. (PL/72)

He must finally resign himself to the sort of broad-spectrum social philosophy voiced by a leading "spokesman" character like the Connatic.

At the close of *The Asutra*, Gastel Etzwane returns from the distant world Kahei convinced that his life-long efforts to thwart first the Anome, then the Rogushkoi and the Asutra, have ended successfully, and satisfied that "for all its misery and black despair, he had lived to his utmost capacity; he had augmented and enriched his life" (As/178). A few pages later he learns from the exasperating Earthman, Ifness, that the Earth-worlds had already enforced peace and co-operation upon the Ka and the Asutra a short while before, so that in retrospect both Etzwane and the reader realize that these extraterrestrial hostiles would have been stopped in any event, and in spite of Etzwane's efforts. Etzwane has simply been the local response to the problem as manifested locally on Durdane, and that as far as Ifness and his colleagues at the Institute were concerned, Durdane could well have been an unfortunate casualty in this far larger crisis. This awareness of Durdane's "local" problem, its relatively minor role and expendability when seen against the vast number of Earth-worlds, leads the completely disillusioned Etzwane to enquire: "Do you require an aide, an assistant?" (As/187).

It is this winding-down at the end of the Durdane saga, an almost anticlimactic conclusion after the personal force and earlier successes, that obscures one important truth. Etzwane *has* lived "to his utmost capacity." He has indeed "augmented and enriched his life," especially in view of what he has been able to achieve as purely a local "response"—and in terms of the ethos supporting Vance's universe, there is no worthier task. It involves the kind of free-thinking detachment that wishes to extend its environment, that is tolerant of unfamiliar folkways, that seeks the overview and challenges the dogma and polemic resisting such a stance, that applauds charity and hospitality.

There emerges out of Vance's novels, then, a firm existentialist credo, of very much the *dum vivimus, vivamus* ("While we live, let us live!") sort. It is a bitter-sweet refrain throughout the "general culture" works. For example, Apollon Zamp reflects:

> The single and only verity was *now*, with wind blowing the reek of water and mud, wet reeds, dingle and black-willow into his face, and the sunlight dancing upon the water. (ShW/15)

He says to his audience:

> "In the meantime, on with the performance! Let us enjoy each instant of our all-too-fugitive lives!" (ShW/148)

This, of course, is an older Vance writing, one who has come to savor more keenly the joys of life and their briefness. In *Maske: Thaery*, Vaidro says to Jubal Droad:

> "While we are alive we should sit among colored lights and taste good wines, and discuss our adventures in far places; when we are dead, the opportunity is past." (M:T/208)

So the refrain continues. An innkeeper says to Jubal: "'Alas, we can't be young forever'" (M:T/8), and we are told of how "Benruth entertained the Droad kindred and celebrated the sweet fugacity of existence" (M:T/4). A row of lights beside the door to a Maseache inn on Durdane spells out: *Never neglect the wonder of conscious existence, which too soon comes to an end!* (BFM/88).

Although perhaps more poignant, more wistful in the later novels, this "existentialist-pantheistic-humanism" has always been another fundamental element of Vance's work.

> Omon Bozhd focused both fractions of his eyes on Farr. He spoke in a reflective key. "Every second of existence is a new miracle. Consider the countless variations and possibilities that await us every second—avenues into the future. We take only one of these; the others—who knows where they go? This is the eternal marvel, the magnificent uncertainty of the second next to come, with the past a steady carpet of denouement.... Our minds become numbed to the wonder of life, because of its very pressures and magnitude." (III/73)

ON THE RELATIVE MERITS OF MUMBO-JUMBO

> "Godogma takes all men."
> —Sivij Suthiro / *Star King*

Compared with such an all-embracing reverence for the total miracle of existence, formalized religion of any kind, rigidly delineated within what is usually an inflexible body of doctrine, is a highly suspect social institution, and is invariably shown as repressing the human spirit and severely limiting the range of life-options open to the members of a community.

So whenever a religion or ideology is presented as an aspect of culture (and rarely is it lacking—the planet Pao being a notable exception), it is always made to seem comical in its doctrinaire self-righteousness and parochial absolutism—to the extent that the Sarkoy pantheon is ruled by a deity significantly called Godogma. But whether it is the violent worship of the Female

Mystery on Tschai; the worship of Finuka on Halma with its devotional-structure of "leaping"; or the unique male-dominated religion of the Chilites in Canton Bashon on Durdane, revering Galexis the Female Principle while maintaining a social system which relies on prostitution to ensure itself of a continuing population, the picture is the same: each organized religion is to be seen as a local manifestation of the awe and exultation experienced at the sheer existence of an infinite universe; one person's most fervent beliefs becoming another's mumbo-jumbo. As Adam Reith tells his Pnumekin companion, Zap 210, having observed certain rites of the Khors: "'It's only religion'" (Pn/70).

Hence we get the whimsical, satirical detachment that views the religious phenomenon as just one more aspect of the overall phenomenon of humanity; a manifestation of yearnings given expression within the social contract, of broad philosophical rather than any vested ideological interest:

> No less an index to thought-processes of a people was their religion. The Dirdir, so Reith knew from conversations with Anacho, were irreligious. The Dirdirmen, to the contrary, had evolved an elaborate theology, based on a creation myth which derived Man and Dirdir from a single primordial egg. The submen of Sivishe patronized a dozen different temples. The observances, as far as Reith could see, followed the more or less universal pattern—abasement, followed by a request for favors, as often as not foreknowledge regarding the outcome of the daily races. Certain cults had refined and complicated their doctrines, their doxology was a metaphysical jargon subtle and ambiguous enough to please even the folk of Sivishe. Other creeds serving different needs had simplified procedures so that the worshippers merely made a sacred sign, threw sequins into the priest's bowl, received a benediction and were off about their affairs. (D/90-91)

And again, one easily overlooked fact filling the background of the Demon Princes novels is the appearance throughout the Oikumene of another major Earth-based religion—the worship of Kalzibah. Christianity is already seen as "the unsubstantiated dogma of a localized religious cult" (SK/101) and, by extension, the cult of Kalzibah is given the same short shrift when regarded from a historical and transcultural perspective. It is reduced, made to seem comical and trivial in its self-importance:

> When the girl was sixteen, they lived in Edmonton, Canada, the goal of hordes of pilgrims who came to gaze upon the Sacred Shin. Navarth reasoned that here, among the interminable festivals, processions and sacerdotal rights, they might live unnoticed. (PL/106)

Later, this worship is contained further and made to seem even more ludicrous when a reference is given to the Tournament of the Gods held at Astropolis to determine which three deities of thirteen cults are to occupy the pre-eminent positions for the next seven years. Kalzibah has won a position on four consecutive occasions. The whole arrangement has about it that quality of good-humored skepticism, that ready-to-oblige syncresis which characterized the polytheistic state religion of the Roman Empire around the time of Nero.

It is not surprising that Vance should use this diversity of metaphysical conviction as a main area of "collision" among his various cultural groups. Nothing exposes the soft underbellies, the unique cultural idiosyncrasies, the limitations, prejudices and doctrines of self-interest more than the religious discourse. Vance uses it to polarize his human types into near-sighted, self-righteous parochials and the true cosmopolitans. A typical conversation on the subject has Anacho the Dirdirman explaining the religion of Gozed to his fellow travelers:

> "At night the scorpions come up from the sea to spawn, which they accomplish by stinging eggs into a

host animal, often a woman left down on the beach for that purpose. The eggs hatch, the 'Mother of the Gods' is devoured by the larva. In the last stages, when pain and religious ecstasy produce a curious psychological state in the 'Mother', she runs down the beach and flings herself into the sea."

"An unsettling religion."

The Dirdirman admitted as much. "Still it appears to suit the folk of Gozed...." (SW/39)

Such is the detachment brought to a local situation by a relatively enlightened cosmopolitan of Tschai. Usually it is taken further, and we have a familiar framework of contention and comparison—the collision of parochial viewpoints. Val Dal Barba asks:

"Why are there only 'Mothers of the Gods'? Why shouldn't those flint-faced men go down on the beach and become 'Fathers of the Gods'?"

The captain chuckled. "It seems as if the honors are reserved for the ladies."

"It would never be thus in Murgen," declared the merchant warmly. "We pay sizable tithes to the priests; they take all the responsibility for appeasing Bisme; we have no further inconvenience."

"A system as sensible as any," agreed Palo Barba. "This year we subscribe to the Pansogmatic Gnosis, and the religion has much virtue to it."

"I like it much better than Tutelanics," said Edwe. "You merely recite the litany and then you are done for the day."

"Tutelanics was a dreadful bore," Heizari concurred. "All that memorizing! And remember that dreadful Convocation of Souls, where the priests were so familiar? I like Pansogmatic Gnosis much better."

> Dordolio gave an indulgent laugh. "You prefer not to become intense. I myself incline in this direction. Yao doctrine, of course, is to some extent a syncresis; or, better to say, in the course of the 'round' all aspects of the Ineffable are given opportunity to manifest themselves, so that, as we move with the cycle, we experience all theopathy." (SW/40-41)

And when, on top of all this, the protagonist Reith is asked what "theosophical insights" he can contribute to the discussion, the answer is typically that of a Vance surrogate:

> "None," said Reith. "Very few, at any rate. It occurs to me that the man and his religion are one and the same thing. The unknown exists. Each man projects on the blankness the shape of his own particular world-view. He endows his creation with his personal volitions and attitudes. The religious man stating his case is in essence explaining himself. When a fanatic is contradicted he feels a threat to his own existence; he reacts violently."
>
> "Interesting!" declared the fat merchant. "And the atheist?"
>
> "He projects no image upon the blank whatever. The cosmic mysteries he accepts as things in themselves; he feels no need to hang a more or less human mask upon them." (SW/41)

So too in an earlier novel does Joe Smith express this same enlightened tolerance:

> "At present," said Joe, "there is no organized religion on Earth. We are free to express our joy at being alive in any way which pleases us. Some revere a cosmic creator—others merely acknowledge the physical

laws controlling the universe to almost the same result." (ST/57)

Such expansiveness is part of that ethical pragmatism displayed by Magnus Ridolph, Gerd Jemasze and many others. That other dynamic surrogate, Kirth Gersen, is no different:

> "As for right and wrong—each man to his own answer. There never has been a true consensus."
> Teehalt smiled sadly. "You espouse a very popular doctrine, ethical pragmatism, which always turns out to be the doctrine of self-interest." (SK/14)

This is an honest viewpoint. It recognizes that as creatures we serve ourselves in any event, regardless of the trappings we choose to conceal such a fact. What becomes important is that we strive to obtain the most infinite and encompassing view for an infinite universe—to be cosmopolitan in that practical sense, permitting sufficient "collisions" for us continually to measure ourselves, and stave off prejudices and assumptions—those "barnacles" on the growing personality.

In noting the "collisions" with which the "general culture" novels are concerned, it becomes clear that Vance is endorsing the flexibility and detachment of this cosmopolitan viewpoint, whether this is manifested in the persons of the Connatic, Miro Hetzel or a character like Matho Lorcas:

> "By an axiom of social anthropology, the more isolated a community, the more idiosyncratic become its customs and conventions. This of course is not necessarily disadvantageous.
> "On the other hand, consider a person such as myself: a rootless wanderer, a cosmopolitan. Such a person tends to flexibility; he adapts himself to his surroundings without qualms or misgivings. His baggage of conventions is simple and natural, the lowest

common denominator of his experience. He evinces a kind of universal culture which will serve him almost anywhere across the Gaean Reach. I make no virtue of this flexibility, except to suggest that it is more comfortable to travel with than a set of conventions, which, if jostled, work emotional strains upon those who espouse them." (M:A/109)

In *Space Opera*, Dame Isobel Grayce says: "Yes; we must not be too parochial..." (p.84); and then proceeds to be just that, steadfastly persisting in going forth to bring cultural enlightenment to the inhabitants of distant worlds. At best, this self-righteous program stands to become an example of that "cultural imperialism" acclaimed by another of Vance's characters as "the only practicable form" (ST/119). It leads to the condescension that sees a world like Swannick's Star as "a charming world, old-fashioned and quaint" (SO/102) on the one hand; or as a "wretched dirty little world reverted to feudalism" (SO/102) on the other.

But there is equal danger in going too far the other way, in becoming so refined and consciously cosmopolitan as to become cynical, over-detached and decadent. We are cautioned by Yao society on Tschai, by the effete Earth-based publication *Cosmopolis* in the Demon Princes novels, or by the quite daunting intellectual community of Olanje on Koryphon:

> Kelse laughed; "Also in passing I might mention that urbane folk make up the membership of the Redemptionist Alliance, the Vitatis Cult, the Cosmic Peace Movement, Panortheism, a dozen more: all motivated by abstractions four or five or six times removed from reality." (GP/52)

Kelse cautions us further:

> "Urban folk, dealing as they do in ideas and abstractions, become conditioned to unreality. Then, whenever the fabric of civilization breaks, these people are as helpless as fish out of water." (GP/51)

This important assertion is later demonstrated in *The Gray Prince* when the erjins rebel. An even more intense warning is voiced by Institute spokesman, Baron Bodissey:

> How common the man of intellect who cannot feel? How trifling are his judgments against those of the peasant who derives his strength, like Antaeus, from the emotional sediment of the race! Essentially the tastes and preferences of the intellectual elite, derived from learning, are false, doctrinaire, artificial, shrill, shallow, uncertain, eclectic, jejune, and insincere. (KM/118)

Vance's protagonists take a middle course. Men like Gerd Jemasze and Kelse Madduc exist in a balanced environment—neither as parochial as the Blues and the Wind-runners nor as over-civilized as the intellectual elite of Olanje. They function within their local environment, cherishing it, but they measure themselves against lifestyles other than their own, seeking to preserve the best of both worlds. They are necessarily impatient with the abstractions, nimble rationalisms and sophistry that so often passes for enlightened, civilized and cultured behavior, for these can produce that curious fool's paradise which is so out of touch as to think itself impervious. It is up to characters like Gerd Jemasze to inject a note of reality into this specious calm:

> "The travesty exists only because reliance upon abstractions has made reality incomprehensible to you. These issues aren't merely local: they extend across the Gaean Reach. Except for a few special cases, title

to every parcel of real property derives from an act of violence, more or less remote, and ownership is only as valid as the strength and will required to maintain it. This is the lesson of history, whether you like it or not." (GP/172)

A RENASCENCE OF SIMPLICITY

"Our refuge is medievalism."
—Navarth / *The Palace of Love*

It is here too that Vance's "medievalism" fulfils its other major role. Apart from supplying old-world settings that are quaint and familiar and permit an easy marriage with contexts and decor normally associated with the favorite elements of sword-and-sorcery/fantasy adventures, we have the endorsement of a lifestyle and philosophical orientation that is benignly medieval, rather in that sense of agreeable "rustication" acclaimed by William Morris in *A Dream of John Ball* (1888).

But balance is once again the keynote. Careful distinctions must be made. Vance is not advocating the sort of medievalism nurtured by Kokor Hekkus on Thamber. As Alusz Iphigenia says: "none of it is real. It is animated myth, archaic scenes from a diorama. It stifles me" (KM/154): in other words, unwholesome, unnatural, and non-viable. Instead, Vance advances the kind of physiological and psychological (not to mention spiritual) communion between humanity and its natural environment that we find characterizing Gilbert Duray's choice of "Home" in "Rumfuddle"; that leads Kirth Gersen to long for "a cottage, with an old-fashioned garden, an orchard in the meadow, a rowboat tied to the riverbank" (SK/191); or that characterizes the Trill lifestyle on Trullion; that of the Alouan land-barons of Koryphon or the Thariots of Maske. Any such rapport is for the good. We see it again in the words of a fulfilled "spokesman" figure like the Sea-National, Shrack:

> "I have seen strange sights, I have known startling experiences of which no city-dweller could be aware, no matter how agile his intellect. The *Clanche* is my home. I love each splinter of her fabric, but I agree that a boat is different from a parcel of land with a cottage, a stream, a meadow, and an orchard of fruit. Better? Or worse? I have known both and I cannot decide." (M:T/57)

Like Shrack, Vance too has known both. It is the same condition that has the mad poet, Navarth, remark precipitously to his fellow travelers en route to the Palace of Love:

> "We are midway along in the journey. Here is where the carelessness, the amplitude, the calm ease depart. The winds arose at our back and hurried us through the woods. Our refuge is medievalism." (PL/144)

Similarly, when Gersen regards an ancient lakeside village on Earth as "bucolic and charming, almost medieval." (PL/90), we have an approbation that clearly comes from Vance himself, a sanctioning of a middle course of enlightened medievalism that is clearly Vance's optimum demographical condition. Even the dissembling Ramus Ymph calls for this shift away from sterile overcomplication, and though his motivations are selfish ones, his words ironically capture the essence of this neo-medieval balance:

> "After all, change is not necessarily equivalent to unwholesome innovation. Subtleties are the curse of our old civilization. If change there must be, I would wish a renascence of simplicity." (M:T/33)

And in "Rumfuddle," Vance has Alan Robertson restate the important views already expressed earlier by the representatives of the Institute. Robertson reminds us:

> Man is a creature whose evolutionary environment has been the open air. His nerves, muscles, and senses have developed across three million years in intimate contiguity with natural earth, crude stone, live wood, wind, and rain. Now this creature is suddenly—on the geological side, instantaneously—shifted to an unnatural environment of metal and glass, plastic and plywood, to which his psychic substrate lack all compatibility. The wonder is not that we have so much mental instability but so little. Add to this the weird noises, electrical pleasures, bizarre colors, synthetic foods, abstract entertainments! We should congratulate ourselves on our durability. (R/94)

But whether it is Robertson or the Institute, the ideological point being made is that humanity must spare itself "the nightmare of the artificial man" (PL/133). The Institute fights a delaying tactic, seeing itself as a "highly active set of antibodies" (PL/133) at work in the human race, striving to resist the supposed "blessings" of too much progress. As always, such a force naturally breeds its own antithesis, and there are those who would see the Institute as preferring "more of Thamber in the daily life of the Oikumene" (KM/146). But whatever the arguments for and against, such a sociological profile remains the philosophical cornerstone upon which Vance's planetary cultures are built, much the same way as it is for writers like Clifford Simak, Theodore Sturgeon or Ursula Le Guin.

Moreover, the extremes are there. Sometimes the medievalism is enforced and regressive, as with Ambroy on Halma or even the Rhune Realms. Sometimes it is almost excessively idyllic, as with the society of Merlank on Trullion. But it is the preferred cultural format for that complex set of reasons we have noted, and it allows adventure story-tellers the best of all possible worlds—allowing them to draw on the modern and ancient, editing out those undesirable aspects of both as they see fit.

AVENUES INTO THE FUTURE

> "The basic law of the cosmos is this: in a situation of infinity, whatever is possible exists in fact."
> —Ifness / *The Asutra*

Along with the important stances of ethical pragmatist, cosmopolitan and enlightened medievalist, there is yet another stance—equally important, and one in terms of which this study must in a sense ultimately damn itself out of excessive scholarly zeal. For when that dynamic pragmatist, Gastel Etzwane, bitterly asserts the practical realities of the cosmos with: "Bah,... Iron is iron, glass is glass, and this is the same here or at the end of the universe" (As/69), the equally pragmatic but more "cosmopolitan" Ifness reminds both Etzwane and ourselves of the need for a conceptual flexibility to keep us in perspective. We are only at one steadily advancing point in an infinite process of development and discovery. As Ifness cautions a suddenly quite philosophically parochial Etzwane: "Conceivably entire disassociated phases of knowledge exist; the field of para-psychology comes to mind" (As/69). Coming from a spokesman for the inherently conservative Institute, this amounts to an important statement indeed, although a name like "Ifness" should alert us to this consideration of possibility.

Elsewhere, cultures and life-forms possessing psionic skills and the gifts of parapsychology are a recurring feature of Vance's universe, and can be seen as having these gifts for more reasons than just adding to the exotic focus or the mystery element.

The paranormal is used, of course, to endow Vance's otherworldly cultures and settings with that *outré* quality and truly exotic flavor. But never far away from this is the attitude of the person introducing it. Vance would remind us of the unknown as an eternal quantity—of the plurality of approaches to the infinite. Initially, psionics and parapsychology are used to bring about a collision between the reader and classifications like "primitive," "sentient" and "sophisticated." The Green Chasch of Tschai, the Gomaz of Maz, and the erjins of Koryphon could all be classified superficially as "noble savages" or as unsophisticated races—but all three utilize telepathy. Vance leaves the possibilities largely unresolved. He will apply terms like "quasi-intelligent" or suggest a highly-developed hive consciousness at work to throw us back on our own taxonomical prejudices, and then go on to show how few meaningful points of connection there are for one sort of intelligence really to understand another. We can observe the crucial role of the fertility hormone *chir* in the lives of the Gomaz, but only as a physical cause-and-effect agency. We cannot grasp anything like the full significance of their "wars of love" and the part played in these by *chir*, except by making the most facile oversimplifications based on an often inadequate understanding of our own procreative drives and processes. When visitors to Axistil on Maz are warned against fraternizing too closely with the indigenous Gomaz and are told:

> The Gomaz are adept telepaths; the extent, however, to which they can comprehend human thought is still a matter of conjecture, (DTA/474)

there is the clear implication that this goes two ways: humans can achieve only a most dubious understanding of the Gomaz. And while, superficially, they present a picture of a feudalistic society constantly engaged in warfare, this is our interpretation of the facts, producing the sort of misconceptions that led to the near-extermination of the entire race of Kokod Warriors in an earlier Magnus Ridolph story (a race distinctly reminiscent of the Gomaz).

But most of all, by giving many of his alien cultures extrasensory powers, Vance reminds us that there is more to the universe and, by implication, so much more within ourselves. There is also the suggestion that in becoming a technologically sophisticated and civilized animal, humanity may have closed certain doors on itself, and possibly cut itself off from a more harmonious and rewarding relationship with the natural world—just cause indeed for the medievalist outlook that seeks to heal this rift.

Vance has always been attuned to the possibility that a higher psychic dimension is available within that "situation of infinity" (As/69) that is the universe, and often, in sharp contrast to his over-civilized human cultures, he will present a technologically primitive but psychically sophisticated race to remind us of these vital alternatives.

As in other aspects of Vance's approach as writer, what the "general culture" novels make a commonplace is solidly anticipated by the earlier works. Among the divergent human races in *The Houses of Iszm*, we hear of the Nenes, "tall slender near-men, agile, voluble and clairvoyant" (p.60).

In *The Dragon Masters* there are the highly sophisticated, calm and meditative sacerdotes of Aerlith, beings who have denied their terrestrial origin altogether. On Pangborn, as we have already seen, the descendants of a highly technological humanity have detoured from the regimens of their ancestors and refined for themselves a most formidable array of mental sciences.

But as always, Vance reminds us of the need for the middle course—for the best possible balance of our powers: mental and physical. The sacerdotes must in the end resort to the physical measures they abhor in order to preserve their way of life. So too are the magicians of Pangborn reminded of the blessings of a more conventional scientific method. The lesson then is that we should locate the optimum condition in which we can develop the total person as much as possible. The incentive for doing this must lie in the hope of achieving purer insights into an infinite cosmos, and of identifying and functioning as closely as possible to one's maximum capacities.

The key point that Vance makes regarding the paranormal is that it is to be considered as a normal part of everyday life. As he says in his Foreword to *Eight Fantasms and Magics* (1969):

> Strange things happen. Almost everyone has had some sort of brush with the paranormal, even the most resistant and skeptical of persons. The range of events is wide and only roughly amenable to classification. In olden times angels and demons were held responsible; to date no-one has produced a more reasonable explanation.
>
> Phenomena such as telepathy and poltergeists may well be manifestations of different and distinct principles; there may be two, three, four, or more such realms of knowledge, each at least as rich and intricate as physics or astronomy. There is little systematic study. Conventional scientists shy away from the field because they are, in fact, conventional; because they fear to compromise their careers; because the subject is difficult to get a grip on; because scientists are as susceptible to awe and eeriness as anyone else. So: the mysteries persist; the lore accumulates, and we know for sure no more than our remote ancestors, if as much. (8F/7)

The important point that emerges out of this is that these "strange things" are part of the phenomenal universe, occurring so often as to have become another facet of that same pragmatism endorsed by Vance. As we have said, the unknown is as integral and matter-of-fact a part of our universe as those properties we allegedly understand. Hence, in Vance's novels, there is always the suggestion of this extra dimension, a dimension which the Vance-surrogate will always respect. In *The Houses of Iszm*, Aile Farr argues with the Iszic house-growers:

> "The knowledge eventually will be duplicated," said Farr, "whether you like it or not. There are too many homeless people in the universe."

"No!" Zhde Patasz snapped his viewer. "The craft cannot be induced rationally—an element of magic still exists."

"Magic?"

"Not literally. The trappings of magic. For instance, we sing incantations to sprouting seeds. The seeds sprout and prosper. Without incantations they fail. Why? Who knows? No one on Iszm. In every phase of growing, training and breaking the house for habitation, this special lore makes the difference between a house and a withered useless vine." (HI/38)

On Sarkovy, we encounter a similar confrontation. The guide, Edelrod, says:

"We are frequently asked why we persist in deriving our poisons from natural sources.... The answer is of course that natural poisons, being initially associated with living tissue, are the more effective."

"I would suggest the presence of catalyzing impurities in the natural poisons," suggested Gersen, "rather than metaphysical association."

Edelrod held up a minatory finger. "Never scoff at the role of the mind! For instance... See there—the little reptile.... This is the meng. From one of his organs comes a substance which can be distributed either as ulgar or as furux. The same substance, mind you! But when sold as ulgar and used as such, the symptoms are spasms, biting off of the tongue and a frothing madness: When sold and used as furux, the interskeletal cartilage is dissolved so that the frame goes limp. What do you say to that? Is that not metaphysics of the most exalted sort?" (PL/14)

And to extend this important trend into the "general culture" works, there are the Waels of Wellas on the planet Maske:

> "You can inspect the boatyards, where every plank is shaped by hand to imaginary plans. They cut the wood into strips and then weld them to the hull with *mais*—'the stuff of life', which they keep in bottles of black glass. What is *mais*? No one knows but the Waels. If they curse a ship, the *mais* loosens in midocean and the ship becomes a tangle of sticks." (M:T/176)

To regard these occurrences as mere superstition is to forget such very real local "realities" as pointing the bone, faith-healing, clairvoyance and harvest rites; everything from voodoo to the blessing of the fishing fleet. These "strange things" are as integral and matter of fact a part of the phenomenal universe as those other more tangible, more demonstrable elements of life, occurring with such uniformity throughout human society as to have rightly become another factor justifying that truly complete pragmatism embraced by Vance and his principal characters. Gerd Jemasze is properly respectful of the ways of Kurgech and his Uldra dependants, the fiaps and rites of the Wind-runners. Whatever ultimate cause and effect might explain these mysteries, they are facts to be observed with the proper degree of circumspection. Our own predicament becomes very much like that facing Elvo Glissam when he says: "I suppose my sensibilities are atrophied" (GP/89), a remark which Gerd Jemasze answers with: "If you live where magic is unknown, you'll never recognize it" (p.91). With Glissam, we are being cautioned as well.

So too does Jubal Droad respect local mysteries whose causality is not evident to his own perceptual processes. When Jubal and Shrack refuse to convey Ramus Ymph back to Wysrod, the Erdstone Factor merely has to remind them of one thing:

> "Your vessel was built here at Erdstone, and fixed with our good *mais*."
> "True," said Shrack, suddenly glum.

> "Do you wish it to convey you safely across the ocean?"
> "Yes indeed; no question about that."
> "Then you will take Ramus Ymph to Wysrod."
> "We will be happy to oblige you," said Shrack. (M:T/193)

In short, the more skeptical and "enlightened" people who ridicule such powers would find their ships falling apart, leaving them to flounder in midocean with only the dubious comfort of their rational viewpoint and scientific method. Again, the extremes are to be shunned—the hidebound, credulous and superstitious on the one hand, the over-refined and dangerously pedantic on the other.

Then, on Marune, we have Skogel, the eccentric healer of Port Maz who qualifies his frank admission of charlatanism with an important and by now familiar reservation:

> "I will reveal a truth," declared Skogel portentously. "Much of my merchandise, on a functional level, is totally ineffective. Psychically, symbolically, subliminally, the story is different! Each item exerts its own sullen strength, and sometimes I feel myself in the presence of elementals. With an infusion of spider grass, mixed perhaps with pulverized devil's eye, I achieve astounding results. The Benkenists, idiots and witlings as they are, aver that only the credulous are affected; they are wrong! Our organisms swim in a paracosmic fluid, which no one can comprehend; none of our senses find scope or purchase, so to speak. Only by operative procedures...can we manipulate this ineffable medium; and by so stating, am I therefore a charlatan?" (M:A/62-63)

And having cautioned us to a tolerant and relativistic outlook, Vance then extends this potential for being attuned to an incomprehensible dimension to a less outwardly "dynamic" race like the Fwai-chi. Skogel continues:

> "I have long speculated that the Fwai-chi interact with the paracosmos somewhat more readily than men, although they are a taciturn race and never explain their feats, or perhaps they take their multiplex environment for granted." (M:A/63)

The ultimate human refinement of this contact with the paracosmos, as we have seen, is probably on Pangborn, where the technologically impoverished humanity is forced along different paths of inquiry into telekinesis and other psionic skills. It is this final area of respect for the unknown which completes the cosmopolitan stance and true pragmatism in Vance's work.

BLIND SPOTS AND OVERSIGHTS

> "Planet-building is a lot of fun."
>
> —Poul Anderson[56]

In his 1976 lecture, Peter Nicholls makes the following comment:

> It has been said that every writer has one obsessive theme to which he constantly returns. This is even more true inside the science fiction field than out of it. It very often happens in sf that the archetypal story by which a writer is remembered came very early or even first in his career. There are obvious exceptions—the writers who started very moderately, often churning out material for the pulps, and then slowly matured.... No, the Monster of Fulfilled Promise is found with those writers who continue, with variations, to write

---

56. Poul Anderson, *Question and Answer*, Introduction.

their first books over and over again...the writer set the pattern with one or more of his first few books, and then cleaved to the pattern ever after.[57]

As examples of this, Nicholls gives Roger Zelazny, Poul Anderson and Larry Niven, among others. He suggests that one of the major reasons for this variation on themes within "the literature of conceptual exploration" (p. 177) is the "very strong commercial pressure to do more of the same" (p.177).

Nicholls is guilty here of the most recurring malady found among those trying to come to grips with the science fiction/fantasy genre. Blind Spot! Limited conception of what science fiction/fantasy is or should be doing. But then, we all tend towards vested interests—even science fiction writers themselves. For instance, here is Larry Niven on the "fantasy" device of time-travel and the alternate universe:

> I *hate* sidewise-in-time travel stories...they're too easy to write. You don't need a brain to write alternate-world stories. You need a good history text.[58]

There! Gone! Dismissed in one broad sweep, everyone from Ward Moore and Keith Roberts to Philip K. Dick and Nabokov. It is Blind Spot, too, that quibbles over categories and classifications to the detriment of the work being considered, and would see a serious hard-core xenographical "adventure" like *The Gray Prince*—to quote one cover blurb—as "a fantasy epic." Little wonder that the "soft" sciences and an author like Vance have been sadly neglected.

To return to Nicholls' earlier comment, we have yet another example of Blind Spot. However well-intentioned, Nicholls failed to take several important factors into account. Firstly,

---

57. Peter Nicholls, *Explorations of the Marvellous*, p.177.

58. Larry Niven, "The Theory and Practice of Time Travel," *All the Myriad Ways* (Ballantine, 1971), p.116.

many authors are committed to a particular field because their sense of wonder works there—it is where they themselves are fascinated and exalted. They tend to be producing the works that they themselves would like to have read. It is just not enough to say that a writer ought to be working along certain lines in order to be forever pushing forward this "conceptual exploration" angle. The authors who are committed to doing this—Dick, Ballard and others—are frequently among the most praiseworthy in the genre, but other less apparently conceptual areas exist. It is this range and diversity that makes the genre the vital force that it is.

A writer like Zelazny *is* fascinated with mythology. His departures from exploring this fascination in fiction are hardly in reaction to the sort of pressure directed at him by commentators like Nicholls or a restless public. The fascination is there, and Zelazny will return to such a preferred area because it gives him pleasure, because there is magic there for him. Similarly, Vance's first love is the exotic mystery that makes possible some sort of cultural analysis—and hence an analysis of the human condition. The critic cannot adopt a comprehensive critical stance without taking this emotional, intellectual and spiritual predilection into account.

Aware of his limitation within his preferred area, the intelligent writer nevertheless abides there, because he awaits the expression of that fascination that he knows *could* come, and which—from his point of view—none of his earlier pieces might have satisfied. We acclaim an author's earlier startlingly original work, and then criticize him for returning to these areas, forgetting that for the author himself that earlier work may not have been satisfactory, may not have adequately expressed the things he wished to convey and crystallize. Perhaps Zelazny needed *This Immortal* (1966) to get *Lord of Light* (1967) and *Creatures of Light and Darkness* (1969) and the Amber novels. Perhaps Vance needed *Big Planet* and *The Dragon Masters* to make possible *Emphyrio* and *The Gray Prince*.

If the author is impelled to try again, he is in a difficult position indeed, for now the process of assessment becomes harder. The earlier works had the benefits of originality and possibly an exuberance in presentation, so that what to the author may be a flawed early expression of his vision is nevertheless a dynamic and momentous one, acclaimed within the genre and possibly outside it as well. Burdened by comparisons, the writer must then contend with accusations of having found a winning formula and of proceeding safely within it.

Considering the fascination impelling the writer to endure within his preferred area, this is a sorry situation indeed. No wonder Vance eschews contact with his public. He reminds us that his stories "were not conceived as argumentative vehicles, but simply reflect my own fascination with the vast and wonderful reaches of the unknown" (8F/8).

To the critics this is hardly acceptable; there is nothing to hang on to. And of course the writer, whether a Patrick White, a Philip Dick or a Jack Vance, cannot easily convey a sense of this motivating vision. Consequently, many authors have been "reduced" by criticism, exposed as poor writers, derivative stylists, inadequate handlers of character, without a single serious attempt to divine the sensibilities that led the writer to produce the work. It is here that literary criticism can virtually become a caricature of itself, playing arbiter without all the necessary perspectives with which to arbitrate.

Furthermore, once we give too much weight to Nicholls' earlier remark, the problem (for critic, writer and reader alike) becomes compounded. For as Zelazny says:

> Newer writers may begin writing for an academic market and aiming some of their pieces at satisfying academic criticism, and lose something of its pure quality as what the writer has basically thought of as entertainment.[59]

---

59. Terry Dowling and Keith Curtis, "A Conversation with Roger Zelazny," *Science Fiction*, I, 2 (1978), p.19.

Let us take a third example of Blind Spot, one much closer to the subject of this study. R.D. Mullen considers the reasons why Vance has not "had a greater success with the general public or with academics," and suggests:

> If in my old-fashioned way one analyses fictions into the five "parts" of language, thought, character (differences between members of the same species, applying not just to persons but to phenomena of all kinds), nature (differences between species; the part that distinguishes SF from mundane fiction, since SF presents not just imaginary individuals but also imaginary species), and plot, then one can say that despite Vance's excellence in language and nature, he remains irredeemably banal in thought, character, and plot. In "The Moon Moth" and perhaps a few other stories he transcends such banality, but not in *The Dragon Masters* nor in any of the other book-length works I have read.[60]

The point here is not to contest such a claim, but to ask what it means for our consideration of the basic standards of assessment that we apply to the genre. For if Mullen's contentions are to be admitted (a difficult task in view of *Emphyrio* alone), then it becomes apparent that those who decided the Hugo Awards for 1963 were careless that year. The very fact that such an award was made at all suggests an important "variable" set of criteria—but how does one begin to discuss merit based on "imagination quotients" and "sense of wonder" factors? The five parts Mullen uses for assessment seem curiously insufficient as yardsticks for the genre, even somewhat arbitrary: the sign of a rear-guard action.

Nevertheless, our elusive genre is quickly decimated by this quinary approach. But if science fiction must heed these five

---

60. R. D. Mullen, "A Bibliography and 49 Reprints," *Science Fiction Studies* 10, III, 3 (1976), pp.303-308.

traditional factors, then Literature must heed a lesson as well: the ancient and infuriating lesson, that new standards of assessment and new values will develop within a dynamic popular movement that do not mean to compete with old forms. They simply disregard them.

THROUGH A GLASS STRANGELY

"...when erudition comes in, poetry departs."
—Unspiek, Baron Bodissey/ *The Killing Machine*

As a writer, Vance has disdained the self-analysis and autobiographica that inevitably attend the majority of writers working in the genre. He says:

> The less a writer discusses his work—and himself—the better. The master chef slaughters no chickens in the dining room; the doctor writes prescriptions in Latin; the magician hides his hinges, mirrors, and trapdoors with the utmost care. (DTA/568)

This desire for solitude leaves Vance quite defenseless (and one would imagine quite oblivious) to his critics, even those who would see his work in a favorable light. He has been accused of producing travelogues, picaresque jaunts and space opera. Others claim that his novels exist for their settings, and that characters are mere stereotypes moving with stylized unreality amidst the amassed exotica. Out of such criticism, and in terms of the conventions of the novel, Vance's fiction (and sf in general) fares very strangely indeed as Literature. Michele Ciaramella says:

> The main feature of a novel is, indeed, that of being a prose narrative, or tale, of a certain length, describing

probable situations and depicting "possible" characters against a background broadly true to life.[61]

Where Vance's novels are concerned, the words "probable" and "possible" come into question (as they inevitably do for any sf work) and "broadly" is taken to its furthest limit. So, where and how are we to classify the xenographical adventures? In a sense, Vance is working outside Literature by writing for entertainment. He means to give his readers, as Howard Frayberg puts it, "the old human angle—glamor, mystery, thrills!" and so any kind of formal analysis becomes somehow inordinate and malapropos.

But the problem remains (for the academic as much as for the writer of entertainment): how to proceed when an entertainer uses the literary form to produce a work that belongs to the representative genre of the twentieth century? He qualifies, but by his own admission of intent does not mean to qualify. He makes no pretensions to being a "Novelist," but then goes on to exasperate critics with ideas and fictions that draw accolades. The critic is nonplussed. To attack is to claim that a work has pretensions to being serious Literature. To ignore it is to turn a blind eye to the vital, elusive and culturally mainstream phenomenon that it is.

How does one rate the ideas writer who has no great literary style—the mathematician or sociologist who has the truly inspiring extrapolation or entertainment to give but surfaces in literary terms as a hack? Is it churlish to discuss shortcomings of style, character development, sophistication of plot and so forth when a work has exalted and provoked the reader? Inevitably, at least in science fiction, the writer's conception far outweighs his expression of it.

We must be prepared to consider a different tack should our dispassionate honesty as critical observers require it. Increasing leisure-time and a whole accelerating physical-mental-spiritual

---

61. Michele Ciaramella, *A Short History of English Literature* (Apollo, 1966), p.107.

world-view guarantees the proliferation of non-Literature-aimed Literature. The niceties of literary discrimination are being severely tested. Statistically, it is in science fiction that those traditionally separate modes of Poetry and Novel most often come together. And science fiction transcends its literary form (as it does film and music) to become something more. As Brian Aldiss said at his Sydney University lecture in April, 1978: "Science fiction is a philosophical necessity to us all."

This leaves us with one final addition to make to the list we have compiled on Vance as xenographer, mystery writer, ethical pragmatist, enlightened medievalist and so forth—the role of poet. For in reflecting his fascination with "the vast and wonderful reaches of the unknown," Vance would also echo the words of fellow xenophile, James White, that:

> ...we humans as a species need contact with strangers who are physically, mentally, and culturally alien to us—and the more alien the better. Such a meeting is vitally necessary if we are to survive and mature as a species, and it may well be that we shall be forced to run before we can walk.[62]

And because, as Attel Malagate tells us in *Star King* (1964), "Men are after all quite parochial" (p.199), our problem is the same one facing Howard Frayberg and Sam Catlin in "Sjambak." Frayberg says:

> "Consider. We sit in this office. We think we know what kind of show we want. We send out our staff to get it. We're signing the cheques, so back it comes the way we asked for it. We look at it, hear it, smell it—and pretty soon we believe it; our version of the universe, full-blown from our brains like Minerva stepping out of Zeus.... It builds up and up—and finally we're like

---

62. Brian Ash (ed.), *The Visual Encyclopaedia of Science Fiction* (Pan, 1977), p.90.

mice in a trap built of our own ideas.... There comes a time in a man's life...when he wants to take stock, get a new perspective." (pp.11-12)

It has always been the poet's task to record the human condition from as many diverse perspectives as possible, and in science fiction—whether it is through a sentient world-ocean like Solaris, a Raman generation-ship or a hybrid humanity lost among the stars—this becomes the ultimate contribution of the xenophilic writer: an extension of cosmic perspective. Suffice to say, then, that the writer who produced "Noise" (1952), *Emphyrio* and such lyrical and optimistic celebrations of the human condition deserves this title of poet above all the rest.

By holding a mirror up to a nature and a humanity that is exotically different, Vance highlights the constants of our own nature and humanity—the basic "themes" on which his variations are founded. By giving us the wonders of other worlds, he helps us to cherish and see anew the wonders of the world we know.

If at one end of the scale Vance is giving us the glamor, the mystery and the thrills in fine style, what he is doing at the other can be best summed up in the words of the poet of *Little Gidding* (1944):

> We shall not cease from exploration
> And the end of all our exploring
> Will be to arrive where we started
> And know the place for the first time.[63]

---

63. T. S. Eliot, *Four Quartets* (Faber and Faber, 1959), p.59.

VANCE FICTION CITED

(An) *The Anome* (Coronet, 1975)
(As) *The Asutra* (Coronet, 1975)
(BFM) *The Brave Free Men* (Coronet, 1975). Note: the reference shown as (BFM/4/*F&SF*) refers to *The Magazine of Fantasy and Science Fiction* version (July 1972)
(BP) *Big Planet* (Coronet, 1977)
(CC) *City of the Chasch* (Mayflower, 1974)
(D) *The Dirdir* (Mayflower, 1975)
(DM) *The Dragon Masters* (Panther, 1967)
(DTA) *The Dogtown Tourist Agency*, *Epoch*, ed, Roger Elwood and Robert Silverberg (Berkley, 1975)
(8F) *Eight Fantasms and Magics* (Collier, 1970)
(Em) *Emphyrio*, *Fantastic* June 1969 and August 1969 —shown as (Em/1) and (Em/2)
(FGB) *The Five Gold Bands* (Ace, 1963)
(FVM) *The Fox Valley Murders* (Bobbs-Merrill, 1966)
(GP) *The Grey Prince* (Avon, 1975)
(HI) *The Houses of Iszm* (Mayflower, 1974)
(KM) *The Killing Machine* (Science Fiction Book Club, 1968)
(M:A) *Marune: Alastor 933* (Ballantine, 1975)
(MC) *The Man in the Cage* (Boardman, 1960)
(MR) *The Many Worlds of Magnus Ridolph* (Ace, 1966)
(M:T) *Maske: Thaery* (Berkley-Putnam, 1976)
(MW) "The Miracle Workers," *Astounding*, October 1958
(MZ) "The Man from Zodiac," *Amazing*, August 1967
(PL) *The Palace of Love* (Dobson, 1968)

(Pn) *The Pnume* (Mayflower, 1976)
(R) "Rumfuddle," *The Best Science Fiction of the Year 5*, ed, Terry Carr (Ballantine, 1974)
(ShW) *Showboat World* (Pyramid, 1975)
(sj) "Sjambak," *Worlds of Infinity*, I, 3. July 1953
(SK) *Star King* (Mayflower, 1973)
(SO) *Space Opera* (Pyramid, 1965)
(SW) *Servants of the Wankh* (Mayflower, 1975)
(ST) *Son of the Tree* (Mayflower, 1974)
(T:A) *Trullion: Alastor 2262* (Ballantine, 1973)
(W:A) *Wyst: Alastor 1716* (DAW, 1978)

CHAPTER SOURCES IN CHRONOLOGICAL ORDER

"The Art of Xenography: Jack Vance's 'General Culture' Novels," by Terry Dowling *Science Fiction: A Review of Speculative Literature* 3 (Vol.1, No.3) 1978 (here slightly revised).

"Science Fiction and the Plight of the Literary Critic," by Kirpal Singh: *Science Fiction: A Review of Speculative Literature* 12 (Vol.4, No.3) 1982.

"The Camera Speaks: *An Unusual Angle* by Greg Egan," by Veronica Brady: *Science Fiction: A Review of Speculative Literature* 14 (Vol.5, No.2) 1983.

"Strangers in an Alien World: Weinbaum's 'A Martian Odyssey' and Le Guin's *The Left Hand of Darkness*," by Barbara Bengels: *Science Fiction: A Review of Speculative Literature* 38 (Vol.13, No.2) 1996 and 25 (Vol.9, No.1) 1987.

"Science Fiction, Parafiction, and Peter Carey," by George Turner: *Science Fiction: A Review of Speculative Literature* 28 (Vol.10:1) 1988.

"*Rats and Gargoyles* by Mary Gentle," by Yvonne Rousseau: *Science Fiction: A Review of Speculative Literature* 33 (Vol.11, No.3) 1992.

"*Solution Three* by Naomi Mitchison," by Helen Merrick: *Science Fiction: A Review of Speculative Literature* 38 (Vol.13, No.2) 1996.

"Carey Goes Cybersurfing," by Marie Maclean: *Science Fiction: A Review of Speculative Literature* 39 (Vol.14, No.1) 1997.

"Postmodernism vs Postcolonialism," by Elizabeth Hardy *Science Fiction: A Review of Speculative Literature* 39 (Vol.14, No.1) 1997.

"The Other in Its Own Home: Aliens in Speculative Fiction," by G. Travis Regier: *Science Fiction: A Review of Speculative Literature* 40 (Vol.14, No.2) 1997.

"Hacking the Spew: Technology and Anxiety in Neal Stephenson's *Snow Crash* and *The Diamond Age*," by Talia Eilon: *Science Fiction: A Review of Speculative Literature* 44 (Vol.16, no.2) 2002.

CONTRIBUTORS

Barbara Bengels is Adjunct Professor of Writing Studies and Composition at Hofstra University in New York, and has taught courses there in The History of SF and Teaching Composition Through SF. Her collaborative work has also taken her into the fields of astronomy and philosophy.

Veronica Brady, now in her 80s, is a Catholic nun, writer and university academic, now Honorary Senior Fellow in English and Cultural Studies at the University of Western Australia. She has held visiting fellowships at the Rockefeller Study Centre in Bellagio, Italy, the University of Oregon at Eugene and at the Coolidge Research Colloquium, Episcopal Divinity School, Harvard University. She has publicly criticized the Vatican's positions on abortion, homosexuality and contraception, been involved in the Aboriginal rights movement and the anti-uranium mining lobby, and supports the ordination of female priests in the Catholic Church.

Damien Broderick holds a Ph.D. from Deakin University, and has published more than 50 novels, scholarly and popular science books on literature, the paranormal, the technological singularity, the prospect of radical life extension, and the very far future. In 2010 he was runner-up for the Theodore Sturgeon short fiction award, and received the A. Bertram Chandler Award. These days he lives in San Antonio, Texas.

Terry Dowling holds a PhD in Creative Writing from the University of Western Australia, and has published many awarded and anthologized stories in all fantastika genres: science fiction (notably his Tom Rynosseros sequence), horror and fantasy. He has created several computer games, and his debut novel *Clowns at Midnight* appeared from PS Publishing in 2010.

Talia Eilon is an actor who starred in the short film *The Murder of Jonathan Ripley*. She holds an Honours degree in English from the University of Western Australia.

Elizabeth Hardy's Honours dissertation and PhD thesis at the University of Western Australia focused on novels by Peter Carey. She also holds diplomas in Information and Library Studies, and in Journalism.

Van Ikin, winner of the inaugural A. Bertram Chandler Award in 1992, is a professor of English at the University of Western Australia, and gained his PhD from Sydney University. He is co-author (with Russell Blackford and Sean McMullen) of *Strange Constellations* and editor of three anthologies of Australian sf (including *Mortal Fire: Best Australian SF*—the first-ever Australian *Best of* collection, co-edited with Terry Dowling in 1993). He has edited and published *Science Fiction: A Review of Speculative Literature* since 1977.

Marie Maclean was a literary scholar in the field of Comparative Literature. She was Senior Research Fellow of Monash University and Fellow of the Australian Academy of the Humanities until her death in 1996.

Helen Merrick holds a PhD in feminist science fiction, and is co-editor with Tess Williams of *Women of Other Worlds: Excursions through science fiction and feminism* (1999). Her notable book *The Secret Feminist Cabal: A Cultural History of*

Science Fiction Feminisms (2009) received the 2010 William Atheling Jr. award for sf criticism. She is Senior Lecturer in Internet Studies at Curtin University.

Gail Travis Regier is a somewhat reclusive writer of fiction, poetry and literary essays. His work has appeared in *Harpers, Atlantic Monthly, Amazing Stories, American Scholar, ploughshares* and *Poetry*.

Yvonne Rousseau lives quietly in Adelaide, South Australia in the large book-crammed house she shared with her late husband John Foyster, reading prodigiously and writing wittily but publishing far too little.

Kirpal Singh, born in Singapore, holds a PhD from the University of Adelaide, and is an Associate Professor with the Singapore Management University. In 1993 and 1994, he was the first Asian director of the Commonwealth Writers' Prize. A notable postcolonial scholar, he was co-editor in 1980 of *The Stellar Gauge: Essays on Science Fiction Writers*.

George Turner, who died in 1997, remains perhaps Australia's most highly regarded if contentious science fiction author and critic. He shared the 1962 Miles Franklin literary award for *The Cupboard Under the Stairs*. His sf novels include *Beloved Son, The Sea and Summer* (*Drowning Towers*), *Brainchild* and *Genetic Soldier*.

INDEX

Ackroyd, Peter, 63
Aegypt, 64
Aldiss, Brian W., 24, 30, 40, 159, 251
Alien Zone, 127
All Judgment Fled, 159
Altmann, Gerry T. M., 126
And Some Were Savages, 159
Anderson, Patrick, 10
Anderson, Poul, 33, 157-64, 180, 213, 244-45
Anome, The, 172, 174, 181, 188, 196, 203, 208-10, 254
Asaro, Catherine, 126
Ash, Brian, 251
Ascent of Babel, The, 126
Asimov, Isaac, 36-9, 54, 157, 165, 168
Assignment Nor'Dyren, 160-62
Asutra, The, 172, 186, 203-05, 208-09, 224-25, 237, 239, 254
Australian Science Fiction, 11
Bad Ronald, 214
Bæcker, Ronald M., 126
Ballard, J. G., 35, 134, 246
Bayley, Barrington J., 161
Bengels, Barbara, 14, 54, 256, 258
Berends, Jan, 112, 118, 126
Big Planet, 169-73, 193, 195, 199, 202, 220, 246, 254
Biggle, Lloyd Jr., 157, 161-62
Blackford, Russell, 12, 259

Blade Runner, 143
Blish, James, 156, 158
Bliss, 15, 146
Blue World, The, 169, 173, 186
Bodies and Culture in the Cyberage, 129
Boundary Disputes, 128
Brave Free Men, The, 172, 254
Brave New World, 20, 45
Brazil, 10, 84
Breaking the Code with Neal Stephenson, 127
Broderick, Damien, 9, 134, 258
Brown, Fredric, 164
Brown, Tanya., 126
Brydon, Diana, 149
Bukatman, Scott, 126-27
Burning Chrome, 85, 99, 127, 130
Burrows, Roger, 127
Buxton, William, 126
Campbell, John W., Jr., 190
Čapek, Karel, 21
Carey, Peter, 11, 15, 132, 142-45, 148, 256, 259
Chance, The, 137
Chaos and Cyberculture, 129
Cherryh, C. J., 40-4, 49
Christie, John R. R., 127
Ciaramella, Michele, 249-50
City of the Chasch, 172, 190, 197, 254
Clarke, Arthur C., 20, 29, 35, 159, 183
Claustrophile, 30
Clement, Hal, 29, 157, 178
Close to Critical, 178
Collins, Helen, 59
Computer 'Virus' as Metaphor, The, 127
Concept of Anxiety, The, 129
Conversation with Neal Stephenson, 126
Conversations With Unicorns, 134

Cooper, Edmund, 33
Coup de Grace, 178, 215, 221
Cowan, James, 154
Crawford, Harriet, 127
Creatures of Light and Darkness, 246
Crowley, John, 64
Curtis, Keith, 248
Cybercultural Politics, 130
Cybernetic Deconstructions, 84, 128
Cybernetics, Information, Life, 128
Cyberpunk, 81, 84, 127-28, 130
Cyberspace and the Technological Real, 129
Cyberspace/Cyberbodies/Cyberpunk, 127
Cycle of Fire, 178
Dawkins, Richard, 127
de Camp, L. Sprague, 162, 179
Deadly Isles, The, 214
Delany, Samuel R., 40-1, 48-52
Demon Princes, 168, 170, 173, 228, 232
Dery, Mark, 127
Desertion, 30
Dialectic of Sex, The, 69
Diamond Age, The, 80, 91, 110-126, 130, 257
Dick, Philip K., 143
Dirdir, The, 172, 177, 183, 196, 218-19, 228, 254
Disch, Thomas M., 133
Do Androids Dream of Electric Sheep, 143
Do You Love Me?, 136
Dogtown Tourist Agency, The, 171, 173, 183, 187, 199, 209, 238, 249, 254
Dorman, Sonya, 31
Dowling, Terry, 11, 12, 16, 156, 248, 256, 259
Dragon Masters, The, 169, 173, 175, 193, 239, 246-47, 254
Dream of John Ball, A, 234
Drexler, K. Eric, 127

Dying Earth, The, 198
Eco, Umberto, 63
Egan, Greg, 73-8, 256
Eight Fantasms and Magics, 239, 247, 254
Electronic Eros, 130
Eliot, T.S., 253
Emphyrio, 156, 172-73, 187, 192-93, 198, 202, 216, 220, 246-47, 252, 254
Empire of the Sun, The, 134
Empire Writes Back, The, 151
Engines of Creation, 127
Escape Velocity, 127
Exotic Pleasures, 134
Eyes of the Overworld, The, 198
Fabulous Feminist Futures and the Lure of Cyberculture, 130
Fat Man in History, The, 15, 133, 146
Fat Man In History, The, 138
Featherstone, Mike, 127
Fifth Head of Cerberus, The, 31
Firestone, Shulamith, 69
First Light, 63
First Men in the Moon, The, 21
Fishing Trip, 159
Five Gold Bands, The, 168-70, 173, 184-85, 254
Forster, E.M., 24
Foster, Thomas, 127
Foucault's Pendulum, 63
Foundation, 165
Four Quartets, 253
Fox Valley Murders, The, 193, 214, 222, 254
Frankenstein, 20
Frietzke's Turn, 157
From Hestia to Homepage, 130
Galatea 2.2, 92, 128
Garments of Caean, The, 161
Gentle, Mary, 14, 61, 256

Gibson, William, 83-5, 96, 98-9, 127, 130, 143
Gibson's Typewriter, 126
Gift of Gab, The, 215-16
Gilliam, Terry, 84
Glass Reptile Breakout, 11
Gods Themselves, The, 36
Goldberg, Michael, 127
Gozzi Jr, Raymond, 127
Gray Prince, The, 171-75, 181-82, 185, 190, 210-11, 222, 233-34, 242, 245-46, 254
Gunkel, David J., 127
Hacking the Brainstem, 92, 129
Halloran, John A., 128
Haraway, Donna, 71, 128
Hardy, Elizabeth, 15, 148, 257, 259
Harper, Mary Catherine, 128
Harrison, Harry, 21, 157
Hayles, N. Katherine, 92, 128
Heinlein, Robert A., 34, 36
Herbert, Frank, 35, 157-58, 179-80
Hiding Place, 159
History, Science, Vision, 19
History, Theory and Virtual Reality, 129
Hollinger, Veronica, 84, 93, 128
Houses of Iszm, The, 189, 223, 226, 239, 240, 254
Howard, Robert E., 193
Huxley, Aldous, 20, 24, 45, 158
Ikin, Van, 11, 13, 259
Illywhacker, 145-46
Imperial Earth, 20
Incurably Alien Other, 128
Information Multiplicity, 128
Interview with Neal Stephenson, 126
Is Language a Virus?, 130
Island of Dr. Moreau, The, 30
Jaynes, Julian, 128

Jenny Haniver approach, 179-81, 191
Johnston, John, 128
Joy, Bill, 128
Kay, Lily E., 128
Kendrick, Michelle, 129
Kierkegaard, Søren, 129
Killing Machine, The, 176, 185-86, 188, 200-04, 233-36, 249, 254
Knight, Damon, 40
Kornbluth, C.M., 161-62, 165
Kramer, Samuel Noah, 129
Kunzru, Hari, 129
Languages of Pao, The, 170
Last Castle, The, 169, 173, 194, 212
Last Continent, The, 33
Laumer, Keith, 157, 170, 200
Lawlor, Robert, 148
Le Guin, Ursula K., 14, 30, 54, 57, 59, 60, 67, 133, 142, 157, 161-64, 193, 236, 256
Leary, Timothy, 129
Left Hand of Darkness, The, 54, 57, 162, 163, 165, 256
Lem, Stanislaw, 159, 179
Lessing, Doris, 24
Lingua ex Machina, 127
Little Gidding, 252
Little, Big, 64
Lord of Light, 246
Maclean, Marie, 15, 142, 256, 259
Magazine of Fantasy and Science Fiction, The, 192, 254
Make Room! Make Room!, 21
Man From Primrose Lane, The, 10
Man from Zodiac, The, 168, 172, 194, 212, 215, 254
Man in the Cage, The, 214, 217, 254
Many Worlds of Magnus Ridolph, The, 178, 185, 215, 221-22, 254
Markley, Robert, 129

Martian Odyssey, A, 32, 54, 159, 165, 256
Marune: Alastor 933, 171, 173, 194, 196-99, 211-13, 216, 222, 232, 244, 254
Maske: Thaery, 172, 175, 185, 193-95, 205, 209, 211, 214, 225-26, 235-36, 242-43, 254
Materiality of Informatics, The, 128
Matrix, The, 84
McMullen, Sean, 12, 259
Measure for Measure, 209
Meat Puppets or Robopaths?, 127
Memoirs of a Spacewoman, 68
Men, Martians and Machines, 165
Midsummer Night's Dream, A, 208
Miller, P.Schuyler, 169, 177, 198, 213
Miracle Workers, The, 173-74, 204-05, 254
Mirrorshades, 81, 130
Mission of Gravity, 29, 178
Mitchison, Naomi, 67-72, 256
Modern Social Science Fiction, 54
Moon Moth, The, 187, 192, 215, 216, 248
Morris, William, 234
Mortal Fire, 11, 259
Mote in God's Eye, The, 159
Moulthrop, Stuart, 92, 95-6, 129
Mullen, R.D., 248, 249
Murnane, Gerald, 73, 77, 78
Mysteries of the Dreaming, 154
Neuromancer, 84, 127
New Images of Sex in Science Fiction, 59
Nicholls, Peter, 178, 244-47
Night Face, The, 162, 164-65
Nineteen Eighty-Four, 21, 133
Niven, Larry, 157, 159, 161, 165, 171, 180, 183, 186, 216, 245
Nixon, Nicola, 129
No War Machine, 92, 95-6, 129
Noble, Jon, 191-92

Noise, 127, 252
Norton, Andre, 157, 186
On the Edge of the Pacific, 130
Origin of Consciousness in the Breakdown of the Bicameral Mind, The, 128
Orwell, George, 21, 133
Oscar and Lucinda, 146
Outburst!, 130
Palace Of Love, The, 186, 202, 206, 217, 221, 223, 228, 234-36, 242, 254
Piercy, Marge, 69
Plains, The, 73
Pnume, The, 172, 177, 181, 190, 217-18, 227, 255
Pohl, Frederik, 161-62, 165
Politics of Neal Stephenson's *The Diamond Age*, 126
Porush, David, 92, 129
Posthumanist Body, The, 92, 128
Pournelle, Jerry, 159
Puzzling Nature of Blue, The, 134
Quest of the Three Worlds, 165
R.U.R., 21
Rabkin, Eric, 19
Rats and Gargoyles, 14, 61-64, 256
Readings in Human-Computer Interaction, 126
Red Planet, 36
Regier, G. Travis, 11, 14-5, 26, 257, 260
Relics (Regier), 36
Rendezvous with Rama, 159
Renner, James, 10
Report on the Shadow Industry, 134
Resnick, Mike, 33
Ribeiro, Gustavo Lins, 129
Ringworld, 165, 216
Rousseau, Yvonne, 14, 61, 256, 260
Rucker, Rudy, 130
Rumfuddle, 194, 235-36, 255

Russ, Joanna, 192
Salverda, Reinier, 130
Schell, Heather, 130
Schmitz, James, 157
Scholes, Robert, 19
Science Fiction Hall of Fame, The, 54
Scott, Melissa, 130
Search the Sky, 162, 165, 168
Selfish Gene, The, 127
Serpent's Reach, 40-1, 51
Servants of the Wankh, 172, 208-09, 229-31, 255
Shakespeare, William, 209
Shelley, Mary, 20
Showboat World, 171, 173, 193, 208, 225, 255
Shreds and Patches, 129
Silverberg, Robert, 30, 54, 157
Simak, Clifford, 26, 30, 178, 236
Singh, Kirpal, 13, 15, 17, 256, 260
Sjambak, 156, 168, 170, 188, 212, 215, 251, 255
Smith, Cordwainer, 30, 157, 161, 165
Smith, E. E. (Doc), 27
Snow Crash, 80- 120, 126, 128-30, 257
Social Science Fiction, 54
Solaris, 159, 179
Solution Three, 67-72, 256
Son of the Tree, 169-70, 176, 186, 189, 194, 231-32, 255
Soylent Green, 21
Space Opera, 211, 232, 255
Springer, Claudia, 130
Squier, Susan, 67, 69
Squires, Judith, 130
Star Beast, The, 36
Star King, 187, 197, 206, 226, 228, 231, 235, 251, 255
Star, Susan Leigh, 130
Stars in My Pocket like Grains of Sand, 40, 48
Stephenson, Neal, 80-127, 130, 257

Sterling, Bruce, 40, 80-1, 98, 130
Strange Constellations, 11, 259
Stranger in a Strange Land, 35
Stranger Station, 40
Sturgeon, Theodore, 30, 236, 258
Sumer and the Sumerians, 127
Sumerians, The, 129
Swarm, 40
Tax Inspector, The, 147
Technobody and its Discontents, The, 128
Terminator, 84
Thief in Heaven, A, 36
This Immortal, 34, 246
Three Suns of Amara, 165, 168
Time Machine, The, 21
To Live Forever, 173
To Open the Sky, 30
Tolkien, J.R.R., 193, 198
Toluzzi, Peter, 192
Tower of Zanid, The, 162, 179
Tragedy for Cyborgs, A, 127
Trouble and Her Friends, 94, 130
Trullion: Alastor 2262, 157-58, 170-73, 183, 193-95 197, 199, 201, 210, 219, 221, 223, 255
Tubb, E. C., 157, 170, 176
Turner, George, 15, 132, 256, 260
Tyrant's Territory, 159
Unabomber's Manifesto, The, 83, 131
Unleashing the Strange, 9
Unusual Angle, An, 73, 79, 256
Unusual Life of Tristan Smith, The, 15, 142, 146, 148, 150
Van Scyoc, Sydney, 157, 160, 162
Van Vogt, A. E., 35, 179
Vance, Jack, 11, 16, 156- 252, 256
Verne, Jules, 158
Virtual Light, 83-4, 127, 143

Voices of the First Day, 148
Voyage of the Space Beagle, The, 165, 179
War Crimes, 133, 140
War of the Worlds, The, 32, 34
Warriors of the Tao, 11
Way Station, 26
Weinbaum, Stanley, 14, 32, 54-7, 159, 165, 256
Wells, H. G., 20-4, 30, 32, 158
When I was Miss Dow, 31
When the Sleeper Awakes, 23
White Inuit Speaks, The, 149
White, James, 159, 251
Who Programs You?, 127
Why the Future Doesn't Need Us, 83, 128
Wild Nature, 127
Windmill in the West, 134
Wolfbane, 179
Wolfe, Gene, 31, 34
Woman on the Edge of Time, 69
Wonder and Awe, 23
Woods, P.F., 159
World Menders, The, 162
World Thinker, The, 169
Wyst: Alastor 1716, 157, 255
Xeno fiction, 11, 12
You Are Borg, 129
Zeitgeist Machine, The, 134
Zelazny, Roger, 34-5, 245-47

www.ingramcontent.com/pod-product-compliance
Lightning Source LLC
Chambersburg PA
CBHW032104090426
42743CB00007B/223